BUDGET OF THE U.S. GOVERNMENT

FISCAL YEAR 2025

EXECUTIVE OFFICE OF THE PRESIDENT

OFFICE OF MANAGEMENT AND BUDGET

Bernan
Press

Lanham • Boulder • New York • London

Published by Bernan Press
An imprint of The Rowman & Littlefield Publishing Group, Inc.
4501 Forbes Boulevard, Suite 200, Lanham, Maryland 20706
www.rowman.com

86-90 Paul Street, London EC2A 4NE

ISBN: 979-8-89205-052-4 (paperback)

∞™ The paper used in this publication meets the minimum requirements of American National Standard for Information Sciences—Permanence of Paper for Printed Library Materials, ANSI/NISO Z39.48-1992.

THE BUDGET DOCUMENTS

Budget of the United States Government, Fiscal Year 2025 contains the Budget Message of the President, information on the President's priorities, and summary tables.

Analytical Perspectives, Budget of the United States Government, Fiscal Year 2025 contains analyses that are designed to highlight specified subject areas or provide other significant presentations of budget data that place the budget in perspective. This volume includes economic and accounting analyses, information on Federal receipts and collections, analyses of Federal spending, information on Federal borrowing and debt, baseline or current services estimates, and other technical presentations.

Appendix, Budget of the United States Government, Fiscal Year 2025 contains detailed information on the various appropriations and funds that constitute the budget and is designed primarily for the use of the Appropriations Committees. The Appendix contains more detailed financial information on individual programs and appropriation accounts than any of the other budget documents. It includes for each agency: the proposed text of appropriations language; budget schedules for each account; legislative proposals; narrative explanations of each budget account; and proposed general provisions applicable to the appropriations of entire agencies or groups of agencies. Information is also provided on certain activities whose transactions are not part of the budget totals.

GENERAL NOTES

1. All years referenced for budget data are fiscal years unless otherwise noted. All years referenced for economic data are calendar years unless otherwise noted.

2. At the time the Budget was prepared, none of the full-year appropriations bills for 2024 had been enacted; therefore, the programs and activities normally provided for in the full-year appropriations bills were operating under a continuing resolution (Public Law 118-15, division A, as amended). References to 2024 spending in the text and tables reflect the levels provided by the continuing resolution.

3. Detail in this document may not add to the totals due to rounding.

Table of Contents

Page

The Budget Message of the President 1

Building the Economy from the Middle Out and Bottom Up 5

Investing in America and the American People 15

Creating a Government that Delivers for the American People 49

Department of Agriculture 55

Department of Commerce 61

Department of Defense 65

Department of Education 69

Department of Energy 73

Department of Health and Human Services 77

Department of Homeland Security 85

Department of Housing and Urban Development 89

Department of the Interior 93

Department of Justice 97

Department of Labor 101

Department of State and Other International Programs 105

Department of Transportation 111

Department of the Treasury 115

Department of Veterans Affairs 117

Corps of Engineers—Civil Works 121

Environmental Protection Agency 123

National Aeronautics and Space Administration 127

National Science Foundation 129

Small Business Administration 131

Social Security Administration 133

Summary Tables 135

OMB Contributors to the 2025 Budget 177

THE BUDGET MESSAGE OF THE PRESIDENT

To the Congress of the United States:

When I was elected President, a pandemic was raging and our economy was reeling. We were in the midst of the most devastating downturn in nearly a century. I came into office determined to fundamentally change things, by rebuilding our economy from the middle out and bottom up, not the top down—because when the middle class does well, the poor have a ladder up and the wealthy still do well. We all do. We can give everyone a fair shot and leave no one behind.

Our work started with the American Rescue Plan, which vaccinated the Nation, delivered immediate economic relief to people who badly needed it, and sent funding to States and cities to keep key services going. It continued with the biggest investment in our Nation's infrastructure since the 1950s. More than 46,000 new projects have been announced to date, rebuilding our roads, bridges, railroads, ports, airports, public transit, water systems, high-speed internet, and more. At the same time, we are making the most significant investment in fighting climate change in the history of the world. I have seen Americans' courage and resilience in the wake of devastating natural disasters, and I will always have their backs as we rebuild and boost resilience to extreme weather. We are building a cleaner, more resilient and sustainable power grid, and making America's biggest investment in rural electricity since the New Deal. We are revitalizing fence-line communities that have shouldered the burden of harmful pollution for generations. We are lowering energy costs for hardworking families and strengthening our energy security with clean energy breakthroughs. Across the board, we are supporting advanced manufacturing, ensuring the industries of the future are made in America by American workers.

Our plan is working. Already, my Investing in America agenda has attracted $650 billion in private investment from companies that are building factories and moving production back to America. We are making things here in America again, with American union workers. We have ignited a manufacturing boom, a semiconductor boom, an electric-vehicle boom, and more. My agenda is creating hundreds of thousands of union jobs, so folks never have to leave their hometowns to find good-paying work they can raise a family on. Today, America once again has the strongest economy in the world. We have created a record 15 million jobs, with unemployment under four percent for the longest stretch in over 50 years. Growth is strong. Wages are rising and inflation is down by two-thirds, with costs having fallen for key household items from a gallon of gas to a gallon of milk. We have more to do, but folks are starting to feel the benefits. Consumer sentiment has surged more in recent months than any time in 30 years. Americans have filed a record 16 million new business applications since I took office; each one of them is an act of hope.

Importantly, we made these historic investments in a fiscally responsible way, while making our tax system fairer. In 2022, I signed a law that imposed a new minimum tax of 15 percent on the Nation's largest corporations, saved $160 billion by giving Medicare the authority to negotiate prescription drug prices and limit price increases, and boosted funding to the Internal Revenue Service to crack down on wealthy and corporate tax cheats. This is just the beginning. My Budget would do more to close loopholes. It would save another $200 billion by enabling

Medicare to negotiate prices on even more drugs and by limiting other drug price increases. It would cut wasteful subsidies to Big Oil and other special interests; and it would introduce a minimum tax on billionaires, which alone would raise $500 billion for the American people.

So far, we have already cut the deficit by $1 trillion since I took office, one of the biggest reductions in history, and I have signed legislation to cut it by $1 trillion more. My Budget would reduce it by another $3 trillion over the next 10 years as well, while continuing to pay for our investments in America.

And we are just getting started.

My Administration will keep fighting to lower costs for working families, on everything from housing to childcare to student loans. After decades of talk in Washington, we beat Big Pharma and capped the cost of insulin for seniors at $35 a month, down from as much as $400. Starting next year, no senior on Medicare will pay more than $2,000 a year in total out-of-pocket prescription drug costs, even for expensive cancer medications that now cost many times more. We are cracking down on price gouging by requiring drugmakers that raise prices of certain drugs faster than inflation to pay a rebate back to Medicare. At the same time, we have protected and expanded the Affordable Care Act, with a record 21 million Americans enrolled in marketplace plans this past year, while saving millions of Americans $800 per year on their premiums. Today, more Americans have health insurance than ever before. My Budget builds on those gains.

I also know that for too many hardworking families, it costs too much to find a good home, so we are working to lower costs and boost supply of housing nationwide. My Budget will make monthly mortgage payments more affordable for middle-class first-time homebuyers by providing a $5,000 annual mortgage relief credit for two years. My Budget will expand rental assistance to hundreds of thousands of additional families, continuing the largest expansion in 20 years. It will also help to ease America's longstanding shortage of affordable housing, including by cutting red tape, so that more builders can get Federal financing to build more affordable housing. Important progress is underway: more families own homes today than before the pandemic; rents are easing; and a record 1.7 million housing units are under construction nationwide.

My Budget also makes key investments in childcare and education, so every child in America can have the strong start they need to thrive. It restores the Child Tax Credit expansion I signed into law, which cut child poverty nearly in half in 2021; and it guarantees the vast majority of families high-quality childcare for no more than $10 a day, while boosting pay for childcare workers. It offers universal free preschool for all four million of America's four-year-olds. Building on the American Rescue Plan's investment in public education, the biggest in history, it also helps States expand tutoring, afterschool, and summer programs; and boosts recruiting to ease teacher shortages.

At the same time, I am keeping my promise to ease the crushing burden of student debt. Despite legal challenges, we have canceled some $138 billion in student debt for nearly four million Americans, including more than 750,000 teachers, nurses, firefighters, social workers, and other public servants. That is freeing people to finally consider buying a home, having a child, or starting that small business they always dreamed of.

We are also working to secure our border. In October, I sent an emergency request for more funding; my Budget renews that request for additional resources, including for 1,300 more Border Patrol agents, 375 immigration judges, and 1,600 asylum officers, and for cutting-edge technology to help detect fentanyl. We need to pass the Senate's bipartisan border deal as well, which would make urgent additional investments to secure the border and help to fix our broken immigration system.

Today, the world is facing an inflection point in history, at home and abroad. My Administration has restored America's leadership on the world stage, rallying more than 50 nations to support Ukraine in the face of brutal Russian aggression, strengthening and expanding NATO, revitalizing our alliances and partnerships in the Indo-Pacific—including with Japan, South Korea, and Australia—and strengthening democracy across the globe. But we need to do more to prove that America can once again be relied on to stand up for freedom. In October, I submitted a national security supplemental request to cover urgent needs, including support for Ukraine and Israel, and humanitarian aid and relief for Palestinians. My Budget reiterates that request and continues other critical support for NATO allies and partners around the world. It strengthens our deterrence capacity in the Indo-Pacific, expanding our capabilities in the region. It also works to keep our military the best-trained, best-equipped fighting force in the world, integrating advanced innovation technologies, and improving overall readiness. My Budget also takes important steps to honor our Nation's most sacred obligation—to protect and equip our troops when they are in harm's way, and to care for them and their families throughout and after their service. Since I took office, I have signed over 30 significant bipartisan bills to support veterans, including the PACT Act, the biggest-ever expansion of benefits for servicemembers exposed to toxic burn pits during their service; and I have issued the most comprehensive executive actions to date to boost economic security for military families. My Budget builds on that work.

The story of America is one of progress and resilience, of always moving forward and never giving up. It is a story unique among nations. We are the only nation that has emerged from every crisis we have entered stronger than we went in. While my Administration has seen great progress since day one, there is still work to do. My Budget will help make that promise real.

JOSEPH R. BIDEN JR.

THE WHITE HOUSE,
  March 2024

BUILDING THE ECONOMY FROM THE MIDDLE OUT AND BOTTOM UP

When the President and Vice President came into office, America faced historic challenges, including a once-in-a-century pandemic and an economy experiencing the most severe downturn since the Great Depression. From day one, the President moved swiftly to tackle these challenges head-on and has delivered long-lasting results. Over the past three years, the President has overseen a strong economic recovery, amassed one of the most successful legislative records in generations, sought to grow the economy by growing the middle class, and delivered important progress for the American people.

Since the President took office, the economy has added about 15 million jobs. That is about 15 million additional Americans who know the peace of mind that comes with a paycheck. The unemployment rate has remained below four percent for 24 months in a row—a more than 50-year record—while inflation has fallen by two-thirds. Our strong labor market has meant higher paychecks, driven by pay increases across the middle class. Workers' paychecks and household wealth are higher now than they were before the pandemic—including after adjusting for inflation. Higher pay has spurred strong consumer spending and business investment. Americans have filed a record 16 million applications to start businesses—the highest number ever over a three-year span. Under President Biden, the Nation has achieved faster growth than any of America's peer nations and now has the lowest core inflation of almost any other major economy.

The President's top economic priority is lowering costs for hardworking Americans. The Administration is working to bring down prescription drug costs, health insurance premiums, utility bills, and costs for everyday goods—all while taking on junk fees that some airlines, banks, and other companies use to rip off Americans.

The President has lowered costs while investing in America and the American people. The President's Investing in America agenda, which includes his landmark legislation—the Infrastructure Investment and Jobs Act (Bipartisan Infrastructure Law), the CHIPS and Science Act (Public Law 117-167), and the Inflation Reduction Act (Public Law 117-169)—is driving record investment and opportunity in communities across the Nation, including those that have been too often left behind. The President has led a historic economic recovery, implemented the Investing in America agenda, and worked to lower costs for Americans, while also keeping Americans safe and promoting democracy at home and abroad.

As the President said, "the story of America is a story of progress and resilience, of always moving forward, of never, ever giving up. It's a story unique among all nations. We're the only country that has emerged from every crisis we've ever entered stronger than we got into it." Under the President's leadership, the Administration is focused on building on this record of progress as we write the next chapter in the great American story.

LOWERING COSTS AND PUTTING MONEY BACK IN AMERICANS' POCKETS

Over the past three years, the global pandemic and Putin's illegal war against the people of Ukraine have led to inflation all over the world. The President has made it his top domestic priority to lower costs and give American families more breathing room. Under the President's leadership, the Nation has seen significant progress in bringing down inflation. Over the last six months of 2023, core inflation was at the pre-COVID-19 pandemic benchmark of two percent—with average hourly earnings adjusted for inflation higher now than before the COVID-19 pandemic and rising faster than inflation over the last year. The Administration has consistently taken steps to lower a range of costs and put more money back into American's pockets.

Lowering Healthcare Costs

The President signed into law the historic Inflation Reduction Act, which is helping millions of Americans save an average of $800 per year on health insurance by extending the Patient Protection and Affordable Care Act (Affordable Care Act) enhanced premium tax credit, helping drive enrollment in Affordable Care Act health insurance to record-breaking highs. The historic legislation also capped the cost of insulin at $35 a month for seniors per insulin prescription, made recommended vaccines free, and is requiring drug companies to pay rebates to Medicare if they raise prices faster than inflation. Under the President's leadership, the Administration has taken on Big Pharma to finally allow Medicare to negotiate for lower prescription drug prices—starting with ten of the costliest, most widely used drugs used to treat blood clots, cancers, arthritis, diabetes, and more. The Administration has also cracked down on surprise medical bills, preventing Americans from receiving more than one million surprise medical bills every month, and is also including an allowance to ban unwarranted "facility fees" for telehealth and certain other outpatient services in commercial insurance.

Bringing Down Energy and Internet Costs

The President has taken action to bring gas prices down—since their peak, average gas prices for Americans have come down more than $1.60 per gallon. The President's historic Inflation Reduction Act is directly investing in communities while also spurring hundreds of billions of dollars in private sector investment—in wind, solar, energy efficiency, electric vehicles, and more—creating economic opportunities, lowering energy costs across the Nation, and improving public health. The Inflation Reduction Act is expected to help families save an average of $500 per year on energy costs once fully implemented. The President's Bipartisan Infrastructure Law created the Affordable Connectivity Program, which has helped 23 million households save more than $500 million per month on internet bills.

Forgiving Historic Amounts of Student Debt and Launching the Most Affordable Repayment Plan Ever

The President has made history by approving a total of over $137 billion in debt cancellation for over 3.7 million Americans through a variety of actions, including by taking on private, for-profit universities that have scammed hard-working Americans. The Administration launched the most affordable student loan repayment plan ever—the Saving on a Valuable Education plan—which will cut undergraduate loan payments in half and prevent student loan balances from growing due to runaway interest. To alleviate the burden of student loan debt for hard-working public servants, the Administration has helped almost 750,000 people access Public Service Loan Forgiveness (PSLF). Prior to the Administration's fixes to PSLF, only about 7,000 borrowers had received forgiveness. The President has also signed legislation increasing the maximum Pell Grant by $900 since the beginning of the Administration—the largest increase in nearly 10 years—making college more affordable.

Lowering Housing Costs

The President and Vice President understand that housing affordability remains a challenge for too many families. However, we are making progress: homeownership is higher now than it was before the COVID-19 pandemic, including for African Americans and Hispanic Americans; rental costs have moderated in the last year; and a record number of apartments are under construction—which should ease the burden of housing costs going forward. With the Housing Supply Action Plan, the Administration is making progress toward reducing the growth of housing costs by increasing supply, including through reducing barriers to housing and offering new and improved financing for affordable housing development. In 2023, the Administration lowered Federal Housing Administration annual mortgage insurance premiums by about one-third, saving more than 400,000 Americans—including many first-time homebuyers—approximately $800 over the first year of the mortgage with continued savings in subsequent years. To lower rental costs for those who need it most, the Administration has secured rental assistance for over 100,000 additional low-income households for the Housing Choice Voucher program, guaranteeing rents at 30 percent of those families' incomes.

Taking on Junk Fees

Junk fees are hidden, surprise fees that companies sneak onto customer bills, costing American families tens of billions of dollars each year and stifling competition across the economy. The President has taken junk fees head on by directing his Administration to use every available tool to address them and lower costs for the American people—including by cracking down on hidden junk fees in airline tickets, banking, investment advice, health insurance, and apartment rentals. The Administration has pushed banks to reduce overdraft and bounced check fees, saving consumers more than $5 billion a year compared to pre-COVID-19 pandemic. The Federal Trade Commission has proposed rules to ban companies from charging hidden and misleading fees and require them to show the full price up front, and to require sellers to make it as easy for consumers to cancel their enrollment as it was to sign up—rescuing consumers from difficulties cancelling unwanted subscriptions like gym memberships. The Consumer Financial Protection Bureau has proposed a rule that would lower credit card late fees from approximately $30 to $8, saving consumers up to $9 billion annually. To help stop conduct like price fixing or price gouging in grocery stores, the Department of Agriculture has announced a new partnership with bipartisan State attorneys general. In addition, the Department of Housing and Urban Development has called on industry, housing providers, and State and local governments to adopt policies that promote greater fairness and transparency of fees faced by renters.

Taking on Unfair Wage Practices to Put Money Back in Americans' Pockets

The Biden-Harris Administration has recovered more than $770 million for more than 485,000 workers across the Nation by enforcing laws that protect these workers from being victims of wage theft and exploitation, including when they were not paid minimum wages or hard-earned overtime wages, were denied their tips, or were misclassified as independent contractors. The Administration has proposed a new rule to extend overtime pay for up to an additional 3.6 million workers by raising the income threshold, meaning workers like fast-food managers or executive assistants could get their well-deserved overtime pay. In addition, the Vice President announced the publication of a final rule that will raise wage standards of construction workers by updating prevailing wage regulations, affecting more than one million workers constructing $200 billion in federally funded or assisted projects.

Delivering on a Commitment to Fiscal Responsibility

The deficit is over $1 trillion lower than when President Biden took office, thanks in large part to a strong economic recovery facilitated by investments that have expanded the Nation's productive capacity and a historic vaccination program that allowed the responsible wind-down of emergency measures. In addition, the President has also enacted another roughly $1 trillion in savings over the next decade through the Fiscal Responsibility Act of 2023, and through the Inflation Reduction Act provisions that empower Medicare to negotiate lower prescription drug prices, cap insulin at $35 per month for seniors, and make the wealthy and large corporations pay more of their fair share. To address the unfairness of 55 of the most profitable U.S. corporations paying zero dollars in Federal income taxes, the President signed into law a 15-percent minimum tax on the profits of the largest corporations—those with over $1 billion in profits. He also signed into law a surcharge on corporate stock buybacks, which encourages businesses to invest in their growth and productivity as opposed to funneling tax-preferred profits to wealthy shareholders. The Inflation Reduction Act also enacted long-overdue investments in rebuilding and modernizing the Internal Revenue Service (IRS), which raise revenue by making wealthy taxpayers and big corporations pay the taxes they owe—while improving customer service and without increasing audit rates relative to historical levels for small businesses and taxpayers making under $400,000 per year. The Budget would build on this progress by increasing the corporate minimum tax rate to 21 percent, quadrupling the surcharge on stock buybacks, extending the IRS investment, and other important reforms, resulting in about $3 trillion of deficit reduction even after financing the Budget's investments.

INVESTING IN AMERICA AND THE AMERICAN PEOPLE

As the President takes action to lower costs and grow the economy from the middle out and bottom up, he is also investing in America and the American people—expanding access to healthcare and improving women's health, building the next generation of American infrastructure, empowering American workers and families, advancing equity across the Nation, delivering on the most ambitious climate agenda in history, and ensuring the dignity of honoring America's sacred obligation to its veterans.

Expanding Access to Healthcare

The President believes healthcare is a right, not a privilege. The Administration continues to build on and strengthen the Affordable Care Act—and Americans are enrolled in record numbers. A record-breaking 21.3 million Americans signed up for healthcare coverage through the Affordable Care Act Marketplaces for 2024, an increase of more than nine million people since the President took office. In addition, over one million people in the four States that have adopted the Affordable Care Act's Medicaid expansion under the President's watch have gained Medicaid coverage, many for the first time. The Vice President has also continued her leadership on addressing the maternal health crisis and its disparate impacts, particularly on Black women. Since taking office, over 40 States have answered her call to extend Medicaid postpartum coverage from two months to 12—expanding access to this essential care for mothers across the Nation.

Investing in Women's Health Research

Despite making up more than half the population, women have historically been understudied and underrepresented in health research. This lack of investment limits the understanding of conditions that are specific to women, predominantly affect women, or affect women differently. In order to give women and their healthcare providers the tools and information that they need to more effectively prevent, diagnose, and treat these conditions, the President and First Lady launched the first-ever White House Initiative on Women's Health Research—which will galvanize the Federal Government and the private and philanthropic sectors to spur innovation, unleash transformative investment to close research gaps, and improve women's health.

Defending and Protecting Reproductive Rights and Healthcare

Twenty-seven million women of reproductive age—more than one in three—live in one of the 21 States with an abortion ban currently in effect. In the last year, women have been denied medical care needed to preserve their health and save their lives. In the wake of the Supreme Court's decision to overturn nearly 50 years of precedent in Roe v. Wade, the President has signed Executive Orders to: protect access to abortion, including medication abortion; strengthen access to contraception; help ensure women receive the medical care they need in an emergency; and support women's ability to travel across State lines to access care. The Administration has also strengthened privacy protections for patients and doctors, and defended in court women's ability to access medication abortion and emergency medical care required under Federal law. The Administration continues to call on the Congress to pass legislation restoring the protections of Roe v. Wade in Federal law.

Ensuring Robust Access to Mental Healthcare

The President believes mental health is health, particularly given the unprecedented mental health crisis impacting people of all ages that was exacerbated by the COVID-19 pandemic. As part of the Administration's Unity Agenda, President Biden released a comprehensive national strategy to transform how mental health is understood, accessed, treated, and integrated in and out of healthcare settings. The Administration has made historic investments in mental healthcare, including nearly $1 billion to support the 988 Suicide and Crisis Lifeline. The Administration is also committed to investing in training more mental health professionals, and is expanding

Certified Community Behavioral Health Clinics nationwide. In addition, the Administration has taken action to improve and strengthen mental health parity requirements for mental health and substance use care, and ensure that more than 150 million Americans with private health insurance can better access mental health benefits under their insurance plan. The Biden-Harris Administration is also implementing the Bipartisan Safer Communities Act—the single largest investment to support student mental health in history, which will help hire and train over 14,000 school-based mental health professionals across the Nation. In addition, the Administration eliminated the first three copays for mental health outpatient visits for veterans using their Department of Veteran Affairs (VA) benefits.

Delivering Critical Resources to Address the Overdose Epidemic

A key pillar of the President's Unity Agenda, the Administration has taken action to counter the overdose epidemic and save Americans' lives. The Administration has made this issue a top priority, and taken historic actions over the past three years to address substance use, enhance public health, strengthen public safety, and save lives. With the President's leadership, the Administration has provided historic funding to States, localities, and Tribes for overdose prevention efforts like access to naloxone and treatment for opioid-use disorder. In addition, the Administration requested $1.6 billion in supplemental funding for 2024 in the Department of Health and Human Services (HHS) to expand substance use prevention, treatment, harm reduction, and recovery support services to address the overdose crisis.

Building the Next Generation of American Infrastructure and Igniting an Economic Resurgence

The President signed the Bipartisan Infrastructure Law, the largest infrastructure bill since the Eisenhower Administration, and has already announced $400 billion for 40,000 infrastructure projects across 4,500 communities throughout every State in the Nation. This includes over $250 billion to improve transportation all across the Nation—from better roads and bridges, to improved airports, to more reliable public transit and rail service. The Bipartisan Infrastructure Law is investing in rural communities alongside urban ones—it invests in affordable, reliable high-speed internet infrastructure, clean drinking water, and reliable electricity.

The President's Inflation Reduction Act has unleashed a manufacturing and clean energy boom—spurring over $600 billion in private sector investments since taking office, including more than $160 billion announced investments in battery and EV supply chains. Clean energy projects that have moved forward since the President signed the historic law are already on track to create more than 210,000 new clean energy jobs across the Nation, and are projected to create more than 1.5 million additional jobs over the next decade, according to estimates by outside groups. In addition, the President signed the bipartisan CHIPS and Science Act, which is creating good jobs and driving American competitiveness in the industries of the future. As part of the implementation of the CHIPS and Science Act, the Department of Commerce announced 31 Tech Hubs that will help communities across the Nation become centers of innovation critical to American competitiveness.

Supporting Workers and Building Pathways to Good Jobs

President Biden is the most pro-worker President in history—and he is committed to building an economy from the middle out and bottom up. Together, he and Vice President Harris have committed to ensuring high labor standards, bringing workers' voices to the decision-making table, and enforcing rules against unfair labor practices—not just here at home, but around the world. Upholding common standards and protecting fundamental rights are key for American

workers and American companies to compete fairly in the global economy. The White House Task Force on Worker Organizing and Empowerment, led by Vice President Harris, has championed the Administration's commitment to worker rights, including the right to a free and fair choice to join a union and to dignity in the workplace. As the President says, "unions built the middle class," and as we rebuild America, they can help rebuild the middle class in the process.

To expand access to the good jobs created by the President's historic legislation, the Administration has invested in pathways to jobs in growing sectors, supporting both critical workforce programs at community colleges and career pathways programs in the K-12 system through the first-ever Career-Connected High Schools grants. The First Lady announced the first five Workforce Hubs in cities with significant public- and private-sector investments and a new initiative to expand pathways to careers in advanced manufacturing, resulting in the launch of new Registered Apprenticeships, community college, and high school programs and partnerships to provide opportunities for more Americans to pursue careers in the industries that will continue to fuel the economy.

Rebuilding Supply Chains

When the President took office, supply chains were severely disrupted as a result of the COVID-19 pandemic. The Administration made supply chain resilience and response a top priority on day one, collaborating with industry and labor to address acute shortages and bottlenecks throughout the economy—and securing critical supply chain investments through the President's Bipartisan Infrastructure Law, Inflation Reduction Act, and bipartisan CHIPS and Science Act. As a result, critical supply chains are significantly more fluid and resilient than they were when the President took office. In addition, the President recently announced a new White House Council on Supply Chain Resilience, which will support the enduring resilience of America's critical supply chains.

Advancing Equity across the Nation

The President signed two Executive Orders on advancing racial equity and support for underserved communities, providing a powerful and unprecedented mandate for all Federal agencies to launch a whole-of-Government approach to equity. Over the past three years, agencies have taken historic steps toward ensuring that Federal programs are supporting communities that have been locked out of opportunity. The Administration's whole-of-Government work on equity has included key steps to decrease the racial wealth gap, including by expanding Federal contracting opportunities for small disadvantaged businesses and taking sweeping action to address racial bias in home valuations to ensure that every American who buys a home has the same opportunities to build generational wealth through homeownership. In addition, the Administration has tackled gender and racial pay gaps, including through salary history bans and pay transparency measures for Federal workers and contractors. The Administration has also deployed record investments to tribal nations and Native communities, including through the historic American Rescue Plan Act of 2021 (American Rescue Plan) and Bipartisan Infrastructure Law. The enactment of advance appropriations for the Indian Health Service for the first time in history will help ensure more stable, predictable funding and improved access to high quality healthcare. The President also continues to expand the reach of Rural Partners Network, which provides a targeted across-Government approach to accessing training, technical assistance, and programs to distressed rural communities, and creates a clear point-of-entry for rural leaders to utilize all Federal agencies' assistance for rural areas.

In Executive Order 14041, "White House Initiative on Advancing Educational Equity, Excellence, and Economic Opportunity through Historically Black Colleges and Universities (HBCUs)," President Biden charged the initiative to "develop new and expand pre-existing national networks of individuals, organizations, and communities to share and implement administrative and programmatic best practices related to advancing educational equity, excellence, and opportunity at HBCUs." HBCUs are central to the Administration's vision of a more inclusive, equitable, and valuable higher education system. Under the President and Vice President's leadership, the Administration has secured tens of billions of dollars in funding for HBCUs and Minority-Serving Institutions to prepare students to contribute to the future in high-demand and high-income fields, like cybersecurity, engineering, biochemistry, and healthcare. The Administration also re-established the White House Initiative on Advancing Educational Equity, Excellence, and Economic Opportunity for HBCUs to increase their participation in Federal programs that offer greater access to funding, ensuring HBCUs can continue to be engines of opportunity in the future.

Supporting K-12 Education

To deliver on the promise of education for all Americans, the Administration secured the largest investment in public education in history to help students get back to school and recover academically from the COVID-19 pandemic, focusing on evidence-based strategies such as addressing chronic absenteeism and increasing student access to tutoring and summer, afterschool, and extended learning programs. The President's leadership has garnered substantial increases for Federal student support programs to meet the needs of historically underserved students. The Administration has provided record funding to Title I schools and made significant investments in the Nation's teachers. These investments are helping States in their efforts to address teacher shortages, which fall hardest on underserved students. Since the President took office, the Nation has added 73,000 public school teachers.

Increasing High-Quality Care and Supporting Caregivers

High-quality early care and long-term care are critical to the Nation's economic growth and economic security. Early care and education give young children a strong start in life, while long-term care helps older Americans and people with disabilities live, work, and participate in their communities with dignity. Unfortunately, too many families and individuals struggle to access the affordable, high-quality care they need. In recognition of this need, the Administration invested over $60 billion from the American Rescue Plan in the care economy, including $24 billion to help child care providers keep their doors open and to provide child care workers with higher pay, bonuses, and other benefits. To date, these efforts have helped over 225,000 child care programs serving as many as 10 million children across the Nation.

The President's Council of Economic Advisers also found that these investments saved families with young children who rely on paid child care approximately $1,250 per child per year by: slowing the rise of child care prices; increasing the real wages of child care workers by 10 percent; and boosting maternal labor-force participation by up to three percent, bringing hundreds of thousands of mothers into the workforce. The President also worked with the Congress to secure an additional $2.1 billion in annual Child Care and Development Block Grant program funding since 2021, a 36-percent increase, to help low-income working families access the child care they need.

The Administration continues to call on the Congress to make significant new investments to give families in this Nation more breathing room when it comes to care. In April 2023, the President signed an Executive Order with the most comprehensive set of executive actions any president has ever taken to improve care for hard-working families while supporting care workers and family caregivers. Executive Order 14095, "Increasing Access to High-Quality Care and Supporting Caregivers" charged agencies with working within their existing authorities to: lower the cost of care for families; boost the supply of high-quality early care and education and long-term care; provide more options for individuals and families increase access to affordable care for families; and improve job quality and support for care workers and caregivers. Agencies have made substantial

progress in implementing this Executive Order. VA launched a pilot program to provide mental health services to roughly 2,300 family caregivers who care for the Nation's heroes.

HHS has proposed major rulemaking to lower costs for families receiving Federal child care assistance and increase the pay for Head Start teachers. In addition, the Administration has also proposed actions to crack down on nursing homes that put seniors at risk, proposing minimum staffing requirements that would ensure every facility has enough nurses to provide necessary care, and expanded payments to clinicians who train caregivers for seniors and people with disabilities.

Honoring Our Sacred Obligation to Ensure the Dignity of America's Veterans, Military Service Members, and Their Families

President Biden believes we have a sacred obligation to care for the Nation's veterans, their families, caregivers, and survivors. Since taking office, the President has signed into law over 30 bipartisan bills that address some of the most important issues facing veterans today, including the Honoring our PACT Act of 2022 (PACT Act), which is the most significant expansion of benefits and services for veterans exposed to toxic substances in more than 30 years. The bipartisan PACT Act delivers better healthcare and benefits to veterans exposed to toxic burn pits during their military service. In addition, the President has called to end veterans' homelessness—and this year alone, the Administration permanently housed over 46,000 veterans, which far exceeded its goal of permanently housing 38,000 veterans. The Administration and the Congress have worked together to expand access to healthcare, improve access to child and long-term care, and support education and workforce opportunity for veterans and their families. In addition, the Administration also continues to deliver on veterans' services—in 2023 alone, VA delivered $163 billion in earned benefits to 6.3 million veterans and survivors.

Meeting the economic, social, and emotional needs of America's military and veteran families as well as military and veteran caregivers and surviving family members is also a national security imperative. As part of her Joining Forces initiative to support military and veteran spouses, military caregivers, and survivors, the First Lady has championed meaningful policy solutions to improve military spouse employment and entrepreneurship, military children's education, and military family mental health and wellbeing. President Biden signed the most comprehensive set of executive actions by any President to advance military family economic security and make the Federal Government the employer of choice for the military-connected community. The Administration: established Dependent Care Flexible Spending Accounts for service members; funded universal pre-school for military children living overseas; expanded child care options for military families; increased the amount of child care fee assistance available to offset costs; and reduced military child development center costs for lower income military families by 30 percent.

Delivering on the Most Ambitious Climate Agenda in History

Since day one, President Biden has delivered on the most ambitious climate, conservation, and environmental justice agenda in history—taking bold action to reduce climate pollution across every sector of the economy, protecting more than 26 million acres of lands and waters, and restoring the vital role of science in guiding Federal decision-making. The President signed the largest investment in climate action ever with the Inflation Reduction Act—resulting in 210,000 new clean energy jobs created by clean energy projects that have moved forward in the year and a half since the passage of the law, according to estimates by outside groups. The President has also taken bold executive action to cut emissions across the economy, including strong final standards to reduce methane pollution from oil and gas operations. As a result of the President's leadership and economic plan, clean energy jobs are on the rise across the Nation, companies have announced hundreds of billions of dollars in clean energy investments, and the United States is on a path toward cutting carbon pollution in half from 2005 levels by 2030 and net zero by 2050. While tackling the climate crisis, the President is using the Justice40 Initiative to embed environmental justice into clean energy and climate programs, ensuring that communities that are on the frontlines benefit from this historic investment in confronting climate pollution. In addition, in September 2023, the Administration announced the launch of the American Climate Corps initiative to mobilize a new, diverse generation of clean energy, conservation, and resilience workers to tackle the climate crisis in communities around the Nation.

KEEPING AMERICANS SAFE AND PROTECTING DEMOCRACY AT HOME AND ABROAD

Since the President took office, he has protected democracy across the globe and restored U.S. leadership on the world stage. In the wake of Putin's brutal invasion and illegal war against Ukraine, he has rallied the world to support Ukraine's defense and stand up against dictatorship. The President continues to secure critical support for Ukraine in the face of continued Russian aggression while also enhancing the collective capabilities and readiness of the United States, our allies, and partners. The President has strengthened alliances across the globe, including winning congressional support to add Finland and Sweden to the North Atlantic Treaty Organization Alliance.

After Hamas's horrific terrorist attacks against Israel, the President has led the United States to support Israel's right to defend its country and protect its people in a way that upholds international humanitarian law, while ensuring the Palestinian people have access to vital humanitarian aid and lifesaving assistance. The President continues to press for congressional support to provide the necessary security assistance to Israel and to extend humanitarian assistance to civilians impacted by conflict in the region, while working toward a future where Palestinians have a state of their own and Israel's security is assured.

Under the President's leadership, the Administration continues to focus on the Nation's strategic competition with the People's Republic of China —and promoting American competitiveness worldwide. The President has advocated for congressional support to invest in the American defense industrial base to ensure military readiness and strengthen integrated deterrence for the growing security requirements in the Indo-Pacific. The President has also increased U.S. foreign assistance to the region in support of a more free, open, secure, and connected Indo-Pacific, while also expanding America's diplomatic presence.

At the same time, the President remains laser-focused on keeping Americans safe at home. The President took on the gun lobby and signed the Bipartisan Safer Communities Act into law, the first significant gun violence legislation in nearly 30 years, which includes background checks for buyers under 21, expanded mental health programs, and support for implementation of red flag laws that keep guns away from dangerous people. The President created the first-ever White House Office of Gun Violence Prevention in American history, overseen by the Vice President, and has announced nearly 40 executive actions to keep guns out of dangerous hands. The Administration has also delivered the most funding ever for the bipartisan Violence Against Women Act Reauthorization Act of 2022 to combat gender-based violence and strengthened this landmark law, in addition to issuing the Nation's first-ever U.S. National Action Plan to End Gender-Based Violence.

To continue to protect and secure the border, the Department of Homeland Security (DHS) has taken action to process noncitizens at record scale and efficiency. On May 12, 2023, DHS returned to processing all noncitizens under Title 8 immigration authorities. Each day since then, DHS has maximized the use of expedited removal, placing more than 900 individuals into the process each day on average, and conducting more than 100,000 credible fear interviews, both of which are record highs. As a result, DHS has removed or returned more than 565,000 noncitizens who did not have a lawful basis to remain in the United States, the vast majority of whom crossed the Southwest land border, since May 12, 2023. Total removals and returns since mid-May of 2023 exceed removals and returns in every full year since 2013. The majority of all individuals encountered at the Southwest land border over the past three years have been removed, returned, or expelled.

The President and Vice President continue to take action to combat hate which undermines democracy, including by releasing the first-ever national strategy to counter Antisemitism, announcing the development of a national strategy to counter Islamophobia and related forms of bias and discrimination, signing legislation to enhance State and local law enforcement's ability to respond to hate crimes, and signing legislation to make lynching a Federal crime. The President and Vice President have continued to speak out against discrimination, racism, sexism, anti-LGBTQI+ hate, and more—so that all Americans can live freely and without fear of attack or harassment. To strengthen the right to vote, a key pillar of our democracy, the President and Vice President have continued pushing for stronger voting rights to make sure every American can make their voice heard.

INVESTING IN AMERICA AND THE AMERICAN PEOPLE

From the first days of the Administration, the President has moved swiftly to deliver results for the American people. While challenges remain, America has made historic progress as we continue to grow the economy from the middle out and bottom up and ensure America can compete to win in the global economy. Since President Biden took office, the economy has added about 15 million jobs—while core inflation fell to two percent over the last six months of 2023. The actions taken by the Administration have supported that progress—and set the stage for a more prosperous, healthier, and safer future.

Under the President's leadership, the Administration has focused on investing in America and the American people, including by signing into law historic legislation such as the American Rescue Plan, the Bipartisan Infrastructure Law, the CHIPS and Science Act, and the Inflation Reduction Act. These investments—by supporting a manufacturing boom, revitalizing American infrastructure, expanding high-quality education and healthcare, and investing in communities too often left behind—have helped to reverse decades of chronic underfunding of vital priorities all while supporting the Nation's greatest resource: the American people. Importantly, their gains are only beginning to be felt. Over the coming years, the consequences of these investments—and the new jobs, innovation, and benefits they will bring—will continue to spread throughout American communities with the ongoing implementation of the landmark legislation the President has signed into law. At the same time, they set the stage for continued progress under the President's leadership to lower costs, create new good-paying jobs, keep families safe and healthy, and bolster the Nation's leadership on the world stage.

The Budget protects and builds on this progress with proposals for responsible, pro-growth investments in America and the American people. The Budget includes proposals that lower costs for the American people, expand access to high-quality healthcare, support America's workforce, confront the climate crisis, expand opportunity, and protect America at home and abroad. The Budget upholds the President's commitment to protecting Medicare and Social Security for this and future generations. The Budget builds on the President's record to date while achieving meaningful deficit reduction through measures that reduce wasteful spending and ask the wealthy and large corporations to pay their fair share.

LOWERING COSTS FOR THE AMERICAN PEOPLE

The President's top economic priority is lowering costs for American families. Thanks to the Inflation Reduction Act, the United States is lowering costs for prescription drugs, healthcare, and energy for tens of millions of Americans, in a fiscally responsible way. The Administration's actions to eliminate junk fees and promote greater competition across the American economy are playing a key role in lowering costs. The Budget builds on this critical work to lower costs and give families more breathing room.

Accelerates Negotiations of Lower Drug Prices and Expands Access to Prescription Drugs. Thanks to action taken by the Administration, millions of seniors are saving money on their drug costs, and the Administration announced the first 10 drugs for which prices will be negotiated as it continues implementation of the Inflation Reduction Act. The Budget builds on this success by significantly increasing the pace of negotiation, bringing more drugs into negotiation sooner after they launch, expanding inflation rebates and $2,000 out-of-pocket prescription drug cost cap beyond Medicare and into the commercial market, and other steps to build on the Inflation Reduction Act drug provisions. In addition, the Budget extends the $35 cost-sharing cap for a month's supply of a covered insulin product to the commercial market. For Medicaid, the Budget includes proposals to ensure Medicaid and the Children's Health Insurance Program (CHIP) are prudent purchasers of prescription drugs, such as authorizing the Department of Health and Human Services (HHS) to negotiate supplemental drug rebates on behalf of interested States in order to pool purchasing power. The Budget also limits Medicare Part D cost-sharing for high-value generic drugs, such as those used to treat hypertension and hyperlipidemia, to no more than $2 per month for Medicare beneficiaries. To speed up development and increase access to safe and affordable biosimilar medicines, the Budget streamlines and modernizes the Food and Drug Administration's (FDA) premarket review. The Budget also includes funding for continued implementation of the No Surprises Act, which protects Americans across the Nation from surprise medical bills.

Lowers Child Care Costs. From the beginning of this Administration, the President and Vice President have been focused on child care costs as a critical challenge for families. When child care is reliable, high-quality, and affordable, parents can make ends meet, advance in their careers, and stay in the workforce—while

children benefit from opportunities to socialize with peers. The President is committed to providing relief to families, and the Budget creates a historic new program under which working families with incomes up to $200,000 per year would be guaranteed affordable, high-quality child care from birth until kindergarten, with most families paying no more than $10 a day, and the lowest income families paying nothing. This would provide a lifeline to the parents of more than 16 million children, saving the average family over $600 per month in care costs, per child, and giving parents the freedom to select a high-quality child care setting. This investment could help hundreds of thousands of women with young children enter or re-enter the workforce more quickly. The President's Council of Economic Advisers found that recent Federal investments in child care have increased labor force participation among mothers with young children by roughly three percentage points, equivalent to over 300,000 more women in the labor force. The President's proposal would also ensure that early care and education workers receive fair and competitive pay. In addition, the Budget provides $8.5 billion for the Child Care and Development Block Grant, a 44-percent increase since the first year of the Administration, which would continue to serve school-age children, while most children under age six would be served through the new program. The Budget also expands a tax credit to encourage businesses to provide child care benefits to their employees.

Reduces the Cost of Education Pathways that Connect to Growing Jobs. Ensuring all Americans benefit from the jobs created by the Investing in America agenda is critical to growing the economy from the middle out and the bottom up. High college prices deter many young people from attending the colleges that would be best for them. The Budget includes a $12 billion mandatory Reducing the Costs of College Fund that would fund three strategies to lower college costs for students. First, the fund would provide competitive awards for public institutions that affordably deliver a quality education, allowing those schools to use those funds either to serve more students or to share best practices so that other schools can become more affordable. Second, the Classroom to Career fund would also provide over $7 billion for States to provide access to at least 12 credits of transferable career-connected dual enrollment credits to students while in high school—credits that can enable students to obtain postsecondary degrees more affordably. Third, the fund would support evidence-based strategies, such as the City University of New York's Accelerated Study in Associated Programs Associate Program model, which increase college graduation rates, reduce cost burdens for students, and lower costs per graduate.

Increases Affordable Housing Supply to Reduce Housing Costs. The President believes that all Americans should be able to afford a quality home. The Budget builds on previous investments and actions by this Administration to boost housing supply and lower housing costs, particularly for lower- and middle-income households. The Budget invests $1.3 billion in the HOME Investment Partnerships Program (HOME) to construct and rehabilitate affordable rental housing and provide homeownership opportunities. To further address the critical shortage of affordable housing in communities throughout the Nation, the Budget provides $20 billion in mandatory funding for a new Innovation Fund for Housing Expansion, which would be a competitive grant program for municipalities and other entities that develop concrete plans for expanding housing supply, with additional funding for housing affordability pilots. The Budget also provides $7.5 billion in mandatory funding for new Project-Based Rental Assistance contracts to incentivize the development of new climate-resilient affordable housing. The Budget expands the existing Low-Income Housing Tax Credit and proposes a new Neighborhood Homes Tax Credit. Together these proposals would expand the supply of safe and affordable housing, bring new units to market, and ultimately help curb cost growth across the broader rental market.

Expands Access to Homeownership and Reduces Down Payments for First-Time and First-Generation Homebuyers. The Budget proposes a new Mortgage Relief Credit to help increase access to affordable housing. The proposal includes a new tax credit for middle-class first-time homebuyers of up to $10,000 over two years to ease affordability challenges. In addition, to unlock starter home inventory for first-time homebuyers and help middle-class families who are "locked in" to their current homes due to lower mortgage rates at the time of purchase, this proposal also includes a credit of up to $10,000 for one year to middle-class families who sell their starter home—a home at or below the area median home price—to another owner-occupant. The Budget also provides $10 billion in mandatory funding for a new First-Generation Down Payment Assistance program to help address homeownership and wealth gaps. In addition, the Budget preserves the Administration's progress in expanding access to homeownership for underserved borrowers, including many first-time and minority homebuyers, through Federal Housing Administration (FHA) and Ginnie Mae credit guarantees. In 2023, first-time homebuyers accounted for over 80 percent of FHA-insured home purchase loans. The Budget also includes up to $50 million for a HOME down payment assistance pilot program that would reduce mortgage down payments for first-generation as well as low wealth first-time homebuyers.

Expands Access to Affordable Rent through the Housing Choice Voucher (HCV) Program. The HCV program currently provides 2.3 million low-income families with rental assistance to obtain housing in the private market, but many families who are eligible do not receive assistance due to limited funding. The Budget proposes $32.8 billion in discretionary funding, an increase of $2.5 billion over the 2023 level, and assumes Public Housing Agencies will draw $963 million from HCV program reserves to maintain and protect critical services for all currently assisted families. The Budget also reflects the Administration's continued commitment to expand assistance, supporting an additional 20,000 households, particularly those who are experiencing homelessness or fleeing, or attempting to flee, domestic violence or other forms of gender-based violence. To further ensure that more households have access to safe and affordable housing, the

Budget includes mandatory funding to support two populations that are particularly vulnerable to homelessness—youth aging out of foster care and extremely low-income (ELI) veterans. The Budget provides $9 billion to establish a housing voucher program for all 20,000 youth aging out of foster care annually, and provides $13 billion to incrementally expand rental assistance for 400,000 ELI veteran families, paving a path to guaranteed assistance for all who have served the Nation and are in need. Since the beginning of this Administration, Department of Housing and Urban Development (HUD) has expanded voucher assistance to over 100,000 additional families, and the Budget continues this progress by expanding voucher access to hundreds of thousands of families.

Reduces Home Heating and Water Costs. The Budget provides $4.1 billion for the Low Income Home Energy Assistance Program (LIHEAP). Reducing household energy and water costs continues to be a priority for the Administration, as reflected in the $7 billion in additional funding the Administration has secured for LIHEAP since 2021. LIHEAP helps families access home energy and weatherization assistance—vital tools for protecting vulnerable families' health in response to extreme weather and climate change. In addition, since the Low Income Household Water Assistance Program expired at the end of 2023, the Budget proposes to allow States the option to use a portion of their LIHEAP funds to provide water bill assistance to low-income households.

Lowers Energy Costs and Catalyzes Clean Energy and Economic Growth in Rural Communities. The Budget builds on the $13 billion provided in the President's historic Inflation Reduction Act for rural development programs at the Department of Agriculture (USDA) to reduce energy bills for families, expand clean energy, transform rural power production, and create thousands of good-paying jobs for people across rural America. Rural communities are critical to achieving the goal of 100 percent clean electricity by 2035. The Budget provides $1 billion for loan guarantees for renewable energy systems and energy efficiency improvements for farmers and rural small businesses, and $6.5 billion in authority for rural electric loans to support additional clean energy, energy storage, and transmission projects that would create good-paying jobs. In addition, the Budget includes $53 million in zero-interest loans for the Rural Energy Savings Program, which would help rural Americans implement durable cost-effective energy efficiency measures in their homes, which lowers energy costs and contributes to the President's clean energy goals. The Budget also provides $10 million in Rural Community Facilities Grants specifically for rural communities making an energy transition away from outdated energy sources, facilitating emerging infrastructure needs.

Connects More Americans to Affordable, High-Speed, and Reliable Internet. The President is committed to ensuring that every American has access to affordable broadband internet. Thanks to the Bipartisan Infrastructure Law: the Affordable Connectivity Program has provided high-speed Internet service to over 23 million eligible low income households at low or no cost; the Department of Commerce (Commerce) has allocated nearly $42 billion in Broadband Equity, Access, and Deployment program funding to all 50 States, the District of Columbia, and five Territories to deploy reliable high-speed Internet service; and USDA has provided $2.3 billion to people living and working across 35 States and Territories, which is expected to expand broadband access to more than 137,000 households. Installing high-speed internet creates high-paying union jobs and strengthens local economies, which leads to increased job and population growth, lower unemployment rates, and new business formation. Reliable internet is also crucial for Americans to access healthcare services through telehealth. Building on the $2 billion for USDA broadband programs provided in the Bipartisan Infrastructure Law for 2023, the Budget provides $112 million for the ReConnect program, which provides grants and loans to deploy broadband to unserved areas, especially tribal areas. Building on the demonstrated successes enabled by the $14 billion provided in the Bipartisan Infrastructure Law, the

Budget includes the Administration's pending supplemental request for $6 billion to continue the Affordable Connectivity Program in 2024 and the Administration will work with the Congress to secure additional funding for this important need in 2025 and beyond.

Eliminates the Origination Fee on Student Loans. The Budget builds on the President's historic actions to reduce student debt and the cost of college by eliminating the origination fees charged to borrowers on every new Federal student loan. These unnecessary fees burden anyone who needs to borrow to help get an education and cost American families billions of dollars.

Bolsters Antitrust Enforcement. The Budget proposes $288 million for the Antitrust Division of the Department of Justice (DOJ), an increase of $63 million over the 2023 enacted level and $103 million over the 2021 enacted level, to strengthen antitrust enforcement efforts to promote vigorous marketplace competition and reduce costs and raise wages for the American people.

STRENGTHENING AMERICANS' RETIREMENT SECURITY BY HONORING THE PROMISE OF MEDICARE AND SOCIAL SECURITY

Prior to the creation of Social Security nearly 90 years ago, almost half of all American seniors lived in poverty—including some seniors who had worked their entire lives. Before Medicare was signed into law almost 60 years ago, many seniors' basic needs went unmet without healthcare to count on. Social Security and Medicare are more than Government programs, they are a promise—a rock-solid guarantee that generations of Americans have counted on—that after a life of hard work, you will be able to retire with dignity and security. As the President has made clear, he will reject any efforts to cut or undermine the Medicare or Social Security benefits that seniors and people with disabilities have earned and paid into their entire working lives. The Budget honors that ironclad commitment by firmly opposing benefit cuts to either program and by embracing reforms that would protect and strengthen these programs. The President remains committed to working with the Congress to protect Medicare and Social Security for this and future generations.

Strengthens Medicare by Requiring High-Income Americans to Contribute Their Fair Share and Reducing Prescription Drug Costs. The Budget extends solvency of the Medicare Hospital Insurance (HI) trust fund indefinitely by modestly increasing the Medicare tax rate on incomes above $400,000, closing loopholes in existing Medicare taxes, and directing revenue from the Net Investment Income Tax into the HI trust fund as was originally intended. Current law allows certain wealthy business owners avoid Medicare taxes on some of the profits they get from passthrough businesses. The Budget closes the loophole that allows certain business owners to avoid paying Medicare taxes on these profits and raises Medicare tax rates on earned and unearned income from 3.8 percent to 5 percent for those with incomes over $400,000. In addition, the Budget directs an amount equivalent to the savings from the proposed Medicare drug reforms into the HI trust fund.

Protects the Social Security Benefits that Americans Have Earned. The Administration is committed to protecting and strengthening Social Security. In particular, the Administration looks forward to working with the Congress to responsibly strengthen Social Security based on the following principles:

- No benefit cuts. The President opposes policies that cut benefits, as well as proposals to privatize Social Security.

- Extending solvency by asking the highest-income Americans to pay their fair share.

The President believes that protecting Social Security should start with asking the highest-income Americans to pay their fair share.

- Improving financial security for seniors and people with disabilities. The President supports efforts to improve Social Security benefits, as well as Supplemental Security Income benefits, for seniors and people with disabilities, especially for those who face the greatest challenges making ends meet.

- Ensuring that Americans can access the benefits they have earned. The President supports investments in Social Security Administration (SSA) services so that seniors and people with disabilities can access the benefits they have earned.

Consistent with the final principle, the Budget invests in staff, information technology (IT), and other improvements at SSA, providing an increase of $1.3 billion, a nine-percent increase from the 2023 enacted level. These funds would improve customer service at SSA's field offices, State disability determination services, and tele-service centers for retirees, individuals with disabilities, and their families. The Budget also adds staff to process more disability claims and reduce the amount of time claimants have to wait for decisions on vital benefits.

Protects Seniors' Health and Dignity. The Budget invests $150 billion over 10 years to strengthen and expand Medicaid home and community-based services, allowing elderly and individuals with disabilities to remain in their homes and stay active in their communities, and improving the quality of jobs for home care workers. The Budget also increases funding for senior nutrition services to ensure seniors continue to receive healthy meals by eight percent above the 2023 level, and 21 percent over the 2021 level. In addition, the Budget proposes to shift funding for nursing home surveys from discretionary to mandatory beginning in 2026, and increase funding to cover 100 percent of statutorily-mandated surveys, which would guard against negligent care and ensure that Americans receive high-quality, safe services within these facilities. The Budget also continues to build on the President's commitment to protect the Nation's seniors through a comprehensive agenda that: improves the safety and quality of nursing home care; addresses the backlog of complaint surveys from nursing home residents; expands financial penalties for under-performing facilities; requires greater transparency of nursing facility ownership; and increases the inspection of facilities with serious safety deficiencies.

PROTECTING AND EXPANDING ACCESS TO HIGH-QUALITY HEALTHCARE AND CREATING HEALTHIER COMMUNITIES

The Administration has achieved monumental gains in its commitment to protect and expand Americans' access to quality, affordable healthcare. Since taking office, the President has: delivered the resources necessary to end the COVID-19 emergency; built on the success of the Affordable Care Act to further close the uninsured gap; reduced Americans' healthcare premiums and prescription drug costs; finally allowed Medicare to negotiate for lower prescription drug prices; acted to protect millions of consumers from surprise medical bills and junk fees; made progress on bold new goals as part of the Biden Cancer Moonshot; and created new efforts dedicated to preventing, detecting, and treating devastating diseases like cancer and Alzheimer's disease. The Administration recognizes that by investing in the health and well-being of the American people, healthier, safer, and more productive communities can be created. The Budget protects the progress this Administration has made while proposing additional investments to address the challenges that remain, including further expanding access to high-quality healthcare, responding to mental health needs, and strengthening America's public health infrastructure.

Putting High-Quality Healthcare Within Reach

Expands Access to Quality, Affordable Healthcare. The President and the Vice President believe that healthcare is a right, not a privilege. With enrollment in marketplace coverage at an all-time high, the Budget builds on the incredible success of the Affordable Care Act by making permanent the expanded premium tax credits that the Inflation Reduction Act extended and providing Medicaid-like coverage to individuals in States that have not adopted Medicaid expansion, paired with financial incentives to ensure States maintain their existing expansions. For Medicaid and CHIP, the Budget allows States to extend the existing 12-month continuous eligibility for all children to 36 months, and allows States to provide continuous eligibility for children from birth until they turn age six. Further, the Budget prohibits enrollment fees and premiums in CHIP. The President also supports eliminating Medicaid funding caps for Puerto Rico and other Territories while aligning their matching rate with States—and moving toward parity for other critical Federal programs including Supplemental Security Income and the Supplemental Nutrition Assistance Program.

Supports Family Planning Services for More Americans. Americans deserve access to the healthcare they need, including contraception and family planning services, which are essential to ensuring control over personal decisions about their own health, lives, and families. For more than 50 years, Title X family planning clinics have played a critical role in ensuring access to a broad range of high-quality family planning and preventive health services. Most Title X clients live in poverty and the uninsured rate of Title X users is twice the national average, making the Title X family planning program a critical part of the public health safety net. The Budget includes $390 million, a 36-percent increase above the 2023 enacted level, for the Title X Family Planning program to increase the number of patients served to 3.6 million.

Promotes Maternal Health and Health Equity. The United States has the highest maternal mortality rate among developed nations, and rates are disproportionately high for Black, American Indian, Alaska Native, and rural women. Since 2021, funding to reduce maternal mortality has grown by over $190 million, demonstrating the Administration's commitment to addressing needs in this area. The Budget continues this progress by including $376 million, an increase of $82 million above the 2023 enacted level to support the ongoing implementation of the *White House Blueprint for Addressing the Maternal Health Crisis*, launched by the Vice President, to reduce maternal mortality and morbidity rates, and address the highest rates of perinatal health disparities. The Budget expands Medicaid maternal health support services during the pregnancy and post-partum period by incentivizing States to reimburse a broad range of providers including doulas, community health workers, peer support initiatives, and nurse home visiting programs. In addition, the Budget builds on the success of the more than 40 States that answered the Vice President's call to extend Medicaid postpartum coverage for 12 months, eliminating gaps in health insurance at a critical time for all women.

Saving Lives by Advancing Behavioral Healthcare

Strengthens Mental Health Parity Protections. The Budget requires all health plans to cover mental health and substance use disorder benefits, ensures that plans have an adequate network of behavioral health providers, and improves the Department of Labor's (DOL) ability to enforce the law. In addition, the Budget includes $275 million over 10 years to increase the Department's capacity to ensure that large group market health plans and issuers comply with mental health and substance use disorder requirements, and to take action against plans and issuers that do not comply.

Expands Coverage and Invests in Behavioral Healthcare Services. In 2022, almost a quarter of adults suffered from mental illness, 13 percent of adolescents had serious thoughts of suicide, and overdose deaths continued near record highs. As a core pillar of his Unity Agenda, the President released a national strategy to transform how to understand and address mental health in America—and the Budget makes progress on this agenda by improving access to care for individuals and communities. The Budget makes significant investments in expanding the 988 Suicide and Crisis Lifeline that is projected to respond to 7.5 million contacts from individuals in distress in 2025 alone. The Budget: expands mental healthcare and support services in schools; expands the Centers for Disease Control and Prevention's (CDC) suicide prevention program to additional States, as well as tribal and territorial jurisdictions; and invests in strengthening the behavioral health workforce—including integration of behavioral health services into primary care settings. The Budget also expands access to behavioral health services through significant investments in Certified Community Behavioral Health Clinics and Community Mental Health Centers. In addition, the Budget provides $1 billion to advance Health IT adoption and engagement in interoperability for certain behavioral health providers. The Administration is also implementing the Bipartisan Safer Communities Act—the single largest investment to support student mental health in history, which would help hire and train over 14,000 school-based mental health professionals across the Nation.

Expands Access to Treatment for Substance Use Disorder. The Administration has made historic advances in expanding access to treatment for opioid use disorder, including signing into law a bipartisan provision to expand the number of medical providers who can initiate buprenorphine treatment for opioid use disorder from 129,000 to nearly two million, a 15-fold increase that can expand treatment to rural and underserved areas. Funding for States, Territories, and Tribes through the Substance Use

Prevention, Treatment, and Recovery Services Block Grant and the State Opioid Response grant program has grown by a combined seven percent since 2021, expanding access to prevention, harm reduction, treatment, and recovery support services nationwide. The Budget builds on these accomplishments by increasing funding for the State Opioid Response grant program, which has provided treatment services to over 1.2 million people and enabled States to reverse more than 500,000 overdoses with over nine million purchased overdose reversal medication kits. The Budget also invests in a new technical assistance center to strengthen health providers' understanding and treatment of women's mental health and substance use.

Driving Healthcare Innovation and Discovering Future Treatments

Advances Progress toward Biden Cancer Moonshot Goals. The President and First Lady reignited the Biden Cancer Moonshot to mobilize a national effort to end cancer as we know it—spurring tremendous action across the Federal Government and from the public and private sectors, and building a strong foundation for the work ahead. To date, the Biden Cancer Moonshot has announced roughly 50 new programs, policies, and resources to address five priority actions including: improving access to cancer screening; understanding and addressing environmental and toxic exposures; making progress on cancer prevention; driving innovation to reach communities and individuals; and boosting support for patients, families, and caregivers. More than 100 private companies, non-profits, academic institutions, and patient groups have also stepped up with new actions and collaborations. The Budget makes significant investments to work toward the President and First Lady's signature Biden Cancer Moonshot goal of reducing the cancer death rate by at least 50 percent over the next 25 years and improving the experience of people who are living with or who have survived cancer. These investments include an increase of more than $2 billion across the National Cancer

Institute, FDA, CDC, cancer projects at the Advanced Research Projects Agency for Health, and additional mandatory funds for the Indian Health Service (IHS) beginning in 2026.

Enhances Biodefense and Public Health Infrastructure. Over the past three years, substantial progress has been made toward developing and implementing transformational capabilities to increase the Nation's ability to respond to and prepare for emerging health threats. Building upon this progress, the Budget invests $9.8 billion in both discretionary and mandatory Prevention and Public Health Fund funding, an increase of $499 million over the 2023 enacted level, to bolster public health capacity to enable CDC to better serve and protect the American public. These resources would continue to strengthen State, tribal, local, and territorial health departments, enhance public health data systems and collection, and improve the core immunization program. In addition, the Budget includes $20 billion in mandatory funding for HHS public health agencies in support of the Administration's biodefense priorities as outlined in the 2022 *National Biodefense Strategy and Implementation Plan for Countering Biological Threats, Enhancing Pandemic Preparedness, and Achieving Global Health Security*.

Invests in the Treatment and Prevention of Infectious Diseases. The Budget invests in the treatment and prevention of infectious diseases, including Hepatitis C, HIV, and vaccine-preventable diseases. The Budget proposes a national program to significantly expand screening, testing, treatment, prevention, and monitoring of Hepatitis C infections in the United States, with a specific focus on populations with high infection levels. To help end the HIV epidemic, the Budget eliminates barriers to accessing pre-exposure prophylaxis—also known as PrEP—for Medicaid beneficiaries and proposes a new mandatory program to guarantee PrEP at no cost for all uninsured and underinsured individuals and provide essential wrap-around services. The Budget also invests in State and local efforts to promote equity and protect civil rights through a new initiative to modernize outdated criminal statutes with a discriminatory impact on HIV-positive individuals. In addition, the Budget proposes a new Vaccines for Adults program to provide uninsured adults with access to routine and outbreak vaccines at no cost. The Budget also expands the Vaccines for Children (VFC) program to include all children under age 19 enrolled in CHIP and covers the vaccine administration fee for all VFC-eligible uninsured children.

SUPPORTING AMERICA'S WORKFORCE AND PREPARING AMERICA'S ECONOMY FOR 21ST CENTURY CHALLENGES

The President's economic strategy is rooted in what has always worked best for this Nation: investing in America and the American people. Since the President took office, the economy has added about 15 million new jobs—including nearly 800,000 manufacturing jobs—more Americans are working than at any point in American history, a record number of Americans have started small businesses, and America continues to outpace its global peers in the speed and breadth of our economic recovery from the COVID-19 pandemic. The President's plan is modernizing and rebuilding America's infrastructure, promoting a flexible and dynamic workforce, empowering workers and creating good jobs here at home, fueling healthy competition in the marketplace, and reinvigorating manufacturing and industry across the Nation. The Budget builds on this proven record of economic success with additional proposals to secure America's position as the strongest economy in the world by: continuing to invest in manufacturing and making more in America; ensuring workers and entrepreneurs have the skills and supports to thrive; and creating good-paying jobs in emerging fields.

Boosting American Manufacturing and Investing in Infrastructure

Continues Implementation of the President's Historic Bipartisan Infrastructure Law. The Budget provides a total of $78.4 billion for highway, highway safety, and transit formula programs, supporting the amounts authorized for year four of the Bipartisan Infrastructure Law. This includes $62.1 billion in obligation limitation funding for the Federal-aid Highways program, an increase of $3.3 billion above the 2023 enacted level and $15.7 billion above the enacted level for 2021, the year prior to enactment of the Bipartisan Infrastructure Law. This funding would support the continued repair and upgrading of the Nation's highways and bridges. The Budget also includes $14.3 billion for Transit Formula Grants, a $645 million increase above the 2023 enacted level, to support core capital and planning programs for transit agencies across the Nation, as well as transit research, technical assistance, and data collection. The Budget also reflects an additional $9.5 billion in advance appropriations provided by the Bipartisan Infrastructure Law for bridge replacement and rehabilitation, electric vehicle charging infrastructure, and other programs to improve the safety, sustainability, and resilience of America's transportation network.

Maintains World Leading Research through the CHIPS and Science Act Investments. The Budget invests $20 billion across major research agencies, an increase of $1.2 billion above the 2023 level, to boost American innovation and re-establish American leadership in research and scientific discovery. At the National Science Foundation (NSF), these investments include support for regional innovation programs, investments in emerging technologies—such as artificial intelligence (AI) and quantum information science—and science, technology, engineering, and mathematics (STEM) workforce programs. Funding for Commerce's National Institute for Standards and Technology would support activities responsive to the Administration's Executive Order 14110, "Safe, Secure and Trustworthy Development and Use of Artificial Intelligence" and fund construction and maintenance of research and development facilities. In the Department of Energy's (DOE) Office of Science, the Budget supports AI, high performance computing to improve climate modeling, clean energy technologies including fusion, and positions the United States to meet the demand for isotopes.

Prioritizes Investment in the Federal Aviation Administration (FAA). The Budget provides $17.5 billion in discretionary budget authority for FAA, an increase of $2.1 billion above the 2023 enacted level, less Congressionally Directed Spending. This funding supports robust hiring and training of air traffic controllers started in 2023, to rebuild the pipeline of new controllers needed to safely meet projected air traffic demands. The Budget also continues FAA's multiyear effort of reforming aircraft certification, as well as increasing its safety oversight capabilities. The Budget proposes a five-year, $8 billion mandatory program to significantly modernize FAA's major facilities and radars. This effort would ensure that the American people and all travelers can continue to depend on a safe, modern, and efficient aviation system. In addition, the Administration proposes to increase the fuel tax for high-end business jets, to better align the costs of the services provided to those users on the system.

Builds on Investments for a Safe and Efficient Passenger and Freight Rail Network. The Budget expands on the Bipartisan Infrastructure Law's already significant investments toward improving the safety and efficiency of the Nation's rail network. This includes $2.5 billion for grants to Amtrak, along with $250 million for the Consolidated Rail Infrastructure and Safety Improvements program, which is in addition to the $13.2 billion in rail funding directly provided by the Bipartisan Infrastructure Law. The Budget also increases funding for critical rail safety programs.

Supports the Administration's Goal of Replacing All Lead Pipes and Invests in Critical Water Infrastructure. To help protect families from the health hazards of lead pipes, the Budget provides a total of $101 million to two Environmental Protection Agency (EPA) grant programs dedicated to remediating lead contamination in drinking water—the Reducing Lead in Drinking Water grant program and the Voluntary School and Child Care Lead Testing and Reduction Grant Program—an increase of $53 million over the 2021 enacted level. This investment, along with other programs at EPA that can be used for lead projects, builds on the historic $15 billion in direct funding for lead pipe replacement through the Bipartisan Infrastructure Law and underscores the President's commitment to ensuring access to safe drinking water and creating good-paying jobs in the process. In addition, the Budget provides a total of $2.4 billion for EPA's State Revolving Funds for drinking water and wastewater infrastructure, an increase of more than $1 billion over the 2023 enacted level for those programs. The Budget also provides $350 million in HUD grants for States, local governments, and nonprofits to reduce lead-based paint and other health hazards, especially in the homes of low-income families with young children. The Budget targets $67 million at HUD specifically to prevent and mitigate lead-based paint and housing-related health hazards, such as fire safety and mold, in public housing, an increase of $2 million above 2023 levels.

Strengthens American Leadership in Space. The Budget includes $7.8 billion for the Artemis program, which would bring astronauts—including the first women, first people of color, and first international astronauts—to the lunar surface as part of a long-term journey of science and exploration. The Budget invests in new systems to assist lunar surface science and exploration activities, including a small lunar rover and a large cargo lander that would be used to deliver larger rovers and habitats to the surface in the 2030s.

Supporting Workers, Entrepreneurs, and Small Businesses

Cuts Taxes for Families with Children and American Workers. The Budget would expand key tax cuts benefitting lower- and middle-income workers and families. The Budget would restore the full Child Tax Credit enacted in the American Rescue Plan, which helped cut child poverty nearly in half in 2021 to its lowest level in history. The Budget would expand the credit from $2,000 per child to $3,000 per child for children six years old and above, and to $3,600 per child for children under six. In addition, the Budget would permanently reform the credit to make it fully refundable, so that it no longer excludes 18 million children in the lowest-income families from receiving the full credit, and allow families to receive monthly advance payments. The President also calls on the Congress to make permanent the Earned Income Tax Credit expansion for workers not raising children in their homes, which would boost the income of 19 million very low-paid workers.

Provides National, Comprehensive Paid Family and Medical Leave and Proposes Paid Sick Days. The vast majority of America's workers do not have access to employer-provided paid family leave, including 73 percent of private sector workers. Among the lowest-paid workers, who are disproportionately women and workers of color, 94 percent lack access to paid family leave through their employers. In addition, as many as one in five retirees leave the workforce earlier than planned to care for an ill family member, which negatively impacts families, as well as the Nation's labor supply and productivity. The Budget proposes to establish a national, comprehensive paid family and medical leave program administered by SSA to ensure that all eligible workers can take up to 12 weeks to bond with a new child, care for a seriously ill loved one, heal from their own serious illness, address circumstances arising from a loved one's military deployment, find safety from domestic violence, dating violence, sexual assault, or stalking—otherwise known as "safe leave"; or up to three days to grieve the death of a loved one. The program would provide workers with progressive, partial wage replacement to take time off for family and medical reasons; include robust administrative funding; and use an inclusive family definition. Further, the President continues to call on the

Congress to require employers to provide seven job-protected paid sick days each year to all workers, and ensure that employers cannot penalize workers for taking time off to address their health needs, or the health needs of their families, or for safe leave.

Empowers and Protects Workers. Workers power America's economic prosperity, building the economy from the middle out and bottom up. To ensure workers are treated with dignity and respect in the workplace, the Budget invests $2 billion in DOL's worker protection agencies. These investments would build upon the nearly $100 million increase in base appropriations for these agencies since the beginning of the Administration, in addition to the $200 million in American Rescue Plan funding the Administration secured for the agencies to address the unprecedented COVID-19 emergency. The Budget would enable DOL to protect workers' wages and benefits, ensure that children are working only in conditions that are safe and legal, address the misclassification of workers as independent contractors, and improve workplace health and safety. Since 2019, DOL has seen an 88-percent increase in children being employed illegally by companies. The Administration is focused on preventing and addressing child labor exploitation, and has assessed more than $16 million in child labor penalties. The Budget also includes additional funding to combat exploitative child labor, including among migrant children, who are particularly vulnerable. For the Equal Employment Opportunity Commission, the Budget supports implementation and enforcement of the Pregnant Workers Fairness Act, and advancement of pay equity through the collection and analysis of employer pay data. The Budget also supports the Agency's work to ensure that employers' use of automated employment systems, including those that incorporate AI, does not result in discrimination against employees or job applicants in any of a wide range of job-related activities, including recruitment, selection, retention, pay, or promotion. The Budget also includes funding to strengthen the National Labor Relations Board's capacity to enforce workers' right to organize and collectively bargain for better wages and working conditions. The Budget proposes instituting and significantly increasing penalties for employers that violate workplace safety and health, wage and hour, child labor, equal opportunity, and labor organizing rules. The Budget also includes funding to implement the significant reforms to employer-sponsored retirement plans enacted in the SECURE 2.0 Act of 2022, helping to ensure that workers' retirement plans are always protected.

Broadens Access to Registered Apprenticeships. The Budget increases support for Registered Apprenticeships, an evidence-based earn-and-learn model that is a critical tool for training future workforces for good jobs in the clean energy, construction, semiconductor, transportation and logistics, education, health, and other growing and in-demand industries. The Budget invests $335 million, a $50 million increase above the 2023 enacted level, and supports expanding existing Registered Apprenticeship programs in clean energy-related occupations. This investment would also be used to increase the number of workers from historically underrepresented groups, including people of color, women, and people with disabilities, who participate in Registered Apprenticeships.

Expands Access to Capital for Small Businesses. Building on the historic growth in small business applications under the President and Vice President's leadership, the Budget supports historic lending levels across the Small Business Administration's (SBA) business lending programs, including: the 7(a) business loan guarantee; capital for major fixed assets, otherwise known as a 504 loan guarantee; the Small Business Investment Company (SBIC) program; and Microloan programs. The over $58 billion in lending provided in the Budget would address the need for greater access to affordable capital, particularly in underserved communities. The Budget proposes a new direct 7(a) lending program, which would further enable SBA to address gaps in access to small dollar lending. In addition, increasing the authorized lending level for the SBIC program by 16 percent to $7 billion would significantly expand the availability of venture capital funding for small businesses.

CONFRONTING THE CLIMATE CRISIS WHILE SPURRING CLEAN ENERGY INNOVATION, INCREASING RESILIENCE, AND PROTECTING NATURAL RESOURCES

Since taking office, the President has delivered on the most ambitious climate, clean energy, conservation, and environmental justice agenda in history by: signing into law the largest investment in climate action ever; protecting more than 26 million acres of lands and water; mobilizing and training the next generation of workers for good-paying jobs in clean energy, conservation and resilience; and advancing the Justice40 Initiative, which directs 40 percent of the overall benefits from key Federal investments to disadvantaged communities. This includes the Administration's work to continue implementation of the Inflation Reduction Act and the Bipartisan Infrastructure Law—the largest investments that any country has made in clean energy, energy security, clean air and water, and combatting climate change in history. The Budget protects and builds on this monumental progress, making pro-growth investments in clean energy across the Nation, cutting energy bills for families, creating good-paying jobs, and safeguarding and modernizing American communities and infrastructure.

Reducing Greenhouse Gas (GHG) Emissions, Advancing Clean Energy, and Investing in Climate Science and Innovation

Reduces GHG Emissions and Tackles the Climate Crisis. The Budget builds on the historic climate investments made in the Inflation Reduction Act and Bipartisan Infrastructure Law, and includes over $2.8 billion in EPA climate-related programs to address the climate crisis by: reducing GHG emissions; expanding upon the GHG Reporting Program and Sinks inventory; implementing provisions in the American Innovation and Manufacturing Act of 2020 to continue phasing out the production and import of hydrofluorocarbons; advancing equitable implementation of EPA authorities and directives in Indian Country; and engaging with the global community to respond to the shared challenge of

building resilience in the face of climate impacts. The Budget includes $10.6 billion in DOE climate and clean energy research, development, demonstration, and deployment programs. This funding advances efforts crucial for achieving the goal of a 50- to 52-percent reduction from 2005 levels of economy-wide net GHG pollution in 2030 and economy-wide net-zero emissions no later than 2050, while also cutting energy bills for American families and building U.S. leadership in the global clean energy economy.

Creates Jobs by Building Clean Energy Infrastructure. The Budget provides $1.6 billion for DOE, more than double above the 2021 enacted level and 29 percent above the 2023 enacted level, to support clean energy workforce and infrastructure projects across the Nation, including: $385 million to weatherize and retrofit homes of low-income Americans; $113 million to create good jobs and ensure reliable supply chains by manufacturing clean energy components here at home; $95 million to electrify tribal homes and transition tribal colleges and universities to renewable energy; and $102 million to support utilities and State and local governments in building a grid that is more secure, reliable, resilient, and able to integrate electricity from clean energy sources. These investments, which complement and bolster the historic funding in the Bipartisan Infrastructure Law and Inflation Reduction Act, create good-paying jobs while driving progress toward the Administration's climate goals, including carbon pollution-free electricity by 2035.

Continues to Advance Clean Energy Development on Public Lands. The Budget includes $142 million, an increase of $31 million above the 2023 enacted level, to continue the Administration's progress in deploying clean energy on public lands and waters, spurring economic development and creating thousands of good-paying jobs. The Budget supports the leasing, planning, and permitting of solar, wind, and geothermal energy projects, and associated transmission infrastructure that would help mitigate the impacts of climate change and support the Administration's goal of deploying 30 gigawatts of offshore wind capacity by 2030 and 25 gigawatts of clean energy capacity on public lands by 2025.

Strengthens and Accelerates Permitting Activities. The Budget supports environmental permitting capacity to ensure the effective and efficient delivery of modernized infrastructure across the Nation while promoting positive environmental and community outcomes. The Budget includes over $1 billion to support environmental review and permitting processes that are effective, efficient, and transparent, guided by the best available science and shaped by early and meaningful public engagement and input. For example, the Budget continues to propose expanding existing transfer authority by enabling Federal agencies to transfer funds provided under the Bipartisan Infrastructure Law to the U.S. Fish and Wildlife Service and National Oceanic and Atmospheric Administration (NOAA) Fisheries to expedite the Endangered Species Act of 1973 consultations.

Builds the Clean Energy Innovation Pipeline. The Budget includes $10.7 billion across DOE, the National Aeronautics and Space Administration (NASA), NSF, Department of Defense (DOD), and other agencies to support researchers and entrepreneurs transforming innovations into commercial clean energy products, including in areas such as: offshore wind; industrial heat; sustainable aviation fuel; and grid infrastructure. Across DOE, the Budget provides over $325 million to support the research, development, and demonstration of technologies and processes to increase the domestic supply of sustainable critical minerals and materials essential for several clean energy technologies. The Budget provides more than $500 million for green aviation at NASA; over $500 million for clean energy research at NSF; and $845 million for DOE Department-wide efforts to accelerate the viability of commercial fusion energy, coordinating academia, national laboratories, and the private sector, which supports the Bold Decadal Vision

for Commercial Fusion Energy. The Budget also funds eight crosscutting DOE Energy Earthshots initiatives which could substantially reduce the cost of energy for the American consumer through innovations in clean energy generation, energy efficiency, and storage. In addition to the amounts above, the Budget includes the Administration's pending supplemental request for $2.2 billion to acquire low-enriched uranium (LEU) and high-assay low-enriched uranium (HALEU), which coupled with a long-term ban on imports of LEU and HALEU from Russia, would prompt sufficient private sector investment to reinvigorate U.S. uranium enrichment and reduce America's current dependence on Russian enriched uranium imports. The Budget also includes the pending supplemental request for $300 million to safeguard the Strategic Petroleum Reserve, which is a critical energy security asset that has historically protected American consumers in times of emergency oil shortages.

Advances Climate Science. The Budget includes $4.5 billion for climate research across NASA, NOAA, NSF, and other agencies. This includes $150 million at NASA to develop the next-generation land-imaging mission, otherwise known as Landsat Next, and more than $600 million for NASA in research grants to enhance understanding of Earth systems, including climate and natural hazards. The Budget includes $900 million for NSF, an increase of $236 million above the 2023 enacted level. This investment supports a broad portfolio of research that includes: atmospheric composition; water and carbon cycles; climate resilience technologies including for communities heavily affected by climate change; and social, behavioral, and economic research on human responses to climate change, among other topics. The Budget also includes $275 million at the Department of the Interior (DOI) to continue to leverage science to better understand the impacts of climate change, and to inform and improve land management practices from the Federal to the local level. The Budget invests $407 million at DOE to support fundamental research, including modeling and scientific user facilities to enable enhanced predictability of dynamically changing climate, environmental, and Earth systems, which includes predictability of climate trends and extremes that influence the design and deployment of next generation energy systems.

Strengthening Resilience

Strengthens Climate Resilience in Communities and Ecosystems. Across America, communities are enduring historic and catastrophic flooding, wildfires, extreme heat, drought, and more, while longer-term changes in temperature affect ecosystems and the economies that depend on them. The intensifying impacts of climate change are costing lives, disrupting livelihoods, and causing billions of dollars in damages. The Budget provides $23 billion in climate adaptation and resilience across Commerce, DOI, the Department of Homeland Security (DHS), USDA, Army Corps of Engineers, EPA, and DOD to address the increasing severity of extreme weather events fueled by climate change. This includes resources for flood hazard mapping, including the development of new data to support future flood conditions so that communities and Americans have the most up-to-date information regarding their flood risk, and investments to mitigate the impacts of extreme heat in low-income and disadvantaged communities. The Budget also provides funding to assist farmers, ranchers, and forestland owners with production goals in the face of a changing climate while conserving, maintaining, and restoring natural resources on their lands. Overall, the Budget supports enhanced and coordinated provision of climate information and tools to support decision making across the Nation.

Invests in America's Brave Wildland Firefighters. The Budget builds on the Administration's historic investments in the wildland firefighting workforce at USDA and DOI by supporting the implementation of permanent and comprehensive pay reform, the enhancement of health services, the hiring of additional permanent and temporary wildland firefighters to increase capacity, and the improvement of Government housing. These investments, totaling $522 million over the comparable

2023 enacted funding levels, would help address long-standing recruitment and retention challenges, increase the Departments' capacity to complete critical risk mitigation work, and further the Administration's commitment to build a more robust and resilient wildland firefighting workforce as the frequency and intensity of catastrophic wildfires continue to increase due to climate change.

Increases Drought Resilience. The Budget helps ensure communities across the West have access to a resilient and reliable water supply by investing in rural water projects, water conservation, development of desalination technologies, and water recycling and reuse projects. The Budget complements the nearly $1.7 billion provided in 2025 for western water infrastructure through the Bipartisan Infrastructure Law, as well as the nearly $4.6 billion provided by the Inflation Reduction Act for drought mitigation and domestic water supply projects through the Bureau of Reclamation.

Reduces Housing Insecurity and Strengthens Climate Resiliency in Rural Communities. Adequate affordable housing has been a long-standing problem in rural communities—one that is exacerbated by low energy efficiency of the aging housing stock, meaning higher costs to families. To help address this, the Budget proposes additional funding for USDA multifamily and single-family housing, and again proposes to eliminate the existing low-income borrower penalty that requires individuals to repay subsidy costs for USDA Single-Family Direct loans—a requirement that only exists for rural housing. The Budget provides strong support for USDA's multifamily housing and housing preservation programs. Through these investments, the Administration advances equity in support of underserved communities by reducing rent burdens for low-income borrowers and preserving low-income tenant-based housing in rural America. The Budget again proposes to reduce operating costs and increase the resiliency of rural housing to the impacts of climate change through a proposal to require energy and water efficiency improvements and green features in USDA's rural housing programs that include construction, such as housing repair loans and grants.

Supports and Expands the American Climate Corps. Last year, the Administration announced the launch of the American Climate Corps (ACC) to mobilize a new, diverse generation of more than 20,000 clean energy, conservation, and climate resilience workers, and this year, the first cohort of ACC members will begin their service. The ACC will provide job training and service opportunities on a wide range of projects that tackle climate change in communities around the Nation. AmeriCorps is supporting this new initiative by standing up an ACC hub to provide centralized coordination across seven agencies—AmeriCorps, USDA, DOI, Commerce, DOE, DOL, and EPA—who are charged with implementing the ACC. The Budget provides $15 million to support and expand AmeriCorps' ACC hub and $23 million to support over 1,700 additional ACC members, as well as $8 billion in mandatory funding to support an additional 50,000 ACC members annually by 2031. This builds on additional investments to support climate-related workforce development and service initiatives across all seven ACC agencies.

Delivering for Communities Often Left Behind. The Administration continues to take bold steps and prioritize efforts to deliver environmental justice in communities across the United States, including implementing the President's Justice40 Initiative and keeping up the momentum of the historic Bipartisan Infrastructure Law and Inflation Reduction Act environmental justice investments. The Budget bolsters these efforts by supporting several key initiatives to accelerate energy equity and justice for historically excluded communities to benefit all Americans, and by investing nearly $1.5 billion across EPA in support of environmental justice efforts, including investments that would support cleaner air and cleaner water in frontline communities. This includes a new $25 million grant to develop Direct Implementation Tribal Cooperative Agreements to carry out crucial EPA programs in Indian Country with an emphasis on addressing the impacts of climate change.

Reduces Health and Environmental Hazards for At-Risk Communities. The Budget provides $8.2 billion to address legacy waste and contamination in communities used during the Manhattan Project and the Cold War for nuclear weapons production, as well as other key investments in programs that reduce environmental hazards like EPA's Superfund program, Brownfields program, and Toxic Substances Control Act enforcement. The Administration would ensure the investments for the management of toxic chemicals, including per-and polyfluoroalkyl substances, cleanup of legacy pollution, and long-term stewardship of these sites align with the Justice40 Initiative to benefit disadvantaged communities.

Invests in Clean Air. The Budget provides a total of $1.5 billion for EPA's Office of Air and Radiation, an increase of $690 million since the beginning of the Administration, to continue the development of national programs, policies, and regulations that control air pollution and radiation exposure. This funding includes a historic $187 million for the Atmospheric Protection Program to support implementation and compliance with GHG emission standards and to tackle the climate crisis at home and abroad. Also included is $100 million for the Diesel Emissions Reduction Act grant program, which funds grants and rebates to reduce harmful emissions from diesel engines, and $70 million for the Targeted Airshed Grants program, which helps reduce air pollution in the most polluted nonattainment areas. The Administration continues to support investment in EPA's work of limiting emissions of harmful air pollutants and tackling the climate crisis.

Doubling Down on America's Global Climate Leadership

Achieves the Administration's Historic Climate Finance Pledge. The Budget provides a path to achieving the President's $11 billion commitment for international climate finance, including $3 billion for the *President's Emergency Plan for Adaptation and Resilience (PREPARE)*.

A signature initiative, PREPARE supports more than half a billion people in developing countries to adapt to and manage the impacts of climate change. The Budget also supports a $500 million 2025 contribution through mandatory funding to finance the Green Climate Fund, as part of the $3 billion multiyear pledge to expand climate adaptation and mitigation projects in developing countries, and $100 million for the Amazon Fund to combat deforestation and preserve the world's largest tropical rainforest. The Budget builds on historic international climate finance progress made over the course of the Administration, in which estimated 2023 levels of $9.5 billion represent a near-six-fold increase from 2021.

EXPANDING OPPORTUNITY, ADVANCING EQUITY, AND DELIVERING FOR COMMUNITIES NATIONWIDE

Since taking office, the President has fought to create opportunity and advance equity—not as a one-year project, but as part of a sustained commitment to make the promise of America real for every American, including rural communities, communities of color, women and girls, tribal communities, Lesbian, Gay, Bisexual, Transgender, Queer, and Intersex individuals, people with disabilities, and communities impacted by persistent poverty. Since day one, the Administration has made significant progress advancing equity across the Federal Government, including by reinvigorating Federal civil rights enforcements, prioritizing the advancement of gender equity and equality, expanding access to opportunities in underserved communities, increasing food security, advancing efforts to end homelessness, improving children's education, upholding the United States' promise to tribal communities, and honoring the Nation's commitment to America's veterans and servicemembers. The Budget builds on that progress by making historic investments to support the advancement of all Americans—especially in underserved communities—and combat racial and gender disparities across the Nation, including in health, education, and economic opportunity.

Investing in American Families

Supports a Strong Nutrition Safety Net. The Budget provides $8.5 billion for critical nutrition programs, including $7.7 billion to fully fund participation in the Special Supplemental Nutrition Program for Women, Infants, and Children (WIC), which is critical to the health of pregnant women, new mothers, infants, and young children. This program helps low-income families put nutritious food on the table and addresses racial disparities in maternal and child health outcomes. In the *Biden-Harris Administration National Strategy on Hunger, Nutrition, and Health*, the Administration set goals to help more individuals experiencing food insecurity access Federal nutrition assistance programs. By investing in outreach and modernization, WIC would reach 800,000 more women, infants, and children each month, providing vital nutrition assistance to nearly seven million individuals, up from 6.2 million in 2021. The Budget supports enhanced benefits for fruits and vegetables to improve nutritional outcomes and reduce food insecurity among children consistent with the recommendations by the National Academies of Science, Engineering, and Medicine. In addition, the Budget includes an emergency contingency fund that would provide additional resources, beyond the $7.7 billion, when there are unanticipated cost pressures. The Budget also includes $15 billion over 10 years to allow more States and schools to leverage participation in the Community Eligibility Provision to provide healthy school meals at no cost to an additional nine million children.

Advances Efforts to End Homelessness. The Budget provides $4.1 billion, an increase of $427 million over the 2023 level, for Homeless Assistance Grants to continue supporting approximately 1.2 million people experiencing homelessness each year and to expand assistance to approximately 25,000 additional households, specifically survivors of domestic violence and homeless youth. In addition, the Administration plans to use approximately $100 million in program recaptures to fund coordinated interventions to support nearly 11,000 additional homeless individuals and families. These new resources support the Administration's commitment to the goals laid out in the *All In: Federal Strategic Plan to Prevent and End Homelessness* and build on efforts that have expanded assistance to roughly 140,000 additional households experiencing homelessness since the President took office. The Budget also provides $505 million, or $6 million above the 2023 level, for Housing Opportunities for Persons with AIDS, serving a population with a disproportionately high rate of homelessness and providing a critical link to services. The Budget further reflects the Administration's commitment to make progress toward ending homelessness by providing $8 billion in mandatory funding for the acquisition, construction, or operation of housing to expand housing options for people experiencing or at-risk of homelessness, as well as $3 billion in mandatory funding for grants to provide counseling and emergency rental assistance to older adult renters at-risk of homelessness.

Expanding Access to Quality Education and Supporting Students

Builds a Strong Foundation for Families with Universal Pre-K and Head Start. The Budget funds voluntary, universal, free preschool for all four million of the Nation's four-year-olds and charts a path to expand preschool to three-year-olds. High-quality preschool would be offered in the setting of the parent's choice—from public schools to child care providers to Head Start. In addition, the Budget increases Head Start funding by $544 million to support the Administration's goal to reach pay parity between Head Start staff and public elementary school teachers with similar qualifications over time. Together these proposals would support healthy child development, help children enter kindergarten ready to learn, and support families by reducing their costs prior to school entry and allowing parents to work.

Addresses Critical Educator Shortages. While the education sector has faced shortages in critical staffing areas for decades, these shortages have grown worse since the COVID-19 pandemic, highlighting the importance of retaining educators and building strong, diverse pipelines into the profession. Since 2021, the Administration has supported schools in addressing educator shortages, including by supporting the expansion of evidence-based pathways such as residencies and grow your own programs, which may be provided through teacher registered apprenticeships. The Budget includes $90 million for Supporting Effective Education Development, $95 million for the Teacher Quality Partnership program, and doubles funding to $30 million for the Hawkins Centers of Excellence program, to expand the number of prospective teachers who have access to comprehensive, high-quality pathways and improve the diversity of the teacher pipeline. The Budget also includes critical investments in recruitment and retention of teachers and school leaders, and provides $173 million for the Teacher and School Leader Incentive Fund.

Increases Support for Children with Disabilities. To support high-quality special education services for over seven million Pre-K through 12 students with disabilities, the Budget provides $14.4 billion for Individuals with Disabilities Education Act (IDEA) State Grants, a $200 million increase over the 2023 enacted level. Since 2021, the Administration has secured a $1.3 billion, or 10-percent increase in annual funding for the program as well as an additional $2.6 billion in American Rescue Plan funds to help students with disabilities recover from the COVID-19 pandemic. The Budget also invests $545 million in IDEA Grants for Infants and Families to provide early intervention services to infants and toddlers with disabilities. To address nationwide special educator shortages, the Budget also invests $125 million, which is $10 million above the 2023 enacted level, in grants to prepare special education and early intervention personnel—addressing another critical educator shortage area.

Supports Students in Schools with High Rates of Poverty. The disruptive effects of the COVID-19 pandemic on student learning and well-being have added new urgency to the work of schools. The Budget includes $8 billion in mandatory funding to provide Academic Acceleration and Achievement Grants to high-need school districts to help close opportunity and achievement gaps and speed the pace of learning recovery. These grants would support evidence-based strategies to increase school attendance, provide high-quality tutoring and student supports, and expand learning time, including both in the summer and in extended day or afterschool programs. To help ensure that every student receives the high-quality education and support they deserve, the Budget also provides $18.6 billion for Title I, a $200 million increase above the 2023 enacted level. This funding amount is $2.1 billion higher than when the President took office, reflecting the President's strong commitment to expanding support for every American student. Title I, which reaches 90 percent of school districts across the Nation, delivers critical funding to public schools in low-income communities so they can provide their students with the learning opportunities needed to recover academically from the COVID-19 pandemic and be successful after graduation.

Improves College Affordability and Provides Free Community College. To help low-and middle-income students overcome financial barriers to postsecondary education, the Budget proposes to increase the discretionary maximum Pell Grant by $100 and thereby expand the reach of the program to over 7.2 million students. The Budget builds on successful bipartisan efforts to increase the maximum Pell Grant award by $900 over the past two years—the largest increase in more than 10 years. The Budget provides a path to double the maximum award by 2029 for students attending public and non-profit institutions. The Budget excludes for-profit institutions from the mandatory increases due to evidence these institutions are least likely to provide

good outcomes for students. The Budget also expands free community college across the Nation through a Federal-State partnership. In addition, the Budget provides two years of subsidized tuition for students from families earning less than $125,000 enrolled in a four-year Historically Black College and University (HBCU), Tribally Controlled College and University (TCCU), or Minority-Serving Institution (MSI).

Expands Institutional Capacity at HBCUs, TCCUs, MSIs—including HSIs—and Community Colleges. The Budget increases institutional capacity at HBCUs, TCCUs, MSIs—including HSIs—and under-resourced institutions, including community colleges, by providing an increase of $93 million above the 2023 enacted level. The Budget funding level is $329 million higher than the 2021 enacted level, underscoring the President's commitment to increasing funding to historically under-served institutions. The Budget also doubles funding by providing $100 million for four-year HBCUs, TCCUs, and MSIs to expand research and development infrastructure at these institutions, a program the President has championed since his first year in office to address historic disparities in Federal research and development funding to HBCUs, TCCUs, and MSIs.

Promotes Equity in STEM Education and Workforce Training. In support of the CHIPS and Science Act's priority of building a diverse, STEM-capable workforce, the Budget provides $1.4 billion for STEM education and workforce development programs at NSF that have an emphasis on diversity, equity, inclusion, and accessibility. The Budget also includes funding for programs focused on increasing the participation of groups historically underrepresented in science and engineering fields, including women and girls and people of color, by supporting: curriculum program design; research on successful recruitment and retention methods; development of outreach or mentorship programs; and fellowships. The Budget also includes $256 million in funding to build capacity for advancing energy research and developing a new energy workforce through programs at HBCUs, TCCUs, MSIs, tribal colleges, community colleges, and emerging research institutions. The Budget also provides $46 million to NASA's Minority University Research and Education Project, to increase competitive awards to MSIs to recruit and retain underrepresented and underserved students in STEM fields.

Bolsters Mental Health Supports for All Students. The mental health of students, teachers, and school staff is essential for their overall well-being and continued academic recovery, and continues to be a high priority of the Administration, which has delivered an additional $2.1 billion to mental health programs since 2021. Research shows that students who receive social, emotional, mental, and behavioral supports have better outcomes, including performing better academically. The Budget provides a combined total of $216 million for mental health programs, including $200 million from the Bipartisan Safer Communities Act, a 900-percent increase in program funding since 2021. These funds would help increase the number of school-based counselors, psychologists, social workers, and other mental health professionals in K-12 schools.

Honoring America's Commitments to America's Veterans and Servicemembers

Expands Healthcare, Benefits, and Services for Environmental Exposures. The Sergeant First Class Heath Robinson Honoring our Promise to Address Comprehensive Toxics Act of 2022 (PACT Act) represented the most significant expansion of Department of Veterans Affairs (VA) healthcare and disability compensation benefits for veterans exposed to burn pits and other environmental exposures in 30 years. As part of the PACT Act, the Congress authorized the Cost of War Toxic Exposures Fund (TEF) to fund increased costs above 2021 funding levels for healthcare and benefits delivery for veterans exposed to certain environmental hazards—and ensure there is sufficient funding available to cover these costs without shortchanging other elements of veteran medical care and benefits

delivery. The Budget continues this commitment and includes $24.5 billion for the TEF in 2025, through funds appropriated by the Fiscal Responsibility Act (FRA), which is $19.5 billion above the 2023 enacted level.

Strengthens VA Medical Care and Invests in Critical Veteran Medical Facilities. The Budget provides a total of $112.6 billion in discretionary medical care funding in 2025, equal to the 2025 advance appropriation request. In addition, the Budget, through funds appropriated by the FRA, includes $21.5 billion in TEF for medical care, bringing the medical care total to $134 billion in 2025, an $11.5 billion increase over the 2023 enacted level. In addition to fully funding inpatient, outpatient, mental health, and long-term care services, the Budget supports programs that enhance VA healthcare quality and delivery, including a $2 billion investment for non-recurring maintenance to improve medical facility infrastructure, and continued efforts to address the opioid and drug overdose epidemic. The Budget also includes $2.8 billion in budgetary resources for construction and expansion of critical infrastructure and facilities.

Prioritizes Mental Health Services, Suicide Prevention, and Sexual Assault Prevention for Military Servicemembers and Veterans. The Budget invests $135 million within VA research programs, together with $17.1 billion within the VA Medical Care program, to increase access to quality mental healthcare, with the goal of helping veterans take charge of their treatment and live full, meaningful lives. In addition, the Budget provides $583 million to further advance the Administration's veteran suicide prevention initiatives, including continued support of the Veterans Crisis Line's 988 and additional support for VA's National Suicide Prevention Strategy. The Budget also includes funding to support DOD's efforts on Suicide Prevention and Response and implements recommendations from the Suicide Prevention and Response Independent Review Committee. This funding would support improving the delivery of mental healthcare, addressing stigma and other barriers to care, revising suicide prevention training, and promoting a culture of lethal means safety within the military. The Budget also includes funding to support DOD's efforts on Sexual Assault Prevention designed to increase awareness, provide support mechanisms to victims, and significantly reduce the environment for, tolerance of, and occurrence of sexual assault in the Joint Force.

Supports Women Veterans' Healthcare. The Budget invests $13.7 billion for women veterans' healthcare, including $1.1 billion toward women's gender-specific care. More women are choosing VA healthcare than ever before, with women accounting for over 30 percent of the increase in enrolled veterans over the past five years. These investments support comprehensive specialty medical and surgical services for women veterans, improve maternal health outcomes, increase access to infertility counseling and assisted reproductive technology, and eliminate copayments for contraceptive coverage. The Budget also improves the safety of women veterans seeking healthcare at VA facilities by supporting implementation of the zero-tolerance policy for sexual harassment and assault.

Bolsters Efforts to End Veteran Homelessness. The President believes that every veteran should have permanent, safe, and sustainable housing with access to healthcare and other supportive services. The Budget invests $3.2 billion to end current veteran homelessness and prevent veterans from becoming homeless in the future. In addition to investments made in VA programs, the Budget for HUD provides $13 billion in mandatory funding to expand the HCV program to reach an additional 400,000 ELI veteran families, paving a path to guaranteed assistance for all who have served the Nation and are in need.

Invests in Overdose Prevention and Treatment Programs. The Budget invests $713 million toward opioid use disorder prevention and treatment programs for veterans, including using predictive analytics to stratify a patient's risk of overdose, provide augmented care as appropriate, and to support programs

authorized in the Jason Simcakoski PROMISE Act. In addition, investments contribute to distribution of naloxone to veterans, which, according to researchers with the VA Palo Alto Health Care System, has demonstrated success in effective utilization of the lifesaving opioid overdose reversal medication, and development of an opioid safety toolkit that provides clinicians materials that aid in decisions related to safe opioid prescribing and non-opioid pain management options.

Fulfills America's Commitment to Military Families. Military families are key to the readiness and well-being of the All-Volunteer Force, and therefore are critical to national security. The Budget continues to support military families by prioritizing programs, including the Secretary of Defense's Taking Care of People initiatives, that seek to increase access to behavioral health providers. The Budget also continues to support the establishment of universal pre-school for military children at DOD Education Activity schools, both stateside and overseas, to ensure no military child faces barriers to accessing early childhood education due to where their parents are stationed. The Budget provides critical funding for the VA Program of General Caregivers Support Services, as well as $2.9 billion for the Program of Comprehensive Assistance for Family Caregivers, which includes stipend payments and support services to help empower family caregivers of eligible veterans.

Supports Economic Security for Military Families. Military families, like their civilian counterparts, increasingly look to rely upon dual incomes. However, the 21-percent unemployment rate experienced by active-duty military spouses makes that a difficult goal to achieve and maintain. The President continues to prioritize efforts to make the Federal Government the employer of choice for military spouses. In addition, the Administration understands that access to high-quality, affordable child care is a necessity for working families, and a military readiness issue. The Budget continues to support increases to high-quality child care for military families via the Child Care Workforce Initiative. The Budget also proposes to increase the income eligibility threshold for the Basic Needs Allowance from 150 percent to 200 percent of the Federal Poverty Guidelines.

Delivering for Tribal Communities

Guarantees Adequate and Stable Funding for IHS. The Administration is committed to upholding the United States' responsibility to tribal nations by addressing the historical underfunding of IHS. The enactment of an advance appropriation for 2024 for IHS was a historic and welcome step toward the goal of securing adequate and stable funding for IHS that will provide needed improvements in access to care and the overall health status of American Indians and Alaska Natives. The Budget requests $8 billion in discretionary resources in 2025, including increases for clinical services, preventative health, facilities construction, contract support costs, and tribal leases. Beginning in 2026, the Budget proposes all resources as mandatory. Mandatory funding would close longstanding service and facility shortfalls over time, improve access to high-quality healthcare, and fund key Administration priorities such as the Biden Cancer Moonshot. The Budget also proposes to reauthorize and increase funding for the Special Diabetes Program for Indians, which has been critical in lowering the prevalence of diabetes in Indian Country.

Honors Commitments to Support Tribal Communities. Incorporating feedback from tribal consultations, the Budget continues to provide robust support for indigenous communities in keeping with U.S. Federal trust responsibilities while working to advance equity. The Budget includes $4.6 billion for DOI's tribal programs, $514 million above the 2023 enacted level and more than $1 billion over the 2021 enacted level, to support public safety and justice, human and social services, and education. The Budget continues to propose reclassification of Contract Support Costs and the Indian Self-Determination Act Section 105(l) leases as mandatory spending, beginning in 2026, to provide certainty for tribal communities in meeting these ongoing

requirements with dedicated funding. Budget resources across DOI's tribal programs build on historic investments in the American Rescue Plan and complement Inflation Reduction Act and Bipartisan Infrastructure Law investments to ensure long-term success in addressing critical infrastructure and climate adaptation needs in indigenous communities. The Budget supports the Administration's commitment to prioritize restoration of healthy and abundant wild salmon, steelhead, and other native fish populations in the Columbia River Basin, and honor the United States' obligations to tribal nations. This includes $145 million through the Corps of Engineers, a 123-percent, or $80 million increase above the 2023 enacted level, $19 million through the Bureau of Reclamation, and $34 million through NOAA to enhance restoration efforts in the watershed.

Invests in Affordable Housing in Tribal Communities. Native Americans are seven times more likely to live in overcrowded conditions and five times more likely to have inadequate plumbing, kitchen, or heating systems than all U.S. households. The Budget provides $1.1 billion, a $33 million increase above the 2023 level, at HUD to support tribal efforts to expand affordable housing, improve housing conditions and infrastructure, and increase economic opportunities for low-income families. Of this total, $150 million would prioritize activities that advance resilience and energy efficiency in housing-related projects.

Commits to Tribal Water Rights Settlements Funding. The Budget builds on Bipartisan Infrastructure Law investments by providing $2.8 billion in additional mandatory funding to the Indian Water Rights Settlement Completion Fund, as well as $226 million in discretionary funding to meet existing settlement obligations. This funding would ensure stable, dedicated funding for tribal water rights settlements, which is crucial for safe, reliable water supplies to improve public and environmental health and support economic opportunity in tribal communities.

PROTECTING AMERICA AT HOME AND ABROAD

From taking action to combat hate in America's communities, tackling gun violence, and strengthening trust in the Nation's democratic institutions, to defending freedom around the globe, and rebuilding key alliances, the Administration has taken decisive action to strengthen America at home and abroad, all with the goal of keeping Americans safe. The Budget builds on this progress with proposals to continue: investing in State, local, tribal, and Federal law enforcement; advancing much-needed reforms to the criminal justice system; reducing gun violence and crime; revitalizing U.S. alliances and partnerships, confronting global threats and strengthening America's military; securing the border and strengthening the U.S. immigration system; advancing U.S. national security to Out-Compete China and counter Russian aggression; and addressing pressing global challenges.

Tackling Crime, Reducing Gun Violence, and Making America's Communities Safer

Invests in Federal Law Enforcement to Combat Gun Violence and Other Violent Crime. The Budget makes significant investments to bolster Federal law enforcement capacity to strengthen public safety. The Budget includes $17.7 billion, an increase of $1.1 billion above the 2023 enacted level and $2.6 billion above the 2021 enacted level, for DOJ law enforcement, including $2 billion for the Bureau of Alcohol, Tobacco, Firearms and Explosives to: effectively investigate and prosecute gun crimes; expand multijurisdictional gun trafficking strike forces; increase regulation of the firearms industry; bolster crime-solving ballistics, gunshot residue, and other forensic technologies as well as analysts; and implement the Bipartisan Safer Communities Act. The Budget includes $1.9 billion for the U.S. Marshals Service (USMS) to support efforts to reduce violent crime, including through fugitive apprehension and enforcement operations. The Budget also provides $51 million to the Federal Bureau of Investigation

(FBI) to support the continued implementation of enhanced background checks, a key provision of the Bipartisan Safer Communities Act. In addition, the Budget provides a total of $2.8 billion for the U.S. Attorneys, which includes funding for 50 new attorneys to prosecute violent crimes. The Budget also requests $15 million for the Jabara-Heyer NO HATE Act, an increase of $5 million over the 2023 enacted level.

Pursues New Mandatory Investments to Combat Violent Crime and Support Victims. The Budget builds upon the Safer America Plan by investing an additional $1.2 billion over five years to launch a new Violent Crime Reduction and Prevention Fund to give Federal, State, local, tribal, and territorial law enforcement the dedicated, seasoned, and full support they need to focus on violent crime. This investment includes hiring new Federal law enforcement agents, prosecutors, and forensic specialists to address violent crime, expand Federal operations to combat fentanyl and apprehend dangerous fugitives, and support for the hiring of 4,700 detectives at the State and local level to solve homicides, non-fatal shootings, and other violent crimes to drive down the high rate of unsolved violent crimes and the lengthy delays that undermine public trust and public safety. In addition, $28 million is provided to expand the USMS's Operation North Star, which has taken more than 6,700 of the most dangerous State and local fugitives off the street since 2021, to 100 more cities over five years, including 20 more cities in 2025 in order to drive down violent crime. This investment also expands Drug Enforcement Administration (DEA) Operation Overdrive, which uses a data-driven, intelligence-led approach to identify and dismantle violent drug trafficking networks, to 50 more cities that are experiencing high rates of gun violence and fentanyl overdoses for 45-day operations. The Budget also requests $7.3 billion to replenish the Crime Victims Fund and ensure a stable and predictable source of funding is available to support critical victim service and compensation programs over the next decade.

Combats Narcotics Trafficking Networks.
The Budget provides $3.3 billion to the DEA to combat drug trafficking, including $1.2 billion to combat opioid trafficking, save lives, and make communities safer. The Budget invests an additional $18 million in Domestic Counter-Fentanyl Threat Targeting Teams at the Drug Enforcement Administration to enhance America's fight against the transnational criminal networks pushing deadly illicit fentanyl in America's communities. These interdisciplinary teams of special agents, intelligence analysts, and data experts would map criminal organizations and build cases that lead to the dismantling of entire drug trafficking networks and the deprivation of hundreds of millions of dollars to the Sinaloa and Jalisco cartels. In addition, the Budget provides $494 million in grants supporting efforts to address substance use, including $190 million for the Comprehensive Opioid, Stimulant, and Substance Use Program, $95 million to support Drug Courts, and $51 million for anti-drug task forces.

Disrupts the International Synthetic Drug Trade. The Budget includes $169 million across the Department of State and the U.S. Agency for International Development (USAID) to counter fentanyl and other synthetic drug production and trafficking, which is 58 percent above 2023 enacted levels. These resources would counter the worldwide flow of fentanyl and other synthetics that endanger public safety and health, and contribute to tens of thousands of drug-overdose deaths in the United States annually.

Supports State, Local, and Tribal Law Enforcement and Public Safety. The Budget provides $3.7 billion in discretionary resources for State and local grants and $30.3 billion in mandatory resources to support State, local, and tribal efforts to protect U.S. communities and promote public safety through the President's Safer America Plan. Through a combination of discretionary and mandatory investments, the Safer America Plan supports the President's goal to recruit, train, support, and hire 100,000 additional police officers for effective, accountable community policing consistent with the standards

of the Executive Order 14074, "Advancing Effective, Accountable Policing and Criminal Justice Practices To Enhance Public Trust and Public Safety." In addition, the Safer America Plan would: fund bonuses for retention of police officers; provide student loan repayment, tuition reimbursement, and higher education grant programs to incentivize service-minded candidates, including women and individuals from under-represented communities to become officers; support pilot programs to explore more flexibility in scheduling and work arrangements; expand mental health and wellness care for police officers; and fund life-saving equipment. The Safer America Plan would further support the evidence-based training of law enforcement on topics including crime control and deterrence tactics, community engagement, use of force, interacting with people with disabilities, and responding to persons in mental health crisis and to domestic violence calls. The Safer America Plan would also further efforts to advance transparency, accountability, and safety to simultaneously strengthen public safety and public trust consistent with the standards of Executive Order 14074 through funding to support the purchase and operation of body-worn cameras, modernize police academies and training, comprehensively reform public safety systems, and combat crime to keep the Nation's streets safe. The Budget, through the Safer America Plan, provides funding for courts around the Nation to clear their backlogs and improve accountability and deterrence for people on pretrial supervision, and supports technology and data systems modernization necessary to ensure that the justice system runs efficiently and with the most current data, such as: case management systems that effectively integrate pretrial services, judicial, and law enforcement records; virtual access and notification systems to facilitate remote check-ins and hearings as appropriate and beneficial for all involved; and scheduling software to manage the increased volume of cases. The Budget also provides funding to support pretrial and post-conviction supervision staffing and systems, ensuring that persons on release are appropriately monitored and given assistance with the employment, health, housing, and other supportive services that reduce the risk of recidivism. Specific discretionary investments include $270 million for the COPS Hiring Program, an increase of $45 million or 20 percent over the 2023 enacted level, and $100 million for Community Violence Intervention (CVI) programs, an increase of $50 million or 100 percent over the 2023 enacted level, to bolster evidence-based strategies for preventing and reducing gun violence in U.S. communities. To achieve the original goals of the Safer America Plan, the Budget requests an additional $1.5 billion in mandatory funding to support CVI programs at the Department over the next 10 years.

Prioritizes Efforts to End Gender-Based Violence. The Budget proposes $800 million to support programs under the Violence Against Women Act of 1994 (VAWA), which was reauthorized and strengthened in 2022. This is a $100 million or 14-percent increase over the 2023 enacted level, which was the highest funding level in history. The Budget supports significant increases for longstanding VAWA programs, including key investments in sexual assault services, transitional housing, and legal assistance for survivors. The Budget strongly supports underserved and tribal communities by providing $15 million for culturally-specific services, $5 million for underserved populations, $25 million to assist enforcement of tribal special domestic violence jurisdiction, $3 million to support tribal Special Assistant U.S. Attorneys, and $10 million for a new special initiative to address missing and murdered indigenous people. The Budget also provides $10 million to address technology-facilitated abuse through funding new VAWA programs that address cybercrimes against individuals. In addition, the Budget provides $55 million to the Office of Justice Programs for the Sexual Assault Kit Initiative to address the rape kit backlog.

Reforms the Federal Criminal Justice System. The Budget leverages the capacity of the Federal justice system to advance criminal justice reform and serve as a model that is comprehensive, evidence-based, and that enhances public safety and equity. The Budget supports key investments in First Step Act (FSA)

implementation, including continuing the historic collaboration between the Bureau of Prisons and DOL to provide comprehensive, intensive, and market-driven workforce development and reentry services for people in the Federal prison system. In total, the Budget continues to invest $409 million in base resources for FSA implementation, to support rehabilitative programming, improve confinement conditions, and hire additional FSA-dedicated staff.

Securing the Border and Strengthening the Immigration System

Reiterates the Administration's Request for Immediate Funding to Secure the Border, Build Capacity to Enforce Immigration Law, and Counter Fentanyl. In October 2023, the Administration transmitted an emergency supplemental request for the Southwest border and migration issues totaling $11.8 billion, of which $8.7 billion was for DHS. The Budget includes, and therefore reiterates the need for, the unmet needs from the October 2023 supplemental request. In addition to urgent requirements, the request includes investments to build longer-term capacity in the areas of border security, immigration enforcement, and countering fentanyl, totaling $2.9 billion for DHS. This amount includes: $405 million to hire 1,300 additional Border Patrol Agents to secure the border; $239 million to hire 1,000 additional U.S. Customs and Border Protection (CBP) Officers to stop fentanyl and other contraband from entering the United States; $755 million to hire an additional 1,600 Asylum Officers and support staff to facilitate timely immigration dispositions; $100 million for Homeland Security Investigations to investigate and disrupt transnational criminal organizations and drug traffickers; and $849 million for cutting-edge detection technology at ports of entry. Taken together, these long-term capacity building investments represent the Administration's vision for ensuring the Nation's border security and immigration system can effectively respond to challenges present along the border. In addition to the Executive Office for Immigration Review (EOIR) investments, the Budget also reiterates the $1.7 billion for DOJ requested in the Administration's October 2023 border, immigration, and countering fentanyl supplement request. Of this amount, $1.3 billion is requested for EOIR to fund the hiring of 375 new immigration judge teams to help reduce the immigration case backlog. In addition, the Administration appreciates the Senate's bipartisan border legislation that would make additional investments in DHS and provide authorities to bolster the Department's efforts to secure and manage the border.

Continues to Invest in Critical Capabilities Needed for Border and Immigration Enforcement. Strengthening border security and providing safe, lawful pathways for migration remain top priorities for the Administration. The Budget builds on the Administration's 2023 October supplemental request to include $25.9 billion for CBP and U.S. Immigration and Customs Enforcement (ICE), an increase of $1.9 billion over the 2023 enacted level when controlling for border management amounts. The Budget includes: funds for CBP to hire an additional 350 Border Patrol Agents and 310 processing coordinators; $127 million for border security technology between ports of entry; and $86 million in air and maritime operational support that is central to efforts to secure the border. The Budget also includes: funds to support 34,000 ICE immigration detention beds; $225 million to address increased transportation and removal costs; and $34 million to combat child exploitation, forced labor, and human trafficking.

Enables Resources to Scale Border Enforcement Capacity for Conditions on the Southwest Border. Given the uncertainty surrounding border conditions in any given year, the Budget proposes a $4.7 billion contingency fund to aid DHS and its components when responding to migration surges along the Southwest border. Modeled on a contingency fund provided for unaccompanied children, each fiscal year the fund would receive appropriations incrementally, and above the base appropriation, as Southwest border encounters reach pre-identified levels. DHS would be limited to obligating funds for surge-related functions, and would transfer funds to CBP, ICE, and Federal Emergency Management Agency accounts for valid surge-related obligations.

Supports America's Promise to Refugees and Care for Unaccompanied Children. The Budget builds on the Administration's October 2023 supplemental request and provides $9.3 billion for the Office of Refugee Resettlement (ORR) to help rebuild the Nation's refugee resettlement infrastructure and support the resettling of up to 125,000 refugees in 2025. The Budget also helps ensure that unaccompanied immigrant children receive appropriate support and services while they are in ORR's care and are unified with relatives and sponsors as safely and quickly as possible. This funding would allow ORR to continue the programmatic improvements the Administration has made, including expanding access to counsel to help children navigate complex immigration court proceedings and enhancing case management and post-release services. In addition, the Budget includes an emergency contingency fund that would provide additional resources, beyond the $9.3 billion, when there are unanticipated increases in the number of unaccompanied children.

Improves Immigration Courts. The Budget invests $981 million, an increase of $121 million above the 2023 enacted level, in EOIR to enhance America's immigration courts and help address the backlog of over 2.4 million currently pending cases. This funding would support 25 new immigration judge teams, which includes the support personnel necessary to ensure efficient case processing. The Budget also invests $30 million for EOIR to partner to with the U.S. Digital Service to develop and implement digital court operations strategies that would maximize each judge's adjudicatory capacity and help reduce the case backlog. In addition to EOIR investments, the Budget also reiterates the $1.7 billion for DOJ requested in the Administration's October 2023 border, immigration, and countering fentanyl supplement request. Of this amount, $1.3 billion is requested for EOIR to fund the hiring of 375 new immigration judge teams to help reduce the immigration case backlog.

Confronting Threats to Global Security and Strengthening America's Military

Reiterates the Administration's Request for Immediate Funding for Urgent National Security Priorities Related to Ukraine, Israel, and the Indo-Pacific. In October 2023, the Administration transmitted an emergency supplemental request totaling $92 billion to the Congress for urgent national security needs through the end of 2024, of which $58 billion was for DOD, $32 billion was for the Department of State and the U.S. Agency for International Development, and $2 billion for the Department of the Treasury (Treasury). This request included $61.4 billion to support Ukraine as it continues to defend itself against Russian aggression, $14.3 billion to support Israel's defense against terrorism, $10 billion for lifesaving humanitarian assistance, including for the Palestinian people, $3.4 billion for the Submarine Industrial Base (SIB), and $4 billion in other national security priorities. The request would also make significant and much needed investments in the American defense industrial base (DIB), benefitting U.S. military readiness and helping to create and sustain jobs across America. Absent congressional action on this emergency request, the United States would not be able to provide the necsssary support to Ukraine, provide urgently needed military support to allies and partners, make critical DIB investments, or sustain lifesaving assistance and development in some of the world's most vulnerable areas. The Administration appreciates the bipartisan supplemental legislation that passed the Senate that would address these urgent needs.

Supports Ukraine, European Allies, and Partners. The Budget continues to provide critical support for Ukraine, the North Atlantic Treaty Organization allies, and other European partner states by prioritizing funding to enhance the capabilities and readiness of U.S., allied, and partner forces in the face of continued Russian aggression. The Budget includes a new capital increase to the European Bank for Reconstruction and Development to maintain support to Ukraine and deliver on multilateral development bank evolution reforms. However, the Budget cannot address the critical support to Ukraine, which requires congressional action on the Administration's October 2023 national security supplemental request.

Promotes Integrated Deterrence in the Indo-Pacific and Globally. To sustain and strengthen deterrence, the Budget provides funding to prioritize China as America's pacing challenge in line with the *2022 National Defense Strategy*. DOD's 2025 *Pacific Deterrence Initiative* highlights some of the key investments the Federal Government is making, focuses on strengthening deterrence in the region, and demonstrates the Administration's long-term commitment to the Indo-Pacific. DOD is building the concepts, capabilities, and posture necessary to meet these challenges, working to integrate deterrence efforts across the U.S. Government and with U.S. allies and partners.

Underpins Commitments to Nuclear Deterrence, Nonproliferation, and Arms Control. Nuclear deterrence remains a top priority for the Nation and is foundational to integrated deterrence. A safe, secure, and effective nuclear force deters strategic attacks and assures allies and partners. To ensure the United States' nuclear deterrent remains responsive to all threats, DOD and DOE continue to modernize the nuclear Triad, nuclear command, control, and communications, and nuclear weapons infrastructure, while strengthening extended deterrence commitments to America's allies. The Budget also supports the President's commitment to reduce nuclear risks and strengthen the global non-proliferation regime by simultaneously pursuing realistic goals for mutual, verifiable arms control and efforts to protect against the existential threats posed by weapons of mass destruction terrorism.

Ensures Readiness across America's Armed Forces. The Budget continues to ensure that U.S. Soldiers, Sailors, Airmen, Marines, and Guardians remain the best trained and equipped fighting forces in the world. The Budget places additional emphasis on foundational investments to sustain current weapon systems and support increased training across DOD, while pursuing technological enhancements to extend the service life of material vital to the warfighter. In addition, the Budget continues the recapitalization and optimization of the four public Naval Shipyards to meet future submarine and carrier maintenance requirements.

Invests in SIB. DOD conducted the 2025 SIB study to determine how to complete the once-in-a-generation recapitalization of the submarine force needed to increase the United States' ability to build and sustain attack submarines to meet U.S. military requirements. The Budget also supports the Administration's commitments under the Australia-United Kingdom-United States enhanced trilateral security partnership, the first major deliverable of which was the historic decision to support Australia acquiring conventionally-armed, nuclear-powered submarines.

Addresses Emerging Cyber Threats. The Budget expands DOJ's ability to pursue cyber threats through investments in FBI's cyber and counterintelligence investigative capabilities. These investments sustain the FBI's cyber intelligence, counterintelligence, and analysis capabilities and include an additional $25 million to enhance those cyber response capabilities. The Budget also includes $5 million to expand a new section within the DOJ's National Security Division to focus on cyber threats. These investments are in line with the *National Cybersecurity Strategy* that emphasizes a whole-of-Nation approach to addressing ongoing cyber threats. The Budget also provides $2 million for DOJ to support implementation of the Executive Order 14110, "Safe, Secure, and Trustworthy Development and Use of Artificial Intelligence."

Combats Terrorism and Corruption and Increases Corporate Transparency. Treasury plays a leading role in monitoring and disrupting corruption, money laundering, terrorist financing, the use of the financial system by malicious actors domestically and abroad, and combatting the trafficking of illicit substances such as fentanyl in American communities. The Budget provides $231 million to the Office of Terrorism and Financial Intelligence, $15 million above the 2023 level, to expand Treasury's capacity to provide financial intelligence and conduct sanctions-related economic analysis while continuing to modernize the sanctions process. These investments would expand Treasury's ability to craft, implement, and enforce sanctions, including the historic sanctions program targeting Russia's illegal war in Ukraine, and sanctions on key Hamas terrorist group members and financial facilitators in Gaza.

Invests in AI. The President issued a landmark Executive Order to ensure that America leads the way in seizing the promise and managing the risks of AI. The Executive Order establishes new standards for AI safety and security, protects Americans' privacy, advances equity and civil rights, stands up for consumers and workers, promotes innovation and competition, advances American leadership around the world, and more. The Budget provides funding to responsibly develop, test, procure, and integrate transformative AI applications across the Federal Government and supports the implementation of the Administration's Executive Order. Specifically, the National Institute of Standards and Technology (NIST) would establish the U.S. AI Safety Institute to operationalize NIST's AI Risk Management Framework by creating guidelines, tools, benchmarks, and best practices for evaluating and mitigating dangerous capabilities and conducting evaluations including red-teaming to identify and mitigate AI risk.

Addressing Pressing Global Challenges

Drives Inclusive and Sustainable Economic Growth and Quality International Infrastructure through the Partnership for Global Infrastructure and Investment (PGI). The Budget advances the President's goal of mobilizing $200 billion for infrastructure investment in low- and middle-income countries by 2027. PGI aims to promote infrastructure development along critical economic corridors to drive inclusive and sustainable economic growth, secure energy supply chains, fortify trusted digital connectivity, and build more resilient food and health systems, as well as critical transport and logistics networks, while advancing gender equality and equity. The Budget includes approximately $50 billion for PGI across all departments and agencies, inclusive of private sector financing leveraged, including $250 million in flexible resources to support strategic, high-quality infrastructure to connect workers to good jobs, allow businesses to grow and thrive, and advance shared national security priorities. To further PGI goals, the Budget includes $2 billion in mandatory funding over five years to establish the International Infrastructure Fund to combat People's Republic of China coercive financing.

Strengthens Health Systems Globally. The Budget provides nearly $10 billion for global health programs, which would increase support for global health programs, strengthening health systems, and pandemic preparedness. The Budget fulfills the President's commitment to the seventh replenishment of the Global Fund to Fight AIDS, Tuberculosis, and Malaria by providing $1.2 billion to match $1 for every $2 contributed by other donors. The Budget also provides more than $900 million for global health security, including $250 million for the Pandemic Fund. The Budget invests $30 million in new resources for the World Bank's Global Financing Facility for Women, Children, and Adolescents, a contribution anticipated to leverage at least $210 million to strengthen health systems, and $20 million for the Administration's Global Health Worker Initiative to better train, equip, and protect the health workforce. In addition, the Budget includes loan guarantees to the World Bank's International Bank for Reconstruction and Development to support investments in global challenges, including pandemic preparedness, which would bolster the impact of these global health activities.

Secures American Presence and Commitment in the Indo-Pacific. The Budget provides over $4 billion to realize a more free, open, secure, and connected Indo-Pacific that bolsters U.S. alliances and partnerships, which is nearly $600 million above the 2023 level. This includes $2.1 billion in bilateral and regional foreign assistance, including $100 million for a standalone request for Taiwan military assistance, and $20 million for the Indo-Pacific Economic Framework. The Budget includes over $62 million in support of the Association of Southeast Asian Nations (ASEAN), demonstrating America's continued commitment to ASEAN centrality. The Indo-Pacific Strategy total also includes $2 billion to support diplomatic presence and programs in the region, including new and planned U.S. diplomatic posts in the Pacific and Indian Oceans. The Budget requests $7.1 billion in mandatory funding for the renewal of the Compact of Free Association relationships with the Federated States of Micronesia, the Republic of the Marshall Islands, and the Republic of Palau. The Budget reflects a substantial commitment to the Indo-Pacific and relies on the $2 billion investment that the Administration requested in the October 2023 national security supplemental request in security assistance to fully address urgent regional security needs and deter acts of aggression.

Provides Lifesaving Humanitarian Assistance and Combats Global Food Insecurity. The Budget provides $10.3 billion in lifesaving humanitarian and refugee assistance to support more than 330 million people in need in more than 70 countries, in addition to the October 2023 emergency supplemental request of $10 billion to address unprecedented global humanitarian needs. The Budget also fully supports the President's commitment to resettle up to 125,000 refugees in the United States, as well as the Enduring Welcome and Safe Mobility Office initiatives. The Budget also provides more than $1 billion to support the President's pledge to alleviate global food insecurity, including $100 million for the Vision for Adapted Crops and Soils, as part of the overall U.S. Government's flagship food security initiative, Feed the Future, which works to build more resilient and sustainable food systems and nutritious food crops in underserved regions. The State Department and USAID would have to reduce lifesaving assistance around the globe without the additional $10 billion in humanitarian assistance requested in the Administration's October 2023 national security supplemental request.

Bolsters Sustainable, Inclusive, and Democratic Global Development. The Budget supports the President's goal to strengthen American development efforts through local expertise and by deploying a more expansive set of development tools. The Budget provides over $3 billion for bolstering global democracy, including $345 million for the President's Initiative for Democratic Renewal to foster transparent and accountable governance. The Budget provides more than $3 billion to advance gender equity and equality worldwide, including $200 million for the Gender Equity and Equality Action Fund. The Budget also includes $110 million in support of internet freedom, including $50 million for the U.S. Agency for Global Media Open Technology Fund. The Budget provides $594 million, an increase of $37 million above the 2023 level, for USAID directed high-impact and lifesaving voluntary family planning and reproductive health

programs and America's voluntary contribution to the United Nations Population Fund. The Budget continues America's commitment to contributions for the United Nations.

Fulfills the President's Commitment to Central America and Strengthens America's Partnership in the Western Hemisphere. The Budget provides approximately $1 billion for Central American programming to meet the President's commitment to invest $4 billion in Central America over four years to address the root causes of migration. The Budget also supports hemispheric programs to advance economic prosperity and regional security through key initiatives such as the Americas Partnership for Economic Prosperity, including $75 million for a capital increase to the Inter-American Investment Corporation—known as IDB Invest—to advance clean energy projects, modernize agriculture, strengthen transportation systems, and expand access to financing. The Budget further reserves $35 million in additional targeted funding for regional migration management, including $25 million for the IDB's Migration Grant Facility to support integration efforts for migrants and host communities and address the root causes of irregular migration.

CUTTING THE DEFICIT BY EXPANDING AMERICA'S PRODUCTIVE CAPACITY AND PROMOTING TAX FAIRNESS

From day one, the Biden-Harris Administration has worked to build an economy from the middle out and bottom up. The President's economic agenda has shown that investing in the Nation can go along with achieving meaningful deficit reduction. The deficit is over $1 trillion lower than when the President took office, thanks in large part to a strong economic recovery facilitated by investments that have expanded the Nation's productive capacity and a historic vaccination program that allowed the responsible wind-down of emergency measures. In addition, the President has also signed into law significant pro-growth investments and deficit-reduction policies that

are already lowering costs for families and reinvigorating American industry and will continue to take full effect in coming years.

Delivering on a Commitment to Fiscal Responsibility.

The President has enacted another roughly $1 trillion in savings over the next decade through the FRA, and through the Inflation Reduction Act provisions that empower Medicare to negotiate lower prescription drug prices, cap insulin at $35 per month for seniors, and make the wealthy and large corporations pay more of their fair share. To address the unfairness of 55 of the most profitable U.S. corporations paying $0 in Federal income taxes, the President signed into law a 15-percent minimum tax on the profits of the largest corporations—those with over $1 billion in profits. He also signed into law a surcharge on corporate stock buybacks, which encourages businesses to invest in their growth and productivity as opposed to funneling tax-preferred profits to wealthy shareholders. The Inflation Reduction Act also enacted long-overdue investments in rebuilding and modernizing the Internal Revenue Service (IRS), which raise revenue by making wealthy taxpayers and big corporations pay the taxes they owe—while improving customer service and without increasing audit rates relative to historical levels for small businesses and taxpayers making under $400,000 per year. The Budget would build on this progress by increasing the corporate minimum tax rate to 21 percent, quadrupling the surcharge on stock buybacks, extending the IRS investment, and other important reforms.

As these investments continue to deliver for working families and communities, the Administration looks forward to building on this progress with responsible investments that continue to grow America's economy from the middle out and bottom up while improving the long-term budget outlook. The Budget proposes another $3 trillion in deficit reduction over the next 10 years by making the wealthy and large corporations pay their fair share, closing tax loopholes, cutting wasteful spending on Big Pharma, Big Oil, and other special interests.

In addition to Medicare tax and prescription drug reforms discussed above, the Budget:

Proposes a Minimum Tax on Billionaires. The tax code currently offers special treatment for the types of income that wealthy people enjoy. While the wages and salaries that everyday Americans earn are taxed as ordinary income, billionaires make their money in ways that are taxed at lower rates, and sometimes not taxed at all. This special treatment, combined with sophisticated tax planning and giant loopholes, allows many of the wealthiest Americans to pay lower rates on their full income than many middle-class households pay. To finally address this glaring inequity, the Budget includes a 25 percent minimum tax on the wealthiest 0.01 percent, those with wealth of more than $100 million.

Ensures Corporations Pay Their Fair Share. The Budget increases the rates that corporations pay in taxes on their profits. Corporations received an enormous tax break in 2017, cutting effective U.S. tax rates for U.S. corporations to a low of less than 10 percent. While their profits soared, their investment in their workers and the economy did not. Their shareholders and top executives reaped the benefits, without the promised trickle down to workers, consumers, or communities. The Budget would set the corporate tax rate at 28 percent, still well below the 35 percent rate that prevailed prior to the 2017 tax law. In addition, the Budget would raise the Inflation Reduction Act's corporate minimum tax rate on billion-dollar corporations from 15 percent to 21 percent, ensuring the biggest corporations pay more of their fair share. These policies are complemented by other proposals to incentivize job creation and investment in the United States and ensure large corporations pay their fair share.

Denies Corporations Deductions for All Compensation Over $1 million Per Employee. Executive compensation has skyrocketed in recent decades, with Chief Executive Officer pay averaging more than 300 times that of a typical worker in 2022. The 2017 tax law's corporate tax cuts only made this problem worse, producing massive boosts to executive compensation while doing nothing for low- and middle-income workers. Current law denies deductions for executive compensation over $1 million only for a small number of highly paid employees at publicly-traded C corporations. The Budget proposes to deny deductions for all compensation over $1 million paid to any employee of a C corporation, which would discourage companies from giving their executives massive pay packages and level the playing field across C corporations.

Stops the Race to the Bottom in International Corporate Tax and Ends Tax Breaks for Offshoring. For decades, countries have competed for multinational business by slashing tax rates, at the expense of having adequate revenues to finance core services. Thanks in part to the Administration's leadership, more than 130 nations signed on to a global tax framework to finally address this race to the bottom in 2021. Many of America's international partners, including many of the world's largest economies, have implemented or will soon implement this transformational agreement. The Budget proposes to do the same by reforming the international tax system to reduce the incentives to book profits in low-tax jurisdictions, stopping corporate inversions to tax havens, and raising the tax rate on U.S. multinationals' foreign earnings from 10.5 percent to 21 percent. These reforms would ensure that profitable multinational corporations pay their fair share.

Quadruples the Stock Buybacks Tax. In 2022, the President signed into law a surcharge on corporate stock buybacks, which reduces the tax advantage for buybacks over dividends and encourages businesses to invest in their growth and productivity as opposed to funneling tax-preferred profits to foreign shareholders. The Budget proposes quadrupling the stock buybacks tax from one percent to four percent to address the continued tax advantage for buybacks and encourage corporations to invest in productivity and the broader economy.

Repeals Tax Cuts for the Wealthy and Reforms Capital Gains Tax to Ensure the Wealthy Pay Their Fair Share. The 2017 tax law lowered rates for the wealthiest Americans, delivering massive tax cuts to the top one percent. The Budget repeals those cuts, restoring the top tax rate of 39.6 percent for single filers making more than $400,000 a year and married couples making more than $450,000 per year. The Budget also proposes taxing capital gains at the same rate as wage income for those with more than $1 million in income and finally closes the carried interest loophole that allows some wealthy investment fund managers to pay tax at lower rates than their secretaries.

Closes Tax Loopholes. The Budget saves billions of dollars by closing other tax loopholes that overwhelmingly benefit the rich and the largest, most profitable corporations. This includes: closing the so-called "like-kind exchange loophole" that lets real estate investors defer tax indefinitely; reforms to tax preferred retirement incentives to ensure that the ultrawealthy cannot use these incentives to amass tax free fortunes; preventing the super-wealthy from abusing life insurance tax shelters; closing a loophole that benefits wealthy crypto investors; and ending a tax break for corporate jets.

Cracks Down on Wealthy Tax Cheats. The Inflation Reduction Act addressed long-standing IRS funding deficiencies by providing stable, multi-year funding to improve tax compliance by finally cracking down on high-income individuals and corporations who too often avoided paying their lawfully owed taxes and improve service for the millions of Americans that do pay their taxes. Already, the IRS is using these resources to crack down on tax evasion by the wealthy and big businesses. For example, the IRS is collecting taxes owed by tax-delinquent millionaires and addressing complex tax schemes used by the largest partnerships and multinational corporations, along with improving customer service and modernizing IT infrastructure. The Budget proposes to restore the full Inflation Reduction Act investment and provide new funding over the long-term to continue cutting the deficit by making sure that wealthy Americans and big corporations pay the taxes they owe.

Addresses Expiring Tax Cuts after 2025. President Trump and congressional Republicans deliberately sunset portions of the Tax Cuts and Jobs Act of 2017 legislation after 2025 to conceal both the true increase in the deficit—much larger than the already-massive $2 trillion cost estimate—and the true size of their tax breaks for multi-millionaires and large corporations. This was one of the most egregious and fiscally reckless budget decisions in modern history. The

President, faced with this fiscally irresponsible legacy, will work with the Congress to address the 2025 expirations, and focus tax policy on rewarding work not wealth, based on the following guiding principles. The President:

- Opposes increasing taxes on people earning less than $400,000 and supports cutting taxes for working people and families with children to give them more breathing room;

- Opposes tax cuts for the wealthy—either extending tax cuts for the top two percent of Americans earning over $400,000 or bringing back deductions and other tax breaks for these households; and

- Supports paying for extending tax cuts for people earning less than $400,000 with additional reforms to ensure that wealthy people and big corporations pay their fair share, so that the problematic sunsets created by President Trump and congressional Republicans are addressed in a fiscally responsible manner.

CREATING A GOVERNMENT THAT DELIVERS FOR THE AMERICAN PEOPLE

To build on the historic progress made under President Biden's leadership, the American people need a modern and effective Government. A high-performing Federal Government—staffed by expert civil servants—plays a critical role in ensuring Americans have reliable services and resources, from helping the American people file taxes and apply for benefits, to confronting the risks and opportunities presented by artificial intelligence (AI).

To help deliver that future, the President's Budget advances the goals of the Biden-Harris Management Agenda (PMA) across three key areas: strengthening and empowering the Federal workforce; delivering excellent, equitable, and secure Federal services and customer experience; and managing the business of Government. This work is critical for bolstering Government's ability to deliver for the American people.

The Right Team and the Right Tools

More than four million Americans serve the Nation, as civilian and uniformed personnel, both at home and overseas. As the Nation's largest employer, the Federal Government is strategically competing for highly-skilled talent to continue carrying out programs and delivering services that benefit the American people. These civil servants need to be equipped with the right tools to do their jobs, including modern information technology (IT). The Budget continues investments to ensure the Federal Government has the right team and tools to deliver for the American people.

Helping Agencies Attract, Retain, and Hire Top Talent. Agencies have made substantial progress in strengthening and empowering the Federal workforce, such as recruiting the wide-range of talent necessary for the implementation of the Bipartisan Infrastructure Law, a once in a generation investment in the Nation's infrastructure and competitiveness that spurred a surge hiring effort of 6,099 targeted positions. The Budget continues to support Office of Personnel Management's (OPM) programs—such as the Hiring Experience Office—in making progress on streamlining hiring. The Budget also directs agencies to take part in collaborative cross-Government shared hiring actions that enable agencies to quickly hire on a larger scale, allowing applicants to submit one Federal job application and be considered for many opportunities. The Budget advances the Administration's focus on the expansion of early career talent pipelines, including the development of strategic and targeted apprenticeships, increased volume of student and early career opportunities, and equitable access to paid internships. The Budget also provides resources to support continued transformation of the personnel vetting mission, and its Trusted Workforce 2.0 Implementation Strategy, which is designed to ensure all Americans can trust the Federal workforce.

Building the Personnel System and Support Required to Make the Federal Government a Model Employer. As the Government faces increasingly complex challenges, the need for Federal leaders, managers, and front-line staff with the right skills in the right jobs has never been greater. The Budget sustains critical investments in OPM to enable the Agency's ability to lead Federal human capital management and serve as a centralized leader in human resources. The Budget further advances work to address Government-wide compensation challenges, and reinforces additional initiatives to enhance personnel systems for critical elements of the workforce.

Modernizing Federal IT Policies and Technology to Better Serve the American People. Technology is a key enabler for the Federal Government and its workforce. The Budget makes key investments to protect the Federal systems from compromises—leveraging the benefits of digital identity and AI while balancing the risks it poses to rights, opportunities, and safety, and redefining security expectations for software and the cloud. To support IT modernization efforts, the Budget also includes an additional $75 million for the Technology Modernization Fund (TMF), an innovative investment program that gives agencies additional ways to deliver services to the American public quickly. TMF manages over $750 million for 48 investments, across 27 Federal agencies, and is particularly well-positioned to make a large impact in the Federal Government's ability to deliver excellent, equitable, and secure services.

Advancing AI Governance, Innovation, and Risk Management. To capitalize on the opportunities and mitigate the risks of AI—including by implementing Section 10 of Executive Order 14110, "Safe, Secure, and Trustworthy Development and Use of Artificial Intelligence,"— the Administration is committed to advancing its management of AI and significantly expanding AI talent in the Federal Government. The Budget provides additional funding for Federal agencies to establish agency Chief AI Officers accountable for their agency's use of AI, to adopt new AI technologies to improve Government services, and to establish minimum safeguards for Government use of AI to protect the rights and safety of the public. In addition to this funding, the Budget also includes an additional $32 million for the U.S. Digital Service (USDS), General Services Administration, and OPM to support the National AI Talent Surge across the Federal Government.

Serving the American People

President Biden set an objective in the PMA that when the American public interacts with Government, they should get a simple, seamless, and secure customer experience that is on par with what they expect in the private sector. The Budget advances this goal by:

Supporting Digital Services Teams. The Budget sustains investment in the USDS to continue bringing world class technology talent into the Federal Government—helping agencies confront some of their hardest issues. USDS staff are centrally recruited into the Government from the private sector and deployed into agencies to assist with the critical projects, buttressing existing personnel with new skills and expertise. Over the past 10 years, USDS has successfully helped agencies to modernize their technical operations and minimize the risk of large IT projects, over 60 percent of which have historically failed without the intervention of USDS. For example, USDS is supporting the Internal Revenue Service in its technology transformation, modernizing decades-old systems and improving taxpayer services, the Department of Health and Human Service (HHS) in streamlining the enrollment and renewal process for Medicaid coverage, including saving half a million children from erroneously losing their health insurance, and the Federal Communications Commission in its efforts to bring affordable, reliable, and high-speed broadband to eligible households.

Increasing Customer Experience Across the Federal Government. The Budget funds the expertise and tools necessary to ensure excellent service delivery and customer experience across the Federal Government. The Budget invests in teams of specialized customer experience and digital services professionals in 10 Federal departments, and critical subagencies that serve millions of customers. The Budget also provides funding for new "Voice of Customer" programs at eight Federal agencies to collect and report performance data on key drivers of customer experience from a broad representation of Americans— which can drive meaningful service improvements. The Budget also supports specific service delivery enhancements, such as the Transportation Security Administration's pilot program to deploy customer experience strategists at airports to streamline passenger screening, and the Department of State's efforts to build online passport renewal.

Designing, Building, and Managing Government Service Delivery for Priority Life Experiences. The Budget advances efforts to better serve the American people by providing funding for interagency teams to build digital service capacity. Following extensive customer experience-focused discovery research and design phase projects and pilots aimed at developing promising solutions, the Budget also specifically supports cross-agency Life Experience projects, including funding for the Health Resources and Services Administration at HHS to help Americans more easily access essential services following the birth of a child. In addition, the Budget invests in shared products and platforms that enable simple, seamless, and secure services across the Federal Government.

Protecting Taxpayer Investment

The Administration has the obligation to invest taxpayer money with care, ensuring that taxpayers get excellent returns on each dollar that is spent. That includes investing in American workers, small businesses, equity efforts, and climate resilience. The Budget invests in improved stewardship of taxpayer funds in the following ways:

Ensuring the Future is Made in America. The President's economic agenda is focused on ensuring the future is made in America. The Administration is delivering on the President's agenda by advancing a whole-of-Government effort to ensure resources and programs advance domestic jobs and industries. The Bipartisan Infrastructure Law included the Build America,

Buy America Act, requiring that all federally funded infrastructure projects use American iron and steel, manufactured products, and construction materials, unless such items are not available, would constitute an unreasonable cost, or meet the requirements of other statutory exemptions. The Office of Management and Budget's (OMB) Made in America Office is working with Federal agencies to improve their capacity to perform supply chain analysis, perform market research, and engage with industry to maximize the use of critical domestic products. These efforts will help to strengthen the U.S. industrial base in critical sectors while increasing the quality and number of good-paying jobs by promoting the domestic production of steel and iron products, manufactured products, and construction materials.

Streamlining Federal Grant-Making and Improving Program Outcomes. In order to reduce administrative burden for Federal agencies and recipients and to improve outcomes of Federal financial assistance programs, OMB is updating its comprehensive Guidance on Grants and Agreements. These updates will represent the most substantial changes to the guidance since its release in 2013, and will reduce unnecessary compliance requirements. In addition, to improve the coordination of Federal financial assistance policy, oversight, and strategic direction, OMB established the Council on Federal Financial Assistance in August 2023. This partnership of Federal grant-making agencies provides a single forum for oversight and management of Federal financial assistance.

Improving Federal Procurement. Under the Better Contracting Initiative, agencies will ensure strong contracting outcomes by making better use of acquisition data and leveraging expertise in acquiring common software and other IT requirements. At the same time, the Administration is working aggressively to create a more resilient supplier base and increase competition by increasing the percent of Federal contract award dollars that go to small disadvantaged businesses—building on historic spend made by agencies to this underserved community on the way to a goal of 15 percent by 2025. In addition, agencies will advance the sustainability of Federal supply chains and achieve net-zero emissions from Federal procurement by 2050.

Managing the Government to Deliver Results that Improve Lives. The Administration continues to drive evidence-based management practices to deliver a more effective Government. OMB and agency leadership conducted strategic review meetings to review progress on agency strategic plans and discuss approaches to strengthening organizational health and organizational performance, following the release of OMB Memorandum M-23-15, Measuring, Monitoring, and Improving Organizational Health and Organizational Performance in the Context of Evolving Agency Work Environments. In December of 2023, agencies established 79 new performance commitments to be achieved through 2025. The public is invited to follow agency progress on *https://Performance.gov*.

Advancing Federal Evidence-Based Policymaking. The President has made clear that the Administration will make decisions guided by the best available science and data. The Budget demonstrates this commitment by investing in evidence-based programs at, and bolstering capacity for, program evaluation. The Budget invests in the Federal statistical system's key role in evidence building by expanding skilled statisticians and infrastructure to equip agencies with tools for ensuring high-quality data and robust data confidentiality protections, as well as creating a seamless data user experience.

Promoting Accountability and Integrity. The Administration is committed to improving program integrity and ensuring effective stewardship of taxpayer dollars, including through implementation of the American Rescue Plan, the Bipartisan Infrastructure Law, the CHIPS and Science Act, and the Inflation Reduction Act. To deliver on those commitments, the Administration has provided agencies with the tools to strengthen program integrity and deliver results. The President has made clear that results, transparency, and accountability go hand-in-hand, which

is why the Budget includes robust legislative and funding proposals that would ensure agencies and their Inspectors General have the resources and authorities they need for appropriate oversight of these programs. For example, the Budget includes new proposals for modernizing, protecting, and strengthening the Unemployment Insurance (UI) program that would help states develop and test fraud-prevention tools and strategies and increase investigations of fraud rings targeting the UI program. Further, the Budget ensures additional resources and time for investigations and prosecution of those engaged in major or systemic pandemic fraud, invests in identity theft and fraud prevention to stop fraud before funds are ever paid out, and provides much-needed help for innocent victims recovering from having their identities and benefits stolen.

Bolstering Federal Cybersecurity. To protect against foreign adversaries and safeguard Federal systems, the Budget bolsters cybersecurity by ensuring every agency is increasing the security of public services. To advance the Administration's commitment to making cyberspace more resilient and defensible, the Budget provides $13 billion in cybersecurity funding across civilian departments and agencies. In addition, the Budget provides an additional $103 million for the Cybersecurity and Infrastructure Security Agency (CISA), for a total of $3 billion to advance the Administration's commitment to making cyberspace more resilient and defensible. This includes: $470 million to deploy Federal network tools, including endpoint detection and response capabilities; $394 million for CISA's internal cybersecurity and analytical capabilities; $41 million for critical infrastructure security coordination, and $116 million for critical infrastructure cyber event reporting.

Transforming Personnel Vetting. The Administration is committed to improving how agencies vet their civilian, military, and contractor personnel—to ensure Government is employing personnel with necessary skillsets. During 2023, the Administration sustained reform momentum by rolling out new training standards for the background investigators and adjudicators implementing policy changes, authorizing the expansion of continuous vetting beyond national security sensitive personnel, and transitioning away from legacy e-QIP software to the more user-friendly eApp platform for individuals entering the personnel vetting process. The Budget instructs agencies to be prepared for further improvements as directed in the Performance Accountability Council's Trusted Workforce 2.0 Implementation Strategy. Among other goals, agencies should expect to continue enrolling their non-sensitive personnel into continuous vetting, expand data collection for enhanced performance metrics, update training and internal processes to reflect reform progress, and adopt additional personnel vetting shared services.

DEPARTMENT OF AGRICULTURE

The U.S. Department of Agriculture (USDA) is responsible for providing nutrition assistance to low-income Americans and a safety net for the farm sector, conserving and preserving private agricultural lands, and sustaining the health and productivity of the Nation's forests. The President's 2025 Budget for USDA: sustains America's advantages in agriculture; strengthens the nutrition safety net and removes barriers to vital assistance; promotes job growth and economic opportunity in rural communities, including more jobs in clean energy to mitigate the effects of greenhouse gas (GHG) emissions; promotes environmental justice; supports historically disadvantaged and underserved producers; and helps farmers, ranchers, and forest landowners adapt to the effects of the climate crisis.

The Budget requests $29.2 billion in discretionary budget authority for 2025, a $2 billion or 7.4-percent increase from the 2023 level, excluding Food for Peace Title II Grants, which are included in the State and International Programs total. Resources provided through the 2025 Budget complement investments in natural resource conservation, national forest and wildland fire management, and broadband deployment provided in the Bipartisan Infrastructure Law and Inflation Reduction Act.

The President's 2025 Budget:

- **Lowers Energy Costs and Catalyzes Clean Energy and Economic Growth in Rural Communities.** The Budget builds on the $13 billion provided in the President's historic Inflation Reduction Act for rural development programs at USDA to reduce energy bills for families, expand clean energy, transform rural power production, and create thousands of good-paying jobs for people across rural America. Rural communities are critical to achieving the goal of 100 percent clean electricity by 2035. The Budget provides $1 billion for loan guarantees for renewable energy systems and energy efficiency improvements for farmers and rural small businesses, and $6.5 billion in authority for rural electric loans to support additional clean energy, energy storage, and transmission projects that would create good-paying jobs. In addition, the Budget includes $53 million in zero-interest loans for the Rural Energy Savings Program, which would help rural Americans implement durable cost-effective energy efficiency measures in their homes, which lowers energy costs and contributes to the President's clean energy goals and the Justice40 Initiative. The Budget also provides $10 million in Rural Community Facilities Grants specifically for rural communities making an energy transition away from outdated energy sources, facilitating emerging infrastructure needs.

- **Connects More Rural Americans to High-Speed, Affordable, and Reliable Internet.** The President is committed to ensuring that every American has access to affordable broadband internet—and thanks to his Bipartisan Infrastructure Law, under the Biden-Harris

Administration, USDA has provided $2.3 billion to people living and working across 35 States and Territories, which is expected to expand broadband access to more than 137,000 households. Installing high-speed internet creates high-paying union jobs and strengthens rural economies, which leads to higher property values, increased job and population growth, lower unemployment rates, and new business formation. Reliable internet is also crucial for rural Americans to access healthcare services through telehealth. Building on the $2 billion for USDA broadband programs provided in the Bipartisan Infrastructure Law for 2023, the Budget provides $112 million for the ReConnect program, which provides grants and loans to deploy broadband to unserved areas, especially tribal areas.

- **Increases Climate Resilience and Other Conservation Practices in Agriculture Production.** Climate change presents real threats to U.S. agricultural production, forest resources, and rural communities. The Budget provides $6 billion for climate-related funding, a $733 million increase over the 2023 enacted level, and $1.3 billion over the 2020 enacted level. This funding includes $985 million for the Natural Resources Conservation Service (NRCS), a $67 million or 7-percent increase above the 2023 enacted level, and a $152 million increase or 18-percent above the 2020 enacted level, to assist farmers, ranchers, and forestland owners with production goals in the face of a changing climate while conserving, maintaining, and restoring natural resources on their lands. The Inflation Reduction Act provided generational investments to increase adoption of voluntary conservation practices that sequester carbon and reduce GHG emissions associated with farming and ranching operations. Increasing conservation in agricultural production supports voluntary environmental services markets, leverages private-sector and other non-Federal investment, and provides additional income opportunities for America's farmers. These practices also help producers adapt to multi-year drought conditions and reductions in water availability. To implement Inflation Reduction Act investments, the NRCS would hire thousands of employees—creating good-paying jobs throughout rural America.

- **Supports a Strong Nutrition Safety Net.** The Budget provides $8.5 billion for critical nutrition programs, including $7.7 billion to fully fund participation in the Special Supplemental Nutrition Program for Women, Infants, and Children (WIC), which is critical to the health of pregnant women, new mothers, infants, and young children. This program helps low-income families put nutritious food on the table and addresses racial disparities in maternal and child health outcomes. In the *Biden-Harris Administration National Strategy on Hunger, Nutrition, and Health*, the Administration set goals to help more individuals experiencing food insecurity access Federal nutrition assistance programs. By investing in outreach and modernization, WIC would reach 800,000 more women, infants, and children each month, providing vital nutrition assistance to nearly seven million individuals, up from 6.2 million in 2021. The Budget supports enhanced benefits for fruits and vegetables to improve nutritional outcomes and reduce food insecurity among children consistent with the recommendations by the National Academies of Sciences, Engineering, and Medicine. In addition, the Budget includes an emergency contingency fund that would provide additional resources, beyond the $7.7 billion, when there are unanticipated cost pressures. The Budget also includes $15 billion over 10 years to allow more States and schools to leverage participation in the Community Eligibility Provision to provide healthy school meals at no cost to an additional nine million children.

- **Invests in America's Brave Wildland Firefighters.** The Budget builds on the Administration's historic investments in the wildland firefighting workforce at the Forest Service and the Department of the Interior, including investments from the Bipartisan Infrastructure Law, by supporting implementation of permanent and comprehensive pay reform, enhancement of health services, hiring of additional permanent and temporary wildland fire-fighters to increase capacity, and improvement of Government housing. These investments, totaling $387 million over the comparable 2023 enacted level for USDA Forest Service, would help address long-standing recruitment and retention challenges, increase the Departments' capacity to complete critical risk mitigation work, and further the Administration's commitment to build a more robust and resilient wildland firefighting workforce as the frequency and intensity of catastrophic wildfires continue to increase due to climate change.

- **Reduces Housing Insecurity and Strengthens Climate Resiliency in Rural Communities.** Adequate affordable housing has been a long-standing problem in rural communities—one that is exacerbated by low energy efficiency of the aging housing stock, meaning higher costs to families. To help address this, the Budget proposes additional funding for rental assistance, multifamily and single-family housing, and again proposes to eliminate the existing low-income borrower penalty that requires individuals to repay subsidy costs for Single-Family Direct loans—a requirement that only exists for rural housing. The Budget provides strong support for USDA's multifamily housing and housing preservation programs. Through these investments, the Administration advances equity in support of underserved communities by reducing rent burdens for low-income borrowers and preserving low-income tenant-based housing in rural America. The Budget again proposes to increase the resiliency of rural housing to the impacts of climate change through a proposal to require energy and water efficiency improvements and green features in USDA's rural housing programs that include construction.

- **Sustains American Leadership in Agricultural Innovation and Research.** The Budget sustains American innovation in agriculture by providing a total of almost $3.8 billion for agricultural research, education, and outreach. This includes $365 million, a 20-percent increase above the 2023 enacted level, for agriculture research, extension, and education grants to minority-serving land grant universities and tribal colleges to increase the productive capacity of small family farms and historically underserved populations, including the responsible application of artificial intelligence to ensure that the entire spectrum of the agriculture sector can reap the economic benefits of this technology. The Budget also includes support for the duties of a Chief Artificial Intelligence Officer, who would promote the safe and responsible application of artificial intelligence in advancing the productivity of the Nation's agriculture sector. The Budget provides $321 million for the Department's core climate-related research and development (R&D) activities, which includes R&D on the carbon cycle and the impacts of weather and water cycle variations on soil, air, and water resources associated with agriculture. This would help to quantify risks and benefits to agriculture from global change so technologies can be developed for harnessing beneficial aspects of global change, adapting agricultural systems to change, and mitigating the Nation's net emissions of GHG.

- **Provides Trade and International Food Security.** America's farmers, ranchers, and producers are feeding the world. The Budget provides funding to fully staff the Foreign Agricultural Service, which supports the marketing and promotion of high-quality, high-value U.S. agricultural products to a variety of overseas markets, creating jobs and income streams throughout the supply chain domestically and internationally. Further, the Budget allows for USDA to engage in international trade and regulatory systems and agreements, creating new markets and ensuring current markets stay open. In addition, the Budget provides food assistance, such as $243 million for the McGovern-Dole International Food for Education and Child Nutrition Program. Lastly, capacity building projects, supported by the Budget, combat global food insecurity, share knowledge around climate-smart agricultural practices, and develop rules- and science-based markets.

- **Supports Better Delivery of Services to Rural America and the Nation's Farmers.** To better serve rural communities and areas that have been previously left behind, the Budget provides funding for USDA to ensure adequate staffing and critical information technology upgrades to improve program delivery. This includes expanding the authority for the Non-recurring Expenses Fund to access expired discretionary funds for projects that would remediate cybersecurity vulnerabilities and improve web-based rural development loan services to provide a more automated experience for borrowers. To make sure that eligible individuals are aware of available Federal support, regardless of their native language, the Budget provides $2 million for a Department-wide Language Access Plan. To expand rural prosperity and economic growth, the Budget includes $10 million for the Rural Partners Network, which continues the collaboration and outreach of 20 Federal agencies and regional commissions to ensure rural communities have equitable access to Federal programs.

- **Supports the Upcoming Farm Bill.** The Budget provides USDA with the staffing resources necessary to seamlessly implement reauthorization of the Farm Bill. The Administration looks forward to working this year with the Congress, partners, stakeholders, and the public to identify shared priorities and build on the historic legislative achievements of the first three years of the Administration. The Farm Bill presents a unique opportunity to transform the food and agricultural system from one that benefits a few to one that benefits many—all while strengthening USDA's nutrition programs, which are among the most effective and far-reaching tools available to improve the health and well-being of Americans. The Nation can achieve meaningful, equitable growth in agriculture and rural economies by creating new revenue streams for American farmers, ranchers, and producers of all sizes through climate smart agriculture and forestry, biobased products, renewable energy, local and regional food systems, increased competition in agricultural markets, and other value-added opportunities, while reducing the paperwork burden for Federal programs and achieving best in Government practices. The Farm Bill is also a critical opportunity to ensure that the wealth created in rural America stays there to empower rural communities with the tools necessary to advance their locally-led vision.

The upcoming Farm Bill is also an opportunity to make progress toward ensuring that all Americans have access to healthy, affordable food, as emphasized in the *Biden-Harris Administration National Strategy on Hunger, Nutrition, and Health*. This is an important moment to protect food assistance benefits that reflect the true cost of a basic, healthy diet, strengthen cross enrollment capabilities across Federal assistance programs, and eliminate barriers to food assistance for vulnerable groups. These barriers make it difficult for underserved groups to succeed, including low-income college students, individuals reentering society and seeking a second chance, youth who have aged out of foster care, kinship families, low-income individuals in the U.S. Territories, and Supplemental Nutrition Assistance Program (SNAP) recipients facing time limits. Rather than reducing obstacles to employment, research demonstrates that time limits on SNAP eligibility amplify existing inequities in food and economic security. Beyond removing barriers to food access, there is also the opportunity to make healthier choices easier by expanding food purchasing options, fruit and vegetable incentives, and local food procurement through Federal nutrition programs, including by building upon efforts already plotted by USDA. The Farm Bill reauthorization process is an opportunity to strengthen program integrity to address new risks and vulnerabilities while ensuring that USDA can continue to support the needs of all eligible households.

The Administration looks forward to working with the Congress to: support new and beginning farmers; shore up the Federal Government's commitment to agricultural research; address climate change by protecting and enhancing investments in conservation, climate-smart agriculture and forestry, and clean energy; strengthen local and regional food supply chains; continue efforts on reducing food loss and waste; support competition by increasing transparency and continuing to support small and independent processors; open new market opportunities and provide a competitive advantage for American producers—including small and historically underserved producers and early adopters. In addition, the Administration supports improvements to crop insurance, proactively managing risk from natural hazards, including the permanent authorization of the cover crop incentive program. These Administration priorities can help create a stronger safety net and better markets for consumers and producers of U.S. agricultural products through the Farm Bill, which is one piece of the puzzle for how USDA helps people across America and the globe.

DEPARTMENT OF COMMERCE

The Department of Commerce (Commerce) is responsible for: promoting job creation; supporting and overseeing international trade; and providing economic, environmental, and scientific information needed by businesses, citizens, and governments. The President's 2025 Budget for Commerce promotes access to good jobs and equitable growth, protects supply chains and national security, bolsters American leadership in manufacturing and responsible innovation, and produces better data about the Nation's economy.

The Budget requests $11.4 billion in discretionary budgetary authority for 2025, a $287 million or 2.4-percent increase above the 2023 level. Resources provided through the 2025 Budget support significant investments in America's innovation economy authorized under the CHIPS and Science Act of 2022.

The President's 2025 Budget:

- **Fosters Economic Development and Creates Good-Paying Jobs.** The Budget provides the U.S. Economic Development Administration (EDA) with $437 million to award grants that help communities across the Nation bolster innovation, competitiveness, and economic development. This represents a significant $131.5 million or 43-percent increase under the Biden-Harris Administration. As part of this historic investment, the Budget provides $41 million to continue the Recompete Pilot Program, a new program established under this Administration to provide flexible, place-based funding to communities working to reduce prime-age employment gaps in the most economically distressed areas. The Budget also proposes $41 million for the Good Jobs Challenge to fund high-quality, locally-led workforce systems that expand career opportunities for hard-working Americans, and $5 million for grants focused exclusively on the economic development needs of tribal governments and indigenous communities.

- **Promotes Leadership and Responsible Innovation in Artificial Intelligence (AI).** The Budget invests $65 million with Commerce to safeguard, regulate, and promote AI, including protecting the American public against its societal risks. This funding would allow Commerce to successfully implement central components of the Administration's Executive Order 14110, "Safe, Secure, and Trustworthy Development and Use of Artificial Intelligence." Specifically, the National Institute of Standards and Technology (NIST) would establish the U.S. AI Safety Institute to operationalize NIST's AI Risk Management Framework by creating guidelines, tools, benchmarks, and best practices for evaluating and mitigating dangerous capabilities and conducting evaluations including red-teaming to identify and mitigate AI risk. The institute would develop technical guidance that would be used by regulators considering rulemaking and enforcement on issues such as authenticating content created by humans, watermarking AI-generated content, identifying and mitigating against harmful algorithmic discrimination, ensuring transparency, and enabling adoption of privacy-preserving AI, and would serve as a driver of the future workforce for safe and trusted AI.

- **Supports Offshore Wind Energy and Climate Resilience.** The Budget provides $53 million to expand offshore wind permitting activities at the National Oceanic and Atmospheric Administration (NOAA), a $31 million increase above the 2023 enacted level. This would support NOAA in its efforts to use the best available science to support the goal of deploying 30 gigawatts of offshore energy by 2030 while protecting biodiversity and promoting sustainable ocean co-use. The Budget also provides $16 million for NOAA's Climate Adaptation Partnerships, which would support collaborative efforts that help communities build equitable climate resilience.

- **Encourages Technological Development and Innovation across the Nation.** The Budget includes $4 billion in mandatory funds for EDA's Regional Technology and Innovation Hubs Program to build on the one-time $500 million investment provided in the Consolidated Appropriations Act, 2023. The Budget also includes $41 million in discretionary funding for smaller grants that enable tech and innovation growth in underrepresented regions. In total, this funding would enable EDA to establish cutting-edge and strategic regional technology hubs that foster the geographic diversity of innovation and create quality jobs in and for underserved and vulnerable communities across the Nation.

- **Advances the Next Generation of Weather Satellites.** The Budget provides $2.1 billion for weather satellites, a $432 million increase above the 2023 enacted level. This investment would maintain the existing fleet of satellites critical for extreme weather forecasts and invest in next generation systems that would provide more accurate forecasts and outlooks as well as new environmental monitoring capabilities as the Nation faces more powerful and frequent storms and extreme weather caused by climate change.

- **Supports Minority-Owned Businesses to Narrow Racial Wealth Gaps.** The Budget provides an additional $10 million to increase the capacity of the Minority Business Development Agency (MBDA) for a total of $80 million. Overall, this funding level reflects a $32 million increase for MBDA since the start of the Administration. This continued investment would bolster services provided to minority-owned, including women of color-owned, enterprises by expanding the Business Center Program, funding the Rural Business Center program, and supporting innovative initiatives to foster economic resiliency.

- **Modernizes Research Facilities.** The Budget invests in the fundamental infrastructure that makes science possible. The Budget provides $312 million for maintenance, renovations, and improvements at NIST research campuses, a $182 million increase above the 2023 enacted level. With these resources, NIST would overhaul the backbone of several electricity, heating, and cooling capabilities to enable its laboratories to continue to advance in measurement sciences and calibration services.

- **Protects High-Priority Natural Resources.** The Budget provides $86 million to support National Marine Sanctuaries and Marine Protected Areas as part of the Administration's America the Beautiful Initiative, which aims to conserve at least 30 percent of U.S. lands and waters by 2030. This is an $18 million increase above the 2023 enacted level, which would expand critical conservation work and support the designation process for additional sanctuaries. In addition, the Budget provides $34 million, a $10 million increase over the 2023 enacted level, to support Mitchell Act hatcheries in the Columbia River Basin. These additional funds are part of the Administration's commitment to prioritize the restoration of healthy and abundant wild salmon, steelhead, and other native fish populations to the Columbia River Basin, and honor the United States' obligations to tribal nations.

- **Improves Economic Data.** The Budget provides $1.6 billion for the Census Bureau, a $93 million increase from the 2023 enacted level. This includes funding to support information technology system modernization to improve the collection and analysis of data, funding to improve how the Census Bureau measures the economic wellbeing of Americans over time, and investments in gathering data about Puerto Rico's people and economy. The Budget provides $138.5 million for the Bureau of Economic Analysis, an $8.5 million increase from the 2023 enacted level, to support economic statistics, including research on environmental-economic statistics.

- **Protects Critical and Emerging Technology.** The Budget provides $223 million to the Bureau of Industry and Security (BIS). These resources would help BIS expand export enforcement domestically and overseas, bolster the Bureau's capacity to identify critical and emerging technologies eligible for export control and evaluate the effectiveness of export controls, and increase regional expertise to enhance cooperation on export controls with allies and partners. In addition, the Budget provides $5 million for the International Trade Administration to effectively implement new requirements under Executive Order 14105, "Addressing United States Investments in Certain National Security Technologies and Products in Countries of Concern."

DEPARTMENT OF DEFENSE

The Department of Defense (DOD) is responsible for the military forces needed to safeguard the United States' vital national interests. The President's 2025 Budget for DOD provides the resources necessary to sustain and strengthen U.S. deterrence, advancing vital national security interests through integrated deterrence, campaigning, and investments that build enduring advantages. The Budget supports America's servicemembers and their families, strengthens alliances and partnerships, bolsters America's technological edge, ensures readiness, preserves economic competitiveness, and combats 21st Century security threats.

The Budget includes $850 billion in discretionary budget authority for 2025, a $34 billion or 4.1-percent increase from the 2023 enacted level. This growth is in alignment with levels agreed to in the Fiscal Responsibility Act of 2023 and enables DOD to make the investments necessary to execute the Administration's 2022 *National Security Strategy* and *2022 National Defense Strategy*.

In addition, the Budget includes a request for unmet needs from the Administration's October 2023 supplemental request for urgent security needs through the end of 2024.

The President's 2025 Budget:

- **Promotes Integrated Deterrence in the Indo-Pacific and Globally.** To sustain and strengthen deterrence, the Budget provides funding to prioritize China as America's pacing challenge in line with the *2022 National Defense Strategy*. DOD's 2025 *Pacific Deterrence Initiative* highlights some of the key investments the Department is making, focuses on strengthening deterrence in the region, and demonstrates the Department's long-term commitment to the Indo-Pacific. The Budget also provides funding to advance the Administration's commitments under the Australia-United Kingdom-United States enhanced trilateral security partnership (AUKUS) dedicated to bolstering security and stability in the region. DOD is building the concepts, capabilities, and posture necessary to meet these challenges, working to integrate deterrence efforts across the U.S. Government and with U.S. allies and partners.

- **Supports Ukraine, European Allies, and Partners.** The Budget continues to provide critical support for Ukraine, North Atlantic Treaty Organization (NATO) allies, and other European partner states by prioritizing funding to enhance the capabilities and readiness of U.S., allied, and partner forces in the face of continued Russian aggression. However, the Budget cannot address the critical support to Ukraine, which requires congressional action on the Administration's October 2023 national security supplemental request.

- **Counters Persistent Threats.** While focused on maintaining robust deterrence against China and Russia, the Budget also provides funding to enable DOD to remain vigilant in the face of other persistent threats including those posed by North Korea, Iran, and violent extremist organizations.

- **Modernizes the Nuclear Deterrent.** The Budget provides funding to maintain a strong nuclear deterrent as a foundational aspect of integrated deterrence, for the security of the Nation and U.S. allies. The Budget supports the U.S. nuclear triad, NATO strategic deterrence, and the necessary ongoing nuclear modernization programs, to include the nuclear command, control, and communication networks.

- **Invests in the Submarine Industrial Base (SIB).** DOD conducted the 2025 SIB study to determine how to complete the once-in-a-generation recapitalization of the submarine force needed to increase the United States' ability to build and sustain attack submarines to meet U.S. military requirements. The Budget builds on the Administration's October 2023 supplemental request supporting the SIB and also supports the Administration's commitments under AUKUS—the first major deliverable of which was the historic decision to support Australia acquiring conventionally-armed, nuclear-powered submarines.

- **Advances U.S. Cybersecurity.** The Budget continues to invest in cybersecurity programs to protect the Nation from malicious cyber actors and cyber campaigns. These investments strengthen cyber protection standards for the defense industrial base (DIB) and cybersecurity of DOD networks.

- **Delivers a Robust Military Pay Raise.** The Budget funds a robust 4.5 percent pay raise for America's servicemembers, continuing to build on the highest pay raise in decades of 5.2 percent in 2024. The Budget also provides servicemembers with annual rate increases for both housing and subsistence allowances.

- **Increases Income Eligibility Threshold for Basic Needs Allowance (BNA).** The Budget proposes to increase the income eligibility threshold for BNA from 150 percent to 200 percent of the Federal Poverty Guidelines.

- **Fulfills America's Commitment to Military Families.** Military families are key to the readiness and well-being of the All-Volunteer Force, and therefore are critical to national security. The Budget continues to support military families by prioritizing programs, including the Secretary of Defense's Taking Care of People initiatives, that seek to increase access to behavioral health providers, continue access to employment opportunities for military spouses, and increase access to high-quality child care for military families via the Child Care Workforce Initiative.

- **Focuses on Suicide and Sexual Assault Prevention and Response Efforts.** The Budget includes funding to support the Department's efforts on Suicide Prevention and Response and implements recommendations from the Suicide Prevention and Response Independent Review Committee. This funding would support improving the delivery of mental healthcare, addressing stigma and other barriers to care, revising suicide prevention training, and promoting a culture of lethal means safety. The Budget also includes funding to support the Department's efforts on Sexual Assault Prevention and Response and implements Secretary-approved recommendations from the Independent Review Commission on Sexual Assault in the Military, designed to increase awareness, provide support mechanisms to victims, and significantly reduce the environment for, tolerance of, and occurrence of sexual assault, sexual harassment, and domestic violence in the Joint Force. The Budget also includes funding to continue implementation of military justice reforms, led by each of the Services' Office for Special Trial Counsel.

- **Promotes Energy Efficiency and Installation Resilience for Warfighting Operations.** The Budget invests in power and energy performance, which makes U.S. forces more agile, efficient, and survivable. The Budget also improves the resilience of DOD facilities and operations to protect mission critical capabilities.

- **Enhances Biodefense and Pandemic Preparedness.** The Budget provides robust funding to support the Administration's *2022 National Biodefense Strategy and Implementation Plan for Countering Biological Threats, Enhancing Pandemic Preparedness, and Achieving Global Health Security*, the National Biotechnology and Biomanufacturing Initiative, and to implement recommendations from DOD's *2023 Biodefense Posture Review*.

- **Ensures Readiness across America's Armed Forces.** The Budget continues to ensure that U.S. Soldiers, Sailors, Airmen, Marines, and Guardians remain the best trained and equipped fighting forces in the world. The Budget places additional emphasis on foundational investments to sustain current weapon systems and support increased training across the Department, while pursuing technological enhancements to extend the service life of material vital to the warfighter. In addition, the Budget continues the recapitalization and optimization of the four public Naval Shipyards to meet future submarine and carrier maintenance requirements.

- **Builds the Air Power Needed for the 21ˢᵗ Century.** The Budget funds the procurement of a mix of highly capable crewed aircraft while continuing to modernize fielded fighter, bomber, mobility, and training aircraft. The Budget also accelerates the development and procurement of uncrewed combat aircraft and the relevant autonomy to augment crewed aircraft. Investing in this mix of aircraft provides an opportunity to increase the resiliency and flexibility of the fleet to meet future threats, while reducing operating costs.

- **Optimizes U.S. Naval Shipbuilding and Modernization.** Maintaining U.S. naval power is critical to reassuring allies and deterring potential adversaries. The Budget includes executable and responsible investments in the U.S. Navy fleet. The Budget also continues the recapitalization of the Nation's strategic ballistic missile submarine fleet while robustly investing in the SIB. In addition, the Budget invests in improving the lethality and survivability of the fleet, particularly improving undersea superiority.

- **Strengthens the U.S. Supply Chain and Industrial Base.** The Budget invests in key technologies and sectors of the U.S. industrial base such as microelectronics, submarine construction, munitions production, and biomanufacturing. The Budget supports DOD's modernization initiatives in its organic industrial base to maintain the Nation's readiness.

- **Supports a Ready and Modern Army.** The Budget maintains a ready Army capable of responding globally as part of the Joint Force through investments in Army modernization initiatives, including critical non-kinetic and long-range strike capabilities. In addition, the Budget modernizes and expands the production capacity of the industrial base to ensure the Army can meet strategic demands for critical munitions.

- **Invests in Long-Range Fire Capabilities.** The safety and security of the Nation requires a strong, sustainable, and responsive mix of long-range strike capabilities. The Budget invests in the development and testing of hypersonic strike capabilities while enhancing existing long-range strike capabilities to bolster deterrence and improve survivability.

- **Increases Space Resilience.** Space is vital to U.S. national security and is integral to modern warfare. The Budget maintains America's advantage by providing funding to improve the resilience of U.S. space architectures, such as in-space sensing and communications, in order to bolster deterrence and increase survivability.

- **Optimizes Force Structure.** In line with the *2022 National Defense Strategy*, the Budget provides funding to optimize force structure in order to build a Joint Force that is lethal, sustainable, resilient, survivable, agile, and responsive.

- **Supports Defense Research and Development (R&D) and the Defense Technology Industrial Base.** DOD plays a critical role in overall Federal R&D that spurs innovation, yields high-value technology, enables America to maintain and build advantages over strategic competitors, and creates good-paying jobs. The Budget sustains high levels of defense R&D, testing, and evaluation funding to invest in breakthrough technologies that drive innovation, support capacity in the defense technology industrial base, ensure American technological leadership, and underpin the development of future defense capabilities.

- **Invests in Artificial Intelligence (AI).** The Budget provides funding to responsibly develop, test, procure, and integrate transformative AI applications across the Department. The Budget also supports the implementation of Executive Order 14110, "Safe, Secure, and Trustworthy Development and Use of Artificial Intelligence."

- **Reiterates the Administration's Request for Urgent National Security Priorities.** In October 2023, the Administration submitted an emergency national security supplemental request to the Congress for urgent security needs through the end of 2024. This request included $58 billion for DOD to provide critical support to Israel and Ukraine, and to strengthen integrated deterrence in the Indo-Pacific. The request would also make crucial investments in the American DIB, benefitting U.S. military readiness and helping to create and sustain jobs across America. Absent congressional action on this emergency request, DOD would not be able to provide this urgently needed support to its allies and partners, or to make these critical DIB investments. The Administration appreciates the bipartisan supplemental legislation that passed the Senate that would address these urgent needs.

DEPARTMENT OF EDUCATION

The Department of Education (ED) is responsible for assisting States, school districts, and institutions of higher education in providing a high-quality education to all students and addressing the inequitable barriers underserved students face in education. The President's 2025 Budget for ED makes critical investments to: spur the Nation's future prosperity; accelerate academic growth; bolster mental health supports for students at all levels; advance the needs of students with disabilities; increase affordability and quality in higher education; and improve connections between the K-12 system, higher education, and the workforce.

The Budget requests $82 billion in discretionary funding for ED in 2025, a $3.1 billion or 3.9-percent increase from the 2023 level.

The President's 2025 Budget:

Preschool to 12th Grade Education

- **Supports Academic Achievement for All Students, Particularly Students in Schools with High Rates of Poverty.** The disruptive effect of the COVID-19 pandemic on student learning has added new urgency to the work of schools. The Budget includes $8 billion in mandatory funding to provide Academic Acceleration and Achievement Grants to close opportunity and achievement gaps and speed the pace of learning recovery. Carrying forward efforts funded by the American Rescue Plan, these grants to school districts would support evidence-based strategies to increase school attendance, provide high-quality tutoring, and expand learning time, including both in the summer and in extended day or afterschool programs. To help ensure that every student receives the high-quality education they deserve, the Budget also provides $18.6 billion for Title I, a $200 million increase above the 2023 enacted level. This funding amount is $2.1 billion higher than when the President took office, reflecting the President's strong commitment to expanding support for every American student. Title I, which reaches 90 percent of school districts across the Nation, delivers critical funding to schools in low-income communities so they can provide their students with the learning opportunities needed to recover academically from the COVID-19 pandemic and be successful after graduation.

- **Expands Access to High-Quality Preschool.** The Budget includes a major new mandatory funding proposal for a Federal-State partnership to provide free, high-quality preschool to four-year olds, offered in the setting of a parent's choice—from public schools to child care providers to Head Start. The proposal gives States the flexibility to expand preschool to three-year-old children once they make high-quality preschool fully available to four-year-old children. Over the next 10 years, this proposal would dramatically expand access to effective early childhood education, ensuring students enter kindergarten ready to learn. This proposal would be administered by the Department of Health and Human Services in collaboration with ED. The Budget also includes $25 million for incentive demonstration grants to create or expand free, high-quality preschool in school or community-based settings for children eligible to attend Title I schools. The incentive demonstration grants, which would require close collaboration among school districts, Head Start, and other community-based providers, would serve as models that could be adopted across the Nation. This program would expand its reach by encouraging districts to leverage Title I funds, along with other Federal, State, and local funds.

- **Bolsters Mental Health Supports for All Students.** The mental health of students, teachers, and school staff is essential for their overall well-being and continued academic recovery, and continues to be a high priority of the Administration, which has delivered an additional $2.1 billion to mental health programs since 2021. Research shows that students who receive social, emotional, mental, and behavioral supports have better outcomes, including performing better academically. The Budget provides a combined total of $216 million for mental health programs, including $200 million from the Bipartisan Safer Communities Act, a 900-percent increase in program funding since 2021. These funds would help increase the number of school-based counselors, psychologists, social workers, and other mental health professionals in K-12 schools.

- **Addresses Critical Educator Shortages.** While the education sector has faced shortages in critical staffing areas for decades, these shortages have grown worse since the COVID-19 pandemic, highlighting the importance of retaining educators and building strong pipelines into the profession. Since 2021, the Administration has supported schools in addressing educator shortages, including by supporting the expansion of evidence-based pathways such as residencies and grow your own programs, which may be provided through teacher registered apprenticeships. The Budget includes $90 million for Supporting Effective Education Development, $95 million for the Teacher Quality Partnership program, and $30 million for the Hawkins Centers of Excellence program, to expand the number of prospective teachers who have access to comprehensive, high-quality pathways and improve the diversity of the teacher pipeline. The Budget also includes critical investments in recruitment and retention of teachers and school leaders, and provides $173 million for the Teacher and School Leader Incentive Fund.

- **Increases Support for Children with Disabilities.** To support high-quality special education services for over seven million Pre-K through 12 students with disabilities, the Budget provides $14.4 billion for Individuals with Disabilities Education Act (IDEA) State Grants, a $200 million increase over the 2023 enacted level. Since 2021, the Administration has secured a $1.3 billion, or 10-percent, increase in annual funding for the program as well as an additional $2.6 billion in American Rescue Plan funds to help students with disabilities recover from the COVID-19 pandemic. The Budget also invests $545 million in IDEA Grants for Infants and Families, to provide early intervention services to infants and toddlers with disabilities. To address nationwide special educator shortages, the Budget also invests $125 million, which is $10 million above the 2023 enacted level, in grants to prepare special education and early intervention personnel—addressing another critical educator shortage area.

- **Expands Full-Service Community Schools.** Community schools continue to be a high priority for the Administration as they play a critical role in providing comprehensive wraparound services to students and their families, including afterschool programs, adult education opportunities, and health and nutrition services, and have been demonstrated to improve academic and other outcomes for students. The Budget provides $200 million for this program, an increase of $50 million above the 2023 enacted level, and a 500-percent, or $120 million, increase in program funding since the beginning of the Administration.

- **Supports Multilingual Learners.** The number of students learning English as a second language continues to grow in the Nation's schools, and multilingualism is a crucial skill that all students should develop to be competitive in a global economy. The Budget provides $940 million for the English Language Acquisition program, an increase of $50 million above the 2023 enacted level, to help students learning English attain English proficiency and achieve academic success. The Budget provides $72 million in dedicated funding to help schools hire more bilingual teachers and allow States and districts to provide professional development on multilingual education for existing teachers and staff.

Education Beyond High School

- **Improves College Affordability and Provides Free Community College.** To help low- and middle-income students overcome financial barriers to postsecondary education, the Budget proposes to increase the discretionary maximum Pell Grant by $100 and thereby expand the reach of the program to over 7.2 million students. The Budget builds on successful bipartisan efforts to increase the maximum Pell Grant award by $900 over the past two years—the largest increase in more than 10 years. The Budget provides a path to double the maximum award by 2029 for students attending public and non-profit institutions. The Budget excludes for-profit institutions from the mandatory increases due to evidence these institutions are least likely to provide good outcomes for students. The Budget also expands free community college across the Nation through a Federal-State partnership. In addition, the Budget provides two years of subsidized tuition for students from families earning less than $125,000 enrolled in a four-year Historically Black College and University (HBCU), Tribally Controlled College and University (TCCU), or Minority-Serving Institution (MSI).

- **Invests in Services for Student Borrowers.** The Budget provides $2.7 billion for the Office of Federal Student Aid (FSA), a $625 million increase above the 2023 enacted level. This additional funding is needed to provide better support to the 46 million student loan borrowers and make additional and necessary improvements to the new servicing system. This increase would allow FSA to continue to modernize its digital infrastructure and ensure the successful administration of its financial aid programs, including the Free Application for Federal Student Aid, through a simplified and streamlined process for students and borrowers.

- **Reduces College Costs for Students.** High college prices deter many young people from attending the colleges that would be best for them. The Budget includes a $12 billion mandatory Reducing the Costs of College Fund that would fund three strategies to lower college costs for students. First, the fund would provide competitive awards for public institutions that affordably deliver a quality education, allowing those schools to use those funds either to serve more students or to share best practices so that other schools can become more affordable. Second, the Classroom to Career fund would also provide over $7 billion for States to provide access to at least 12 credits of transferable career-connected dual enrollment credits to students while in high school—credits that can enable students to obtain postsecondary degrees more affordably. Third, the fund would support evidence-based strategies, such as the City University of New York's Accelerated Study in Associate Programs model, which increase college graduation rates, reduce cost burdens for students, and lower costs per graduate.

- **Eliminates the Origination Fee on Student Loans.** The Budget builds on the President's historic actions to reduce student debt and the cost of college by eliminating the origination fees charged to borrowers on every new Federal student loan. These unnecessary fees burden anyone who needs to borrow to help get an education and cost American families billions of dollars.

- **Reimagines the Transition from High School to Higher Education.** Reimagining traditional educational pathways to higher education is critical to improving outcomes for all students. The Budget doubles the funding provided in 2023 for national activities in career and technical education, including a focus on the Career-Connected High Schools initiative, which seeks to increase the integration and alignment of the last two years of high school and the first two years of higher education by expanding access to dual enrollment programs, work-based learning, college and career advising, and the opportunity to earn industry-recognized credentials while in high school.

- **Supports Students through Graduation.** The Budget supports strategies to improve the enrollment, retention, transfer, and completion rates of students by investing in the Federal TRIO Programs and Gaining Early Awareness and Readiness for Undergraduate Programs, and by more than doubling funding for the Postsecondary Student Success Grants Program. The Budget also promotes student success through investments to support students' basic needs, including funding to help students access non-student aid public benefits and to provide affordable child care for low-income student parents.

- **Expands Institutional Capacity at HBCUs, TCCUs, MSIs—including Hispanic Serving Institutions (HSIs)—and Community Colleges.** The Budget increases institutional capacity at HBCUs, TCCUs, MSIs—including HSIs—and under-resourced institutions, including community colleges, by providing an increase of $93 million above the 2023 enacted level. The Budget funding level is $329 million higher than the 2021 enacted level, underscoring the President's commitment to increasing funding to historically under-served institutions. The Budget also doubles funding by providing $100 million for four-year HBCUs, TCCUs, and MSIs to expand research and development infrastructure at these institutions, a program the President has championed since his first year in office to address historic disparities in Federal research and development funding to HBCUs, TCCUs, and MSIs.

Other Key Priorities

- **Strengthens Civil Rights Enforcement.** The Budget provides $162 million to ED's Office for Civil Rights (OCR), a $22 million increase above the 2023 enacted level. This funding would ensure that OCR has the personnel it needs to carry out its mission to protect equal access to education through the vigorous enforcement of civil rights laws.

- **Advances Opportunities and Manages Risks of Artificial Intelligence (AI).** AI has the potential to provide transformational academic programming and career opportunities for the Nation's students, but it also poses significant risks to the privacy, opportunity, and well-being of students and educators. To support implementation of Executive Order 14410, "Safe, Secure, and Trustworthy Development and Use of Artificial Intelligence," the Budget includes additional resources to enhance the capacity of Department staff, schools, and postsecondary institutions to achieve the promise of AI while managing inherent risks.

DEPARTMENT OF ENERGY

The Department of Energy (DOE) is responsible for supporting the Nation's prosperity by addressing its climate, energy, environmental, and nuclear security challenges through transformative science and technology solutions. The President's 2025 Budget for DOE builds on the Bipartisan Infrastructure Law and the Inflation Reduction Act; invests in innovation for the energy economy; advances basic research and scientific infrastructure; creates jobs building clean energy infrastructure; supports the Nation's energy and environmental justice goals; and modernizes and ensures the safety and security of the nuclear weapons stockpile.

The Budget requests $51 billion in discretionary budget authority for 2025, a $3.6 billion or 7.5-percent increase from the 2023 level.

The President's 2025 Budget:

- **Creates Jobs by Building Clean Energy Infrastructure and Lowers Energy Prices for American Families.** The Budget provides $1.6 billion for DOE, more than double the 2021 enacted level and 29 percent above the 2023 enacted level, to support clean energy workforce and infrastructure projects across the Nation, including: $385 million to weatherize and retrofit homes of low-income Americans; $95 million, $73 million above the 2021 enacted level, to electrify tribal homes, provide technical assistance to advance tribal energy projects, and transition tribal colleges and universities to renewable energy; $113 million for the Office of Manufacturing and Energy Supply Chains to strengthen domestic clean energy supply chains; and $102 million to support utilities and State and local governments in building a grid that is more secure, reliable, resilient, and able to integrate electricity from clean energy sources. These investments, which complement and bolster the historic funding in the Bipartisan Infrastructure Law and Inflation Reduction Act, create good-paying jobs while driving progress toward the Administration's climate goals, including producing carbon pollution-free electricity by 2035. The Budget also provides dedicated funding for the Interagency Working Group on Coal and Power Plant Communities and Economic Revitalization to facilitate a whole-of-Government approach to workforce training, community engagement, and identification of Federal resources to spur economic revitalization in hard-hit energy communities that have powered the Nation for generations. In addition to building clean energy infrastructure, the Budget also assumes enactment of the Administration's request for $300 million in supplemental funding for 2024 to safeguard the Strategic Petroleum Reserve, which is a critical energy security asset that has historically protected American consumers in times of emergency oil shortages.

- **Advances Critical Climate Goals.** The Budget includes $10.6 billion in DOE climate and clean energy research, development, demonstration, and deployment programs, an increase of 12 percent above the 2023 enacted level. Notably, these investments include over $1 billion to improve technologies to reduce pollution from industrial facilities, nearly $900 million to commercialize technologies like sustainable aviation fuel and zero-emission trucks to reduce emissions from the transportation sector, and over $2.4 billion in clean energy research and development to improve carbon-free electricity generation, transmission, distribution, and storage technologies for reliability, resilience, and decarbonization. Specifically, within the Office of Energy Efficiency and Renewable Energy, the Budget includes $502 million for the Vehicle Technologies Office, $280 million for the Bioenergy—including Sustainable Aviation Fuel—Technologies Office, $318 million for the Solar Energy Technologies Office, $199 million for the Wind Energy Technologies Office, $179 million for the Hydrogen and Fuel Cell Technologies Office, and over $500 million for the Advanced Materials and Manufacturing Office and the Industrial Efficiency and Decarbonization Office. In addition, the Budget invests in advancing climate modeling within the Biological and Environmental Research program in the Office of Science. Overall, this funding advances efforts crucial for achieving the goal of a 50- to 52-percent reduction from 2005 levels of economy-wide net greenhouse gas pollution in 2030 and economy-wide net-zero emissions no later than 2050, while also reducing energy bills for American families.

- **Builds the Clean Energy Innovation Pipeline.** The Budget includes $8.5 billion across DOE to support researchers and entrepreneurs transforming innovations into commercial clean energy products, including in areas such as: offshore wind; industrial heat; sustainable aviation fuel; and grid infrastructure. Across DOE, the Budget provides $325 million to support the research, development, and demonstration of technologies and processes to increase the domestic supply of sustainable critical minerals and materials essential for several clean energy technologies. The Budget supports $76 million to advance technologies that can enable earlier detection of methane leaks and integrate across a network of methane monitoring sensors for more reliable measurement and mitigation and $150 million to make small quantities of high-assay, low-enriched uranium (HALEU) available for ongoing advanced nuclear reactor demonstrations. The Budget also assumes enactment of the Administration's request for $2.2 billion in 2024 supplemental funding to procure low-enriched uranium (LEU) and HALEU, which—coupled with a long-term ban on imports of LEU and HALEU from Russia—would prompt sufficient private sector investment to reinvigorate U.S. uranium enrichment and reduce America's current dependence on Russian imports for roughly 20 percent of LEU used in civilian nuclear power reactors. The $8.5 billion also includes $845 million, an $81 million increase above the 2023 enacted level, for a Department-wide initiative to accelerate the viability of commercial fusion energy, coordinating academia, national laboratories, and the private sector, which supports the Bold Decadal Vision for Commercial Fusion Energy. The Budget funds eight crosscutting DOE Energy Earthshots initiatives which could substantially reduce the cost of energy for the American consumer through innovations in clean energy generation, energy efficiency, and storage. In addition, the Budget provides $30 million to accelerate commercial demonstration projects through a new national laboratory effort.

- **Reduces Health and Environmental Hazards for At-Risk Communities.** The Budget provides $8.2 billion to address legacy waste and contamination in communities used during the Manhattan Project and the Cold War for nuclear weapons production, including $3.1 billion to continue cleanup progress at the Hanford site in Washington. The Budget also supports $205 million to ensure cleanup remedies at Cold War sites remain protective of human health and the environment. The Administration would ensure the investments for the cleanup of legacy pollution and long-term stewardship of these sites align with the Justice40 Initiative to benefit disadvantaged communities.

- **Advances Energy Justice and Equity.** The Budget supports several key initiatives to accelerate equity and justice for historically excluded communities to benefit all Americans, including: $55 million for Community Capacity Building grants to address areas impacted by persistent poverty around DOE sites; $105 million to plan, design, and demonstrate community-scale energy solutions to mitigate extreme heat in low-income and disadvantaged communities; and $256 million to build capacity for advancing energy research and developing a new energy workforce through programs at Historically Black Colleges and Universities, Minority Serving Institutions, tribal colleges, community colleges, and emerging research institutions. The Budget also supports systematic implementation of the Justice40 Initiative and the Department's equity action plan strategies.

- **Maintains World Leading Research through the CHIPS and Science Act and Invests in Climate Innovation.** The Budget invests $8.6 billion for the Office of Science to boost American innovation and sustain American leadership in research and scientific discovery, advancing toward the CHIPS and Science Act full authorization level. These investments support: cutting-edge research at the national laboratories and universities as well as building and operating world-class scientific user facilities; identifying and accelerating novel technologies for clean energy solutions; improving predictability of climate trends and extremes using high performance computing; providing new computing insight through quantum information; and positioning the United States to meet the demand for isotopes. The Budget also assumes enactment of the Administration's request for $98 million in 2024 supplemental funding for increased domestic operational capacity for development and production of isotopes. This funding would decrease U.S. dependence on a foreign supply chain for isotopes which are critical for the public health, energy, and national security sectors and would increase U.S. competitiveness in the global market for isotopes.

- **Strengthens Artificial Intelligence (AI), Cybersecurity, and Resilience of the Energy Sector.** The Budget provides $455 million to extend the frontiers of AI for science and technology and to increase AI's safety, security, and resilience. These investments enhance the Department's computing capabilities and support the development of AI testbeds to build foundation models for energy security, national security, and climate resilience as well as tools to evaluate AI capabilities to generate outputs that may represent nuclear, nonproliferation, biological, chemical, critical-infrastructure, and energy security threats or hazards. The funding also invests in continued support for training new researchers from a diverse array of backgrounds capable of meeting the rising demand for AI talent.

- **Protects the Nation from Weapons of Mass Destruction (WMD) Terrorism.** The Budget enhances DOE capabilities to prevent and respond to WMD terrorist attacks by non-state actors at home and abroad. The Budget also supports DOE's long-standing efforts to advance nuclear and radioactive material security, enhancing U.S. national security, health, and economic interests. In addition, the Budget continues investments to develop the next generation of arms control technologies and experts to help mitigate against emerging and evolving national security risks.

- **Strengthens the Nation's Nuclear Deterrent.** The Budget provides $19.8 billion for Weapons Activities, $4.5 billion above the 2021 enacted level, to prioritize implementation of the *2022 National Defense Strategy* and Nuclear Posture Review by modernizing the Nation's nuclear deterrent to keep the American people safe. The Budget supports a safe, secure, reliable, and effective nuclear stockpile and a resilient, responsive nuclear security enterprise necessary to protect the U.S. homeland and allies from growing international threats.

- **Powers the Nuclear Navy.** DOE's Naval Nuclear Propulsion Program ensures safe and reliable operation of reactor plants in nuclear-powered submarines and aircraft carriers. The Budget prioritizes infrastructure modernization and investments to develop, refine, and deliver new technologies to the Navy and maintain America's advantage over its adversaries.

DEPARTMENT OF HEALTH AND HUMAN SERVICES

The Department of Health and Human Services (HHS) is responsible for protecting the health and well-being of Americans through its research, public health, and social services programs. The President's 2025 Budget for HHS: expands access to quality, affordable healthcare while lowering costs; dramatically improves access to early care and learning; advances the Biden Cancer Moonshot; transforms behavioral healthcare; enhances public health infrastructure and capabilities to improve health outcomes; bolsters maternal health; advances health equity; and transforms child welfare.

The Budget requests $130.7 billion in discretionary budget authority for 2025, a $2.2 billion or 1.7-percent increase from the 2023 level. This request includes appropriations for the 21st Century Cures Act and the program integrity cap adjustment.

The President's 2025 Budget:

Reduces Drug and Other Healthcare Costs for All Americans

- **Negotiates Lower Drug Prices and Expands Access to Prescription Drugs.** Thanks to action taken by this Administration, millions of seniors are saving money on their drug costs, and the Administration announced the first 10 drugs for which prices will be negotiated by Medicare as it continues implementation of the Inflation Reduction Act. The Budget builds on this success by: significantly increasing the pace of negotiation; bringing more drugs into negotiation sooner after they launch; expanding the Inflation Reduction Act's inflation rebates and $2,000 out-of-pocket prescription drug cost cap beyond Medicare and into the commercial market; and by taking other steps to build on the Inflation Reduction Act drug provisions. In addition, the Budget extends the $35 cost-sharing cap for a month's supply of a covered insulin product to the commercial market. For Medicaid, the Budget includes proposals to ensure Medicaid and the Children's Health Insurance Program (CHIP) are prudent purchasers of prescription drugs, such as authorizing HHS to negotiate supplemental drug rebates on behalf of interested States in order to pool purchasing power. The Budget also limits Medicare Part D cost-sharing for high-value generic drugs, such as those used to treat hypertension and hyperlipidemia, to no more than $2 for Medicare beneficiaries. To speed development and increase access of safe and affordable biosimilar medicines, the Budget streamlines and modernizes the Food and Drug Administration's (FDA) premarket review.

- **Expands Access to Quality, Affordable Healthcare.** The President and Vice President believe that healthcare is a right, not a privilege. With enrollment in marketplace coverage at an all-time high, the Budget builds on the incredible success of the Affordable Care Act by making permanent the expanded premium tax credits that the Inflation Reduction Act extended and providing Medicaid-like coverage to individuals in States that have not adopted

Medicaid expansion, paired with financial incentives to ensure States maintain their existing expansions. Further, the Budget includes an allowance to ban unwarranted "facility fees" for telehealth and certain outpatient services in commercial insurance. The Budget also includes funding for continued implementation of the No Surprises Act, which protects Americans across the Nation from surprise medical bills. For Medicaid and CHIP, the Budget allows States to extend the existing 12-month continuous eligibility for all children to 36 months, and allows States to provide continuous eligibility for children from birth until they turn age six. Further, the Budget prohibits enrollment fees and premiums in CHIP. The President also supports eliminating Medicaid funding caps for Puerto Rico and other Territories while aligning their matching rate with States and moving toward parity for other critical Federal programs including Supplemental Security Income and the Supplemental Nutrition Assistance Program.

Honors America's Commitment to Seniors and Americans in Need

- **Protects and Strengthens Medicare and Medicaid.** The Budget extends solvency of the Medicare Hospital Insurance (HI) trust fund indefinitely by ensuring that high-income individuals contribute their fair share and directing revenue from the Net Investment Income Tax into the HI trust fund as was originally intended. In addition, the Budget directs an amount equivalent to the savings from the Budget's proposed Medicare drug reforms into the HI trust fund. The Budget proposes to limit the portion of Medicaid and CHIP managed care dollars spent on administration and incentivize more investments in quality healthcare services by establishing a medical loss ratio.

- **Protects Seniors' Health and Dignity.** The Budget invests $150 billion over 10 years to improve and expand Medicaid home and community-based services, which allow older adults and individuals with disabilities to remain in their homes and stay active in their communities, and improve the quality of jobs for home care workers. In addition, the Budget proposes to shift funding for nursing home surveys from discretionary to mandatory beginning in 2026, and increase funding to cover 100 percent of statutorily-mandated surveys, which would guard against negligent care and ensure that Americans receive high-quality, safe services within the facilities. The Budget also continues to build on the President's commitment to protect the Nation's seniors through a comprehensive agenda that: improves the safety and quality of nursing home care; addresses the backlog of complaint surveys from nursing home residents and their families; expands financial penalties for underperforming facilities; requires greater transparency of nursing facility ownership; and increases the inspection of facilities with serious safety deficiencies.

Invests in the Health and Well-Being of Families and the Next Generation

- **Strengthens Families—and the Economy—by Investing in High-Quality Child Care.** From the beginning of this Administration, the President and Vice President have been focused on child care costs as a critical challenge for families. When child care is reliable, high-quality, and affordable, parents can make ends meet, advance in their careers, and stay in the workforce. Children benefit from early childhood experiences that support healthy child development and provide opportunities to socialize with peers. The President is committed to providing relief to families and the Budget creates a historic new program under which working families with incomes up to $200,000 per year would be guaranteed affordable, high-quality child care from birth until kindergarten, with most families paying no more than $10 a day, and the lowest income families paying nothing. This would provide a lifeline to the parents of more than 16 million children, saving the average family over $600 per month in care costs, per child. Parents would have the freedom to select a high-quality child care setting.

This investment could help hundreds of thousands of women with young children enter or re-enter the workforce more quickly. The President's Council of Economic Advisers found that recent Federal investments in child care have increased labor force participation among mothers with young children by roughly three percentage points, equivalent to over 300,000 more women in the labor force. The President's proposal would also ensure that early care and education workers receive fair and competitive pay. The Budget also provides $8.5 billion for the Child Care and Development Block Grant, a 44-percent increase since 2021, which would continue to serve school-age children, while most children under age six would be served through the new program.

- **Builds a Strong Foundation for Families with Universal Pre-K and Head Start.** The Budget funds voluntary, universal, free preschool for all four million of the Nation's four-year-olds and charts a path to expand preschool to three-year-olds. High-quality preschool would be offered in the setting of the parent's choice—from public schools to child care providers to Head Start. In addition, the Budget increases Head Start funding by $544 million to support the Administration's goal to reach pay parity between Head Start staff and public elementary school teachers with similar qualifications over time. Together these proposals would support healthy child development, help children enter kindergarten ready to learn, and support families by reducing their costs prior to school entry and allowing parents to work.

- **Supports Family Planning Services for More Americans.** Americans deserve access to the healthcare they need, including contraception and family planning services, which are essential to ensuring control over personal decisions about their own health, lives, and families. For more than 50 years, Title X family planning clinics have played a critical role in ensuring access to a broad range of high-quality family planning and preventive health services. Most Title X clients live in poverty and the uninsured rate of Title X users is twice the national average, making the Title X family planning program a critical part of the public health safety net. The Budget includes $390 million, a 36-percent increase above the 2023 enacted level, for the Title X Family Planning program to increase the number of patients served to 3.6 million.

- **Reduces Home Energy and Water Costs.** The Budget provides $4.1 billion for the Low Income Home Energy Assistance Program (LIHEAP). Reducing household energy and water costs continues to be a priority for the Administration, as reflected in the $7 billion in additional funding the Administration has secured for LIHEAP since 2021. LIHEAP helps families access home energy and weatherization assistance—vital tools for protecting vulnerable families' health in response to extreme weather and climate change. As part of the Justice40 Initiative, HHS plans to continue its efforts to prevent energy shutoffs and increase support for households with young children and older people, especially those that have high energy burdens. The Budget also proposes to expand LIHEAP to advance the goals of both LIHEAP and the Low Income Household Water Assistance Program. Specifically, the Budget gives States the option to use a portion of their LIHEAP funds to provide water bill assistance to low-income households.

- **Advances Child and Family Well-Being in the Child Welfare System.** With the overarching goal of keeping families safely together, reducing the number of children entering foster care, and achieving better outcomes for children, the Budget proposes to expand and incentivize the use of evidence-based foster care prevention services. The Budget provides States with support and incentives to place more foster children with relatives or other adults who have an existing emotional bond with the children instead of in group homes and institutions, and provides additional funding to support youth who age out of care without a permanent caregiver. The Budget proposes to nearly double flexible funding for States through the Promoting Safe and Stable Families Program, and proposes new provisions to expand access to legal representation for children and families in the child welfare system. The Budget provides competitive grants for States and localities to advance reforms that would reduce the overrepresentation of children and families of color in the child welfare system and address the disparate experiences and outcomes of these families. The Budget also respects the rights of Lesbian, Gay, Bisexual, Transgender, Queer, and Intersex individuals and provides more families with the support they need to remain safely together. In addition, the Budget provides $195 million for States and community-based organizations to respond to and prevent child abuse.

- **Supports America's Promise to Refugees and Care for Unaccompanied Children.** The Budget builds on the Administration's October 2023 supplemental request and provides $9.3 billion for the Office of Refugee Resettlement (ORR) to help rebuild the Nation's refugee resettlement infrastructure and support the resettling of up to 125,000 refugees in 2025. The Budget also helps ensure that unaccompanied immigrant children receive appropriate support and services while they are in ORR's care and are unified with relatives and sponsors as safely and quickly as possible. This funding would allow ORR to continue the programmatic improvements the Administration has made, including expanding access to counsel to help children navigate complex immigration court proceedings and enhancing case management and post-release services. In addition, the Budget includes an emergency contingency fund that would provide additional resources, beyond the $9.3 billion, when there are unanticipated increases in the number of unaccompanied children.

Transforms Behavioral Healthcare

- **Invests in Behavioral Healthcare.** In 2022, almost a quarter of adults suffered from mental illness, 13 percent of adolescents had serious thoughts of suicide, and overdose deaths continued near record highs. As a core pillar of his Unity Agenda, the President released a national strategy to transform how to understand and address mental health in America—and the Budget makes progress on this agenda by improving access to care for individuals and communities. The Budget makes significant investments in expanding the 988 Suicide and Crisis Lifeline that is projected to respond to 7.5 million contacts from individuals in distress in 2025 alone. In addition, the Budget: expands mental healthcare and support services in schools; expands the Centers for Disease Control and Prevention's (CDC) suicide prevention program to additional States, and tribal and territorial jurisdictions; increases funding for the Children's Mental Health Initiative by $50 million; doubles funding for the Mental Health Crisis Partnership Program; and invests in strengthening the behavioral health workforce—including integration into primary care settings. The Budget also expands access to behavioral health services through significant investments in Certified Community Behavioral Health Clinics and Community Mental Health Centers. In addition, the Budget provides $1 billion to advance health information technology adoption and engagement in interoperability for certain behavioral health providers.

- **Expands Coverage of Behavioral Healthcare Services.** The Budget further builds on the President's Unity Agenda by increasing access to behavioral health services through expanded coverage. For Medicare beneficiaries, the Budget ensures parity of coverage between behavioral and physical conditions, expands access to a broader range of behavioral health provider types, and reduces costs for patients receiving behavioral health services. The Budget also proposes to extend incentive payment programs for Medicare providers in areas with clinician shortages to a broader set of clinicians, including behavioral health clinicians. For people with commercial insurance, the Budget expands coverage of mental health benefits and strengthens the network of behavioral health providers.

- **Expands Access to Treatment for Substance Use Disorder.** The Administration has made historic advances in expanding access to treatment for opioid use disorder, including signing into law a bipartisan provision to expand the number of medical providers who can initiate buprenorphine treatment for opioid use disorder from 129,000 to nearly two million, a 15-fold increase that can expand treatment to rural and underserved areas. Funding for States, Territories, and Tribes through the Substance Use Prevention, Treatment, and Recovery Services Block Grant and the State Opioid Response grant program have grown by a combined seven percent since 2021, expanding access to prevention, harm reduction, treatment, and recovery support services nationwide. The Budget builds on these accomplishments by increasing funding for the State Opioid Response grant program, which has provided treatment services to over 1.2 million people and enabled States to reverse more than 500,000 overdoses with over nine million purchased overdose reversal medication kits. The Budget also invests in a new technical assistance center to strengthen health providers understanding and treatment of women's mental health and substance use.

Invests in Medical Innovation, Scientific Breakthroughs, and the Treatments of Tomorrow

- **Advances Progress toward Biden Cancer Moonshot Goals.** The President and First Lady reignited the Biden Cancer Moonshot to mobilize a national effort to end cancer as we know it—spurring tremendous action across the Federal Government and from the public and private sectors and building a strong foundation for the work ahead. To date, the Biden Cancer Moonshot has announced roughly 50 new programs, policies, and resources to address five priority actions including: improving access to cancer screening; understanding and addressing environmental and toxic exposures; making progress on cancer prevention; driving innovation to reach communities and individuals; and boosting support for patients, families, and caregivers. More than 100 private companies, non-profits, academic institutions, and patient groups have also stepped up with new actions and collaborations. The Budget makes significant investments to work toward the President and First Lady's signature Biden Cancer Moonshot goal of reducing the cancer death rate by at least 50 percent over the next 25 years and improving the experience of people who are living with or who have survived cancer. These include an increase of more than $2 billion across the National Cancer Institute, FDA, CDC, cancer projects at the Advanced Research Projects Agency for Health, and additional mandatory funds for the Indian Health Service (IHS) beginning in 2026.

- **Closes Research Gaps in Women's Health.** The President and the First Lady launched the first-ever White House Initiative on Women's Health Research, recognizing that women have been understudied and underrepresented in health research for far too long. The Initiative is working across Government to better integrate women's health within the Federal research portfolio and catalyze significant private and philanthropic commitments to increase funding for women's health research. The Administration proposes to transform the way the Government funds women's health research at the National Institutes of Health (NIH), including by creating a new nationwide network of centers of excellence and innovation in women's health. The Budget would also double existing funding for the Office of Research on Women's Health at NIH. These new resources would make investments that maximize the ability to prevent, diagnose, and treat health conditions in women and ensure women get the answers they need when it comes to their health.

Advances Health Equity

- **Promotes Maternal Health and Health Equity.** The United States has the highest maternal mortality rate among developed nations, and rates are disproportionately high for Black, American Indian and Alaska Native, and rural women. Since 2021, funding to reduce maternal mortality has grown by over $190 million, demonstrating this Administration's commitment to addressing needs in this area. The Budget continues this progress by including $376 million, an increase of $82 million above the 2023 enacted level to support the ongoing implementation of the *White House Blueprint for Addressing the Maternal Health Crisis*, launched by the Vice President, to reduce maternal mortality and morbidity rates, and address the highest rates of perinatal health disparities. The Budget expands Medicaid maternal health support services during the pregnancy and postpartum period by incentivizing States to reimburse a broad range of providers including doulas, community health workers, peer support initiatives, and nurse home visiting programs. In addition, the Budget builds on the success of the more than 40 States that answered the Vice President's call to extend Medicaid postpartum coverage by requiring all States to provide continuous Medicaid coverage for 12 months postpartum, eliminating gaps in health insurance at a critical time for all women.

- **Guarantees Adequate and Stable Funding for IHS.** The Administration is committed to upholding the United States' responsibility to tribal nations by addressing the historical underfunding of IHS. The enactment of an advance appropriation for 2024 for IHS was a historic and welcome step toward the goal of eventually securing adequate and stable funding for IHS that will provide needed improvements in access to care and the overall health status of American Indians and Alaska Natives. The Budget requests $8 billion in discretionary resources in 2025, a 12-percent increase over the 2021 enacted level. Included increases are for clinical services, preventative health, facilities construction, contract support costs, and tribal leases. Beginning in 2026, the Budget proposes all resources as mandatory. Mandatory funding would: close longstanding service and facility shortfalls over time; improve access to high-quality healthcare; and fund key Administration priorities, such as the Biden Cancer Moonshot. The Budget also proposes to reauthorize and increase funding for the Special Diabetes Program for Indians, which has been critical in lowering the prevalence of diabetes in Indian Country.

- **Advances Rural Health.** With over 60 million Americans living in rural areas, the Budget invests in direct primary care and mental healthcare services, expanded infrastructure, and assistance for rural hospitals to remain open and provide high-quality services in these critical communities.

Protects and Strengthens Public Health and Health Infrastructure

- **Helps Communities Respond to and Recover from Gun Violence.** Gun violence is a significant public health problem in the United States and is the leading cause of death for children and teens. The effects of gun violence extend beyond victims and their families. Gun violence can overwhelm communities and lead to short- and long-term needs. The Budget invests a total of $2.5 billion in discretionary and mandatory funds over 10 years in CDC to support an evidence-based community violence initiative. The initiative would address the causes of violence in communities and help reduce the health inequities that characterize such violence across the United States. The Budget also includes $60 million for gun violence research across CDC and NIH.

- **Enhances Biodefense and Public Health Infrastructure.** Over the past three years, substantial progress has been made toward developing and implementing transformational capabilities to increase the Nation's ability to respond to and prepare for emerging health threats. Building upon this progress, the Budget invests $9.8 billion in both discretionary and mandatory Prevention and Public Health Fund funding, an increase of $499 million over the 2023 enacted level, to bolster public health capacity that would enable CDC to better serve and protect the American public. These resources would continue to strengthen State, tribal, local, and territorial health departments, enhance public health data systems and collection, and improve the core immunization program. In addition, the Budget includes $20 billion in mandatory funding for HHS public health agencies in support of the Administration's biodefense priorities as outlined in the 2022 *National Biodefense Strategy and Implementation Plan for Countering Biological Threats, Enhancing Pandemic Preparedness, and Achieving Global Health Security*.

- **Strengthens Domestic Medical and Food Supply Chains.** The Administration has made historic investments over the past three years to increase the resiliency of America's supply chains. Using Defense Production Act authorities, HHS expanded domestic manufacturing capacity of medical countermeasures to make access to lifesaving drugs and vaccines more reliable and quickly scalable to respond to future threats. The Budget builds on this progress by investing $75 million in the Administration for Strategic Preparedness and Response to manufacture more essential medicines, medical countermeasures, and critical inputs in the United States and $12 million to strengthen FDA's capacity to identify and address potential disruptions and shortage threats. The Budget also expands end-to-end supply chain visibility to priority FDA-designated essential medicines and devices to prepare for and mitigate potential shortages. The Budget institutionalizes HHS's supply chain resilience and shortage mitigation efforts in a new office to coordinate Department-wide activities, strategy, and guidance for drugs, biologics, medical devices, and critical foods.

- **Invests in the Treatment and Prevention of Infectious Diseases.** The Budget invests in the treatment and prevention of infectious diseases, including Hepatitis C, HIV, and vaccine-preventable diseases. The Budget proposes a national program to significantly expand screening, testing, treatment, prevention, and monitoring of Hepatitis C infections in the United States, with a specific focus on populations with high infection levels. To help end the HIV epidemic, the Budget eliminates barriers to accessing pre-exposure prophylaxis—also known as PrEP—for Medicaid beneficiaries and proposes a new mandatory program to guarantee PrEP at no cost for all uninsured and underinsured individuals and provide essential wrap-around services. The Budget also invests in State and local efforts to promote equity and protect civil rights through a new initiative to modernize outdated criminal statutes with a discriminatory impact on HIV-positive individuals. In addition, the Budget proposes a new Vaccines for Adults program to provide uninsured adults with access to routine and outbreak vaccines at no cost. The Budget also expands the Vaccines for Children (VFC) program to include all children under age 19 enrolled in CHIP and covers the vaccine administration fee for all VFC-eligible uninsured children.

- **Invests in Healthcare Cybersecurity.** Cyber attacks on the healthcare system disrupt patient care and put patient safety at risk, and the healthcare system continues to be a target for cyber criminals. From 2018 to 2022, there was a 95-percent increase in large data breaches reported to HHS, including ransomware attacks. In line with the *National Cybersecurity Strategy*, which emphasizes a whole-of-Nation approach to addressing the ongoing cyber threat, the Budget invests in protecting the Nation's healthcare system from cyber threats. The Budget includes funding for the Administration for Strategic Preparedness and Response to coordinate HHS's cybersecurity efforts. The Budget provides $800 million to help high-need, low-resourced hospitals cover the upfront costs associated with implementing essential cybersecurity practices, and $500 million for an incentive program to encourage all hospitals to invest in advanced cybersecurity practices. The Budget also provides $141 million to continue strengthening HHS's ability to protect and defend HHS systems and information while supporting the Healthcare and Public Health Sector, including $11 million to expand and enhance HHS's capacity to protect the privacy and security of health information through Health Insurance Portability and Accountability Act of 1996 modernization. The Budget also invests in HHS's role in promoting the use of artificial intelligence in healthcare and public health while protecting against its risks.

- **Modernizes Organ Donor Systems and Networks.** In 2023, the President signed into law the Securing the U.S. Organ Procurement and Transplantation Network Act to overhaul and break up the monopoly that controlled the organ transplant system for decades. This law will help modernize the organ transplant system used to allocate and distribute donor organs to individuals waiting for transplants. The Budget includes critical funding that would support lifesaving reforms to the system to make it more agile, user friendly, accountable, and equitable, resulting in increased access to donor organs. The Budget also helps to facilitate and encourage transplants for Medicare beneficiaries through expanded support for living organ donors.

DEPARTMENT OF HOMELAND SECURITY

The Department of Homeland Security (DHS) is responsible for: protecting the United States from threats and hazards by preventing terrorism; securing the Nation's land and maritime borders; enforcing U.S. immigration laws; protecting the President and other key officials; securing Federal cyberspace and critical infrastructure; and ensuring disaster resilience, response, and recovery. The President's 2025 Budget for DHS advances climate resilience, Federal cybersecurity, maritime security, and humane border enforcement. Resources in the 2025 Budget build on prior-year investments in the DHS workforce, cybersecurity, border security, and hazard mitigation.

The Budget requests $62.2 billion in discretionary budget authority for 2025, a 2-percent increase above the 2023 level, when controlling for a proposal to use a greater portion of Passenger Security Fees to offset the Transportation Security Administration's (TSA) topline. The Budget also includes a proposed $4.7 billion Southwest Border Contingency Fund to respond to changing conditions on the Southwest border, which, if fully accessed, would increase the DHS request to 10 percent above the 2023 level.

In addition, the Budget includes a request for unmet needs from the Administration's October 2023 border and disaster supplemental requests, including investments to build additional DHS border and immigration capacity to better address conditions at the border and counter illegal fentanyl trafficking.

The President's 2025 Budget:

- **Reiterates the Administration's Request for Immediate Funding to Secure the Border, Build Capacity to Enforce Immigration Law, and Counter Fentanyl.** In October 2023, the Administration transmitted an emergency supplemental request for the Southwest border and migration issues totaling $11.8 billion, of which $8.7 billion was for DHS. The Budget includes, and therefore reiterates the need for, the unmet needs from the October 2023 supplemental request. In addition to urgent requirements, the request includes investments to build longer-term capacity in the areas of border security, immigration enforcement, and countering fentanyl, totaling $2.9 billion for DHS. This amount includes: $405 million to hire 1,300 additional Border Patrol Agents to secure the border; $239 million to hire 1,000 additional U.S. Customs and Border Protection (CBP) Officers to stop fentanyl and other contraband from entering the United States; $755 million to hire an additional 1,600 Asylum Officers and support staff to facilitate timely immigration dispositions; $100 million for Homeland Security Investigations to investigate and disrupt transnational criminal organizations and drug traffickers; and $849 million for cutting-edge detection technology at ports of entry. Taken together, these long-term capacity-building investments represent the

Administration's vision for ensuring the Nation's border security and immigration system can effectively respond to challenges present along the border. In addition, the Administration appreciates the Senate's bipartisan border legislation that would make additional investments in DHS and provide authorities to bolster the Department's efforts to secure and manage the border.

- **Continues to Invest in Critical Capabilities Needed for Border and Immigration Enforcement.** Strengthening border security and providing safe, lawful pathways for migration remain top priorities for the Administration. The Budget builds on the Administration's October 2023 supplemental request to include $25.9 billion for CBP and U.S. Immigration and Customs Enforcement (ICE), an increase of $1.9 billion over the 2023 enacted level when controlling for border management amounts. The Budget includes: funds for CBP to hire an additional 350 Border Patrol Agents and 310 processing coordinators; $127 million for border security technology between ports of entry; and $86 million in air and maritime operational support that is central to efforts to secure the border. The Budget also includes: funds to support 34,000 ICE immigration detention beds; $225 million to address increased transportation and removal costs; and $34 million to combat child exploitation, forced labor, and human trafficking.

- **Enables Resources to Scale Border Enforcement Capacity to Conditions on the Southwest Border.** Given the uncertainty surrounding border conditions in any given year, the Budget proposes a $4.7 billion contingency fund to aid the Department and its components when responding to migration surges along the Southwest border. Modeled on a contingency fund provided for unaccompanied children, each fiscal year the fund would receive appropriations incrementally, and above the base appropriation, as Southwest border encounters reach pre-identified levels. DHS would be limited to obligating funds for surge-related functions, and would transfer funds to CBP, ICE, and Federal Emergency Management Agency (FEMA) accounts for valid surge-related obligations.

- **Supports Refugee Processing.** As part of the Administration's commitment to welcome 125,000 refugees annually, the Budget proposes $145 million for U.S. Citizenship and Immigration Services (USCIS) International Refugee Affairs Division.

- **Protects the Homeland from the Threat of Weapons of Mass Destruction (WMD) Terrorism.** To ensure the security of the homeland from all types of terrorism threats, the Budget provides $418 million for Countering Weapons of Mass Destruction (CWMD). The CWMD office works across Federal, State, local, tribal, and territorial governments and the private sector to prevent WMD use against the homeland and promote readiness against chemical, biological, radiological, and nuclear threats. The Budget enhances the ability of high-risk urban areas across the United States to detect and prevent terrorist attacks using nuclear or other radiological material, through critical protection programs such as the Global Nuclear Detection Architecture, Securing the Cities, Radiation Portal Monitor Program, and Mobile Deployment Detection Program.

- **Supports Cybersecurity and Infrastructure Security.** To make U.S. cyberspace more resilient and secure, the Budget provides $3 billion for the Cybersecurity and Infrastructure Security Agency (CISA), an increase of $103 million over the 2023 enacted level. This includes: $470 million to deploy Federal network tools, including endpoint detection and response capabilities; $394 million for CISA's internal cybersecurity and analytical capabilities; $41 million for critical infrastructure security coordination; and $116 million for critical infrastructure cyber event reporting.

- **Deploys Artificial Intelligence (AI) Responsibly.** Recognizing that rapid advancements in AI and machine learning bring with them both opportunities and the potential for misuse, the Budget includes $5 million to open an office at DHS responsible for: coordinating the Department's use of AI; promoting AI innovation; and managing risks from the use of AI, including risks to rights and safety. Additional AI funds are also requested for existing programs in ICE, CBP, and FEMA to ensure investment and expansion of the DHS AI mission, in support of Executive Order 14110, "Safe, Secure, and Trustworthy Development and Use of Artificial Intelligence."

- **Invests in Climate and Natural Disaster Resilience.** As part of the Administration's efforts to build a climate resilient Nation, the Budget provides $4.4 billion for DHS's climate resilience programs. This is in addition to $1 billion provided by the Bipartisan Infrastructure Law for 2025. The Budget helps State and local communities, Tribes, and Territories build climate resilience through various FEMA grant and technical assistance programs, in support of the *National Climate Resilience Framework*. The Budget includes $531 million for flood hazard mapping, including the development of new data to support future flood conditions so that communities and Americans have the most up-to-date information regarding their flood risk.

- **Supports State, Local, Tribal, Territorial, and Community Preparedness.** The Budget proposes $3.2 billion for FEMA grants that support jurisdictions to prevent, protect against, mitigate, respond to, and recover from terrorism and natural disasters. The Budget increases funds for priority grant programs including: $770 million for firefighter grants, which is $50 million above the 2023 enacted level; $375 million for Emergency Management Performance Grants, which is $20 million above the 2023 enacted level; and $385 million for the Nonprofit Security Grant Program, which is $80 million above the 2023 enacted level, and provides vital security assistance to threatened nonprofits, including houses of worship.

- **Reiterates the Need for Additional Disaster Relief and Security Amounts.** In October 2023, the Administration transmitted an emergency supplemental request for domestic requirements totaling $56 billion, of which $9.2 billion was for DHS. The Budget includes, and therefore reiterates the need for, the unmet needs for FEMA from the October 2023 domestic supplemental request. This amount includes $9 billion for the Disaster Relief Fund to address ongoing recovery needs in communities that have suffered major disasters, and close the gap between disaster costs and available funding in 2024. The Budget also reiterates the supplemental request for $200 million for FEMA's Nonprofit Security Grant Program to support nonprofit institutions at risk of terrorist attacks.

- **Enhances America's Presence in the Indo-Pacific Region.** Increasing America's presence in the Indo-Pacific region is critical to strengthening security and prosperity in Asia. The Budget includes $263 million to increase Coast Guard presence in the Indo-Pacific: $200 million to procure two additional Fast Response Cutters; and $63 million to support training, partnerships, and regional engagement. This investment contributes to: building a more stable, free, and open region with unrestricted access to the maritime commons for all nations; advancing the existing rules-based international order; and solidifying the United States as a trusted partner in the region.

- **Supports Presidential Campaign and Special Event Security.** The Budget includes $2.9 billion for the Secret Service, including funds to meet both protective and investigative mission requirements. Of this amount, the Budget includes $70 million for security related to the 2024 Presidential Campaign and inauguration and $16 million to begin security preparations for the 2026 World Cup.

- **Modernizes TSA Pay and Workforce Policies.** The TSA workforce deserves to be fairly compensated at rates comparable with their peers in the Federal workforce. The Budget includes an additional $1.5 billion to fully fund the TSA pay equity initiative. Since implementing pay parity in July 2023, TSA has already seen an 11-percent reduction in attrition, and is making gains in retaining what has historically been a workforce with high turnover.

DEPARTMENT OF HOUSING AND URBAN DEVELOPMENT

The Department of Housing and Urban Development (HUD) is responsible for creating healthy, safe, sustainable, and inclusive communities and affordable homes. The President's 2025 Budget for HUD: protects and expands rental assistance for low-income families; provides new projects to prevent and reduce homelessness; takes steps to address affordable housing supply shortages; protects vulnerable populations from housing instability and health hazards; and prevents and redresses housing-related discrimination.

The Budget requests $72.6 billion in discretionary budget authority for 2025, a nearly $500 million, or 0.7-percent increase from the 2023 level. In recognition of challenges in the housing market, the Budget also includes significant mandatory and tax proposals to prioritize and expand rental assistance, homeownership, and affordable and climate resilient housing supply across the Nation.

The President's 2025 Budget:

- **Expands Access to Affordable Rent through the Housing Choice Voucher (HCV) Program.** The HCV program currently provides 2.3 million low-income families with rental assistance to obtain housing in the private market. The Budget proposes $32.8 billion in discretionary funding, an increase of $2.5 billion over the 2023 level, and assumes Public Housing Agencies will draw $963 million from HCV program reserves to maintain and protect critical services for all currently assisted families. The Budget also reflects the Administration's continued commitment to expand assistance, supporting an additional 20,000 households, particularly those who are experiencing homelessness or fleeing, or attempting to flee, domestic violence or other forms of gender-based violence. To further ensure that more households have access to safe and affordable housing, the Budget includes mandatory funding to support two populations that are particularly vulnerable to homelessness—youth aging out of foster care and extremely low-income (ELI) veterans. The Budget provides $9 billion to establish a housing voucher program for all 20,000 youth aging out of foster care annually, and provides $13 billion to incrementally expand rental assistance for 400,000 ELI veteran families, paving a path to guaranteed assistance for all who have served the Nation and are in need. Since the beginning of this Administration, HUD has expanded voucher assistance to over 100,000 additional families, and the Budget continues this progress by expanding voucher access to hundreds of thousands of families.

- **Increases Affordable Housing Supply to Reduce Housing Costs.** Access to safe and affordable housing is a critical foundation of the President's economic vision. The Budget builds on previous investments and actions by the Administration to boost housing supply and lower housing costs, particularly for lower- and middle-income households. The Budget invests $1.3 billion in the HOME Investment Partnerships Program (HOME) to construct and rehabilitate affordable rental housing and provide homeownership opportunities. To further address the critical shortage of affordable housing in communities throughout the Nation, the Budget provides $20 billion in mandatory funding for a new Innovation Fund for Housing Expansion, which would be a competitive grant program for municipalities and other entities that develop concrete plans for expanding housing supply, with additional funding for housing affordability pilots. The Budget also provides $7.5 billion in mandatory funding for new Project-Based Rental Assistance contracts to incentivize the development of new climate-resilient affordable housing. The Budget expands the existing Low-Income Housing Tax Credit and proposes a new Neighborhood Homes Tax Credit. Together these proposals would expand the supply of safe and affordable housing, bring new units to market, and ultimately help curb cost growth across the broader rental market.

- **Advances Efforts to End Homelessness**. The Budget provides $4.1 billion, an increase of $427 million over the 2023 level, for Homeless Assistance Grants to continue supporting approximately 1.2 million people experiencing homelessness each year and to expand assistance to approximately 25,000 additional households, specifically survivors of domestic violence and homeless youth. In addition, the Administration plans to use approximately $100 million in program recaptures to fund coordinated interventions to support nearly 11,000 additional homeless individuals and families. These new resources support the Administration's commitment to the goals laid out in the *All In: Federal Strategic Plan to Prevent and End Homelessness* and build on efforts that have expanded assistance to roughly 140,000 additional households experiencing homelessness since the President took office. The Budget also provides $505 million, or $6 million above the 2023 level, for Housing Opportunities for Persons with AIDS, serving a population with a disproportionately high rate of homelessness and providing a critical link to services. The Budget further reflects the Administration's commitment to make progress toward ending homelessness by providing $8 billion in mandatory funding for the acquisition, construction, or operation of housing to expand housing options for people experiencing or at-risk of homelessness, as well as $3 billion in mandatory funding for grants to provide counseling and emergency rental assistance to older adult renters at-risk of homelessness.

- **Supports Economic Development and Removes Barriers to Affordable Housing**. The Budget provides $2.9 billion for the Community Development Block Grant program to assist communities in modernizing infrastructure, investing in climate resilience and economic development, creating parks and other public amenities, and providing social services. Within this amount, up to $100 million is provided to expand Pathways to Removing Obstacles to Housing, a competitive program that builds upon ongoing HUD research on land use and affordable housing by rewarding State, local, and regional jurisdictions that make progress in removing barriers to affordable housing developments, such as restrictive zoning. States and localities that embrace efforts to increase their supply of housing would ease cost growth for renters and homebuyers in those areas.

- **Reduces Lead and Other Home Health Hazards for Vulnerable Families**. The Centers for Disease Control and Prevention identifies the risk for lead exposure as greatest for children from racial and ethnic minority groups and children in families living below the poverty level. To help protect families from these health hazards, the Budget provides $350 million for States, local governments, and nonprofits to reduce lead-based paint and other health hazards, especially in the homes of low-income families with young children, as part of the Administration's Justice40 Initiative. To more efficiently deliver assistance, the Budget transforms how States and local governments receive funds through a new formula grant program to more effectively fund lead and other home health hazard mitigation efforts for the most vulnerable and at-risk families across the Nation. The Budget targets $67 million specifically to prevent and mitigate lead-based paint and housing-related health hazards, such as fire safety and mold, in public housing, an increase of $2 million above the 2023 level.

- **Expands Access to Homeownership and Reduces Down Payments for First-Time and First-Generation Homebuyers.** The Budget proposes a new Mortgage Relief Credit to help increase access to affordable housing. The proposal includes a new tax credit for middle-class homebuyers of up to $10,000 over two years to ease affordability challenges. In addition, to unlock starter home inventory for first-time homebuyers and help middle-class families who are "locked in" to their current homes because of lower mortgage rates at the time of purchase, the proposal also includes a credit of up to $10,000 for one year to middle-class families who sell their starter home—a home at or below the area median home price—to another owner-occupant. The Budget also provides $10 billion in mandatory funding for a new First-Generation Down Payment Assistance program to help address homeownership and wealth gaps. In addition, the Budget preserves the Administration's progress in expanding access to homeownership for underserved borrowers, including many first-time and minority homebuyers, through Federal Housing Administration (FHA) and Ginnie Mae credit guarantees. In 2023, first-time homebuyers accounted for over 80 percent of FHA-insured home purchase loans. The Budget also includes up to $50 million for a HOME down payment assistance pilot program that would reduce mortgage down payments for first-generation as well as low wealth first-time homebuyers.

- **Supports Eviction Prevention Efforts.** The Budget provides $3 billion in mandatory funding for competitive grants to promote and solidify State and local efforts to reform eviction policies by providing access to legal counsel, emergency rental assistance, and other forms of rent relief. The Budget also includes $10 million for the Eviction Protection Grant Program, which provides legal assistance to low-income tenants at risk of or subject to eviction.

- **Advances Equity by Preventing and Redressing Housing Discrimination and through Other Government-Wide Priorities.** The Budget provides $86 million, equal to the 2023 level, to support State and local fair housing enforcement organizations and to further education, outreach, and training on rights and responsibilities under Federal fair housing laws. The Budget also preserves robust funding for HUD staffing and technical assistance to affirmatively further fair housing, improve access to affordable housing, address gender-based violence, and combat housing discrimination, including discrimination in tenant and homebuyer screening and advertising in furtherance of Executive Order 14110, "Safe, Secure, and Trustworthy Development and Use of Artificial Intelligence."

- **Improves the Quality of HUD-Assisted Housing.** The Budget provides $26.5 billion in funding to support HUD-assisted multifamily properties and Public Housing to serve 2.2 million low-income families. In addition to ongoing efforts to make HUD-assisted multi-family housing more resilient and energy efficient—the Green and Resilient Retrofit Program, the Budget includes $112 million for preservation and greening of HUD-assisted housing via the Rental Assistance Demonstration. The Budget also centralizes funding for inspections for these properties, which would enhance HUD's ability to identify and address financial and physical risks and would complement HUD's modernized National Standards for Physical Inspection of Real Estate building maintenance standards. To further complement these efforts, the Budget provides $7.5 billion in mandatory funding for comprehensive modernization of targeted Public Housing communities.

- **Invests in Affordable Housing in Tribal Communities**. Native Americans are seven times more likely to live in overcrowded conditions and five times more likely to have inadequate plumbing, kitchen, or heating systems than all U.S. households. The Budget provides $1.1 billion, a $33 million increase above the 2023 level, to support tribal efforts to expand affordable housing, improve housing conditions and infrastructure, and increase economic opportunities for low-income families. Of this total, $150 million would prioritize activities that advance resilience and energy efficiency in housing-related projects.

DEPARTMENT OF THE INTERIOR

The Department of the Interior (DOI) manages and conserves the Nation's natural resources and cultural heritage, and supports the Administration's efforts to address the climate crisis and transition the Nation to clean energy. The President's 2025 Budget for DOI: protects environmental resources by investing in ecosystem restoration, wildfire management, and public land resilience to ensure healthy lands and waters; enhances programs that advance racial and economic justice and honors commitments to tribal nations; and supports development in U.S. Territories and freely associated states.

The Budget requests $17.8 billion in discretionary budget authority for 2025, a $0.8 billion or 4.8-percent increase from the 2023 level. The 2025 Budget advances DOI's mission through investments in wildfire management, tribal programs, ecosystem restoration, national park operations, western water infrastructure, and climate resilience. The Budget demonstrates the continued support of the Compacts of Free Association with Palau, the Federated States of Micronesia, and the Marshall Islands, which are critical to U.S. national security.

The President's 2025 Budget:

- **Honors Commitments to Tribal Communities.** Incorporating feedback from tribal consultations, the Budget continues to provide robust support for indigenous communities and upholds Federal trust responsibilities while working to advance equity. The Budget includes $4.6 billion for DOI's tribal programs, $514 million above the 2023 enacted level and more than $1 billion over the 2021 enacted level, to support public safety and justice, human and social services, and education. The Budget continues to propose reclassification of Contract Support Costs and the Indian Self-Determination Act Section 105(l) leases as mandatory spending, beginning in 2026, to provide certainty for tribal communities in meeting these ongoing requirements with dedicated funding. Budget resources across DOI's tribal programs build on historic investments in the American Rescue Plan and complement Inflation Reduction Act and Bipartisan Infrastructure Law investments to ensure long-term success in addressing critical infrastructure and climate adaptation needs in indigenous communities.

- **Invests in Key Tribal Programs.** The Budget includes over $700 million in Tribal Public Safety and Justice funding at DOI, a $71 million increase over the 2023 enacted level, to support critical law enforcement and tribal court needs in Indian Country. The Budget supports and protects funding for economic development and other tribal community programs and proposes increases over the 2023 enacted level, including: an increase of $26 million for climate resilience and natural resources management; a $77 million increase for education programs across Bureau of Indian Education schools; a $38 million increase for tribal human services programs; and an increase of $12 million for native language and cultural revitalization programs addressing needs highlighted by the Federal Boarding School Initiative and its recently concluded Road to Healing Tour. To strengthen tribal land management and promote tribal sovereignty through tribal co-stewardship, the Budget includes a new $8 million allocation of mandatory funding from the Land and Water Conservation Fund to support tribal land acquisition for conservation and outdoor recreation.

- **Strengthens Climate Resilience in Communities and Ecosystems.** Across America, communities are enduring historic and catastrophic flooding, wildfires, extreme heat, drought, and more, while longer-term changes in temperature will continue to affect ecosystems and the economies that depend on them. The intensifying impacts of climate change are costing lives, disrupting livelihoods, and causing billions of dollars in damages. The Budget provides $5.5 billion in climate adaptation and resilience to address the increasing severity of extreme weather events fueled by climate change. As a key steward of America's public lands and waters, and with a primary responsibility to uphold the Nation's commitments to American Indians and Alaska Natives, DOI plays a critical role in combating the climate crisis. The Budget provides DOI the resources to invest in community partnerships and science-based land management. The Budget complements the historic Bipartisan Infrastructure Law and the Inflation Reduction Act, which dedicate more than $50 billion across the Federal Government to advance climate resilience strategies in every community in America, including in support of the Justice40 Initiative to ensure that these investments reach communities that need them the most.

- **Advances Climate Science.** The Budget includes $275 million at DOI to continue to leverage science to better understand the impacts of climate change and to inform and improve land management practices from the Federal to the local level. The Budget includes additional funding for the U.S. Geological Survey's Climate Adaptation Science Centers, which partners scientists with natural and cultural resource managers and local communities to help fish, wildlife, water, land, and people adapt to climate change. The Budget also provides increases for science that would support land management decisions, including funding to better map migration corridors for big game populations and to develop actionable science and tools for drought response.

- **Invests in America's Brave Wildland Firefighters.** The Budget builds on the Administration's historic investments in the wildland firefighting workforce at DOI and the Department of Agriculture, including investments from the Bipartisan Infrastructure Law, by supporting implementation of permanent and comprehensive pay reform, enhancement of health services, hiring of additional permanent and temporary wildland firefighters to increase capacity, and improvement of Government housing. These investments, totaling $135 million over the comparable 2023 enacted level for DOI, would help address long-standing recruitment and retention challenges, increase the Departments' capacity to complete critical risk mitigation work, and further the Administration's commitment to build a more robust and resilient wildland firefighting workforce as the frequency and intensity of catastrophic wildfires continue to increase due to climate change.

- **Continues to Advance Clean Energy Development on Public Lands.** The Budget includes $142 million, an increase of $31 million above the 2023 enacted level, to continue the Administration's progress in deploying clean energy on public lands and waters, spurring economic development and creating thousands of good-paying jobs, while conserving biodiversity. The Budget supports the leasing, planning, and permitting of solar, wind, and geothermal energy projects, and associated transmission infrastructure that would help mitigate the causes of climate change and support the Administration's goal of deploying 30 gigawatts of offshore wind capacity by 2030 and 25 gigawatts of clean energy capacity on public lands by 2025.

- **Commits to Tribal Water Rights Settlements Funding.** The Budget builds on Bipartisan Infrastructure Law investments to provide $2.8 billion in additional mandatory funding to the Indian Water Rights Settlement Completion Fund, as well as $226 million in discretionary funding to meet existing settlement obligations. This funding would ensure stable, dedicated funding for tribal water rights settlements, which is crucial for safe, reliable water supplies to improve public and environmental health and support economic opportunity in tribal communities.

- **Increases Drought Resilience.** The Budget helps ensure communities across the West have access to a resilient and reliable water supply by investing in rural water projects, water conservation, development of desalination technologies, and water recycling and reuse projects. The Budget complements the nearly $1.7 billion provided in 2025 for western water infrastructure through the Bipartisan Infrastructure Law, as well as the nearly $4.6 billion that was provided by the Inflation Reduction Act for drought mitigation and domestic water supply projects through the Bureau of Reclamation. The Budget provides funding to address the ongoing drought in the western United States, including along the Colorado River System, which remains near historically low levels, and also for other western river sheds that are experiencing similar adverse impacts due to climate change. The Budget also funds Reclamation's research and development activities and the WaterSMART program which converts unusable water resources into useable water supplies, conserve water, and increase drought resiliency.

- **Invests in Columbia and Snake River Salmon Recovery**. The Budget includes $22 million for technical support, studies, and habitat restoration activities to restore healthy and abundant populations of fish in the Columbia and Snake River basins. The Budget provides additional funding for a study to evaluate the potential success of reintroducing anadromous fish above the Grand Coulee Dam.

- **Supports Biodiversity, Ecosystem Health, and Visitor Experiences.** The Budget recognizes the critical importance of biodiversity and ecosystem health across the Nation. In order to enhance the President's America the Beautiful initiative to support locally designed and community-driven conservation, the Budget supports high-priority biodiversity programs including: the Endangered Species Act of 1973 implementation; the National Wildlife Refuge System; and migratory bird, fish, and aquatic conservation. The Budget includes: $602 million for the National Wildlife Refuge System with increased support for refuge law enforcement activities to improve safety and the visitor experience; and $111 million, an increase of $19 million above the 2023 enacted level, for law enforcement programs enhancing wildlife and plant protections. In addition, the Budget also includes increases for natural resource stewardship and increased recreation access at America's National Conservation Lands and other Bureau of Land Management recreation areas, and to help advance the National Seed Strategy across DOI.

- **Increases Access to National Parks.** The Budget provides $3.6 billion for the National Park Service, an increase of $461 million since the start of the Administration. Investments include $11 million to create a more inclusive and representative National Park System and to strengthen tribal co-stewardship. The Budget also includes $11 million to support new sites that preserve the stories of the cultures and history across America. In addition, the Budget provides $125 million for the Outdoor Recreation Legacy Program to develop high-quality recreation opportunities in economically disadvantaged urban communities, which advances the Justice40 Initiative.

- **Strengthens and Streamlines Permitting Activities.** The Budget supports environmental permitting capacity to accelerate delivery of modernized infrastructure across the Nation. For example, the Budget includes nearly $200 million for Endangered Species Act of 1973 environmental planning and consultation and migratory bird permitting, an increase of more than $40 million above the 2023 enacted level. The Budget continues to propose expanding existing transfer authority by enabling Federal agencies to transfer funds provided under the Bipartisan Infrastructure Law to the U.S. Fish and Wildlife Service and National Oceanic and Atmospheric Administration Fisheries to expedite Endangered Species Act of 1973 consultations. Together with existing law, this proposal would facilitate timely development of priority infrastructure projects and energy solutions while minimizing negative environmental impacts.

DEPARTMENT OF JUSTICE

The Department of Justice (DOJ) is responsible for defending the interests of the United States and protecting the rights and safety of all Americans. The President's 2025 Budget for DOJ invests in: combating gun violence and other violent crime, terrorism, violence against women, child exploitation, and cyber threats; countering narcotics; protecting civil rights; implementing Federal, State, and local criminal justice reforms; improving the immigration court system; and bolstering antitrust enforcement.

The Budget requests $37.8 billion in discretionary budget authority for 2025, a $235 million or 0.5-percent increase from the 2023 level.

The President's 2025 Budget:

- **Invests in Federal Law Enforcement to Combat Gun Violence and Other Violent Crime.** The Budget makes significant investments to bolster Federal law enforcement capacity to strengthen public safety. The Budget includes $17.7 billion, an increase of $1.1 billion above the 2023 enacted level and $2.6 billion above the 2021 enacted level, for DOJ law enforcement, including $2 billion for the Bureau of Alcohol, Tobacco, Firearms and Explosives to effectively investigate and prosecute gun crimes; expand multijurisdictional gun trafficking strike forces, increase regulation of the firearms industry, bolster crime-solving ballistics, gunshot residue, and other forensic technologies as well as analysts; and implement the Bipartisan Safer Communities Act. The Budget includes $1.9 billion for the U.S. Marshals Service (USMS) to support efforts to reduce violent crime, including through fugitive apprehension and enforcement operations. The Budget also provides $51 million to the Federal Bureau of Investigation (FBI) to support the continued implementation of enhanced background checks, a key provision of the Bipartisan Safer Communities Act. In addition, the Budget provides a total of $2.8 billion for the U.S. Attorneys, which includes funding for 50 new attorneys to prosecute violent crimes. The Budget further requests $15 million for the Jabara-Heyer NO HATE Act, an increase of $5 million over the 2023 enacted level.

- **Pursues New Mandatory Investments to Combat Violent Crime and Support Victims.** The Budget builds upon the Safer America Plan by investing an additional $1.2 billion over five years to launch a new Violent Crime Reduction and Prevention Fund to give Federal, State, local, tribal, and territorial law enforcement the dedicated, seasoned, and full support they need to focus exclusively on violent crime. This includes: hiring new Federal law enforcement agents, prosecutors, and forensic specialists to address violent crime; expanding Federal operations to combat fentanyl and apprehend dangerous fugitives; and hiring 4,700 detectives at the State and local level to solve homicides, non-fatal shootings, and other violent crimes to drive down the high rate of unsolved violent crimes and the lengthy delays that undermine public trust and public safety. In addition, $28 million is provided to expand the USMS's Operation North Star, which has taken more than 6,700 of the most dangerous State and local fugitives off the street since 2021, to 100 more cities over five years, including 20 more cities in 2025 in order to drive down violent crime. This investment also expands the Drug Enforcement Administration's (DEA) Operation Overdrive, which uses a data-driven, intelligence-led approach to identify and dismantle violent drug trafficking networks, to 50 more cities that are experiencing high rates of gun violence and fentanyl overdoses for 45-day operations. The Budget further requests $7.3 billion to replenish the Crime Victims Fund and ensure a stable and predictable source of funding is available to support critical victim services and compensation programs over the next decade.

- **Combats Narcotics Trafficking Networks.** The Budget also provides $3.3 billion to DEA to combat drug trafficking, including $1.2 billion to combat opioid trafficking, save lives, and make communities safer. The Budget invests an additional $18 million in Counter-Fentanyl Threat Targeting Teams at DEA to enhance America's fight against the transnational criminal networks pushing deadly illicit fentanyl in America's communities. These interdisciplinary teams of special agents, intelligence analysts, and data experts would map criminal organizations and build cases that lead to the dismantling of entire drug trafficking networks and the deprivation of hundreds of millions of dollars to the Sinaloa and Jalisco cartels. In addition, the Budget provides $494 million in grants supporting efforts to address substance use, including $190 million for the Comprehensive Opioid, Stimulant, and Substance Use Program, $95 million to support Drug Courts, and $51 million for anti-drug task forces.

- **Reinvigorates Federal Civil Rights Enforcement.** In order to address longstanding inequities and strengthen civil rights protections, the Budget invests $201 million, an increase of $11 million over the 2023 enacted level, in the DOJ Civil Rights Division. These resources would support police reform via pattern-or-practice investigations, prosecuting hate crimes, enforcing voting rights, and ensuring access to justice.

- **Improves Immigration Courts.** The Budget builds on the Administration's October 2023 supplemental request and invests $981 million, an increase of $121 million above the 2023 enacted level, in the Executive Office for Immigration Review (EOIR) to enhance America's immigration courts and help address the backlog of over 2.4 million currently pending cases. This funding would support 25 new immigration judge teams, which includes the support personnel necessary to ensure efficient case processing. The Budget also invests $30 million for EOIR to partner to with the U.S. Digital Service to develop and implement digital court operations strategies that would maximize each judge's adjudicatory capacity and help reduce the case backlog.

- **Supports State, Local, and Tribal Law Enforcement and Public Safety.** The Budget provides $3.7 billion in discretionary resources for State and local grants and $30.3 billion in mandatory resources to support State, local, and tribal efforts to protect U.S. communities and promote public safety through the President's Safer America Plan. Through a combination of discretionary and mandatory investments, the Safer America Plan supports the President's goal to recruit, train, support, and hire 100,000 additional police officers for effective, accountable community policing consistent with the standards of Executive Order 14074, "Advancing Effective, Accountable Policing and Criminal Justice Practices To Enhance Public Trust and Public Safety." In addition, the Safer America Plan would: fund bonuses for retention of police officers; provide student loan repayment, tuition reimbursement, and higher education grant programs to incentivize service-minded candidates, including women and individuals from underrepresented communities to become officers; support pilot programs to explore more flexibility in scheduling and work arrangements; expand mental health and wellness care for police officers; and fund life-saving equipment. The Safer America Plan would further support the evidence-based training of law enforcement on topics including crime control and deterrence tactics, community engagement, use of force, interacting with people with disabilities, and responding to persons in mental health crisis and to domestic violence calls. The Safer America Plan would also further efforts to advance transparency, accountability, and safety to simultaneously strengthen public safety and public trust consistent with the standards of the Executive Order 14074 through funding to support the purchase and operation of body-worn cameras, modernize police academies and training, comprehensively reform public safety systems, and combat crime to keep the Nation's streets safe. The Budget, through the Safer America Plan provides: funding for courts around the Nation to clear their backlogs and improve accountability and deterrence for people on pretrial supervision, and likewise supports technology and data systems modernization necessary to ensure that the justice system runs efficiently and with the most current data, such as case management systems that effectively integrate pretrial services, judicial, and law enforcement records; virtual access and notification systems to facilitate remote check-ins and hearings as appropriate and beneficial for all involved; and scheduling software to manage the increased volume of cases. The Budget also provides funding to support pretrial and post-conviction supervision staffing and systems, ensuring that persons on release are appropriately monitored and given assistance with the employment, health, housing, and other supportive services that reduce the risk of recidivism. Specific discretionary investments include $270 million for the COPS Hiring Program, an increase of $45 million or 20 percent over the 2023 enacted level, and $100 million for Community Violence Intervention (CVI) programs, an increase of $50 million or 100 percent over the 2023 enacted level, to bolster evidence-based strategies for preventing and reducing gun violence in U.S. communities. To achieve the original goals of the Safer America Plan, the Budget requests an additional $1.5 billion in mandatory funding to support CVI programs at the Department over the next 10 years.

- **Prioritizes Efforts to End Gender-Based Violence.** The Budget proposes $800 million to support programs under the Violence Against Women Act of 1994 (VAWA), which was reauthorized and strengthened in 2022. This is a $100 million or 14-percent increase over the 2023 enacted level, which was the highest funding level in history. The Budget supports significant increases for longstanding VAWA programs, including key investments in sexual assault services, transitional housing, and legal assistance for survivors. The Budget strongly supports underserved and tribal communities by providing $15 million for culturally-specific services, $5 million for underserved populations, $25 million to assist enforcement of tribal special domestic violence jurisdiction, $3 million to support tribal Special Assistant U.S. Attorneys, and $10 million for a new special initiative to address missing and murdered indigenous people. The Budget also provides $10 million to address technology-facilitated abuse through funding new VAWA programs that address cybercrimes against individuals. In addition, the Budget provides $55 million to the Office of Justice Programs for the Sexual Assault Kit Initiative to address the rape kit backlog.

- **Promotes Equity Across the Justice System.** The Budget includes over $10 million in the Office of the Access to Justice to support its work to increase the availability of legal assistance and eliminate barriers to legal access based on economic, demographic, and geographic factors. In addition, the Budget continues to invest in the Office of Environmental Justice to protect overburdened and disadvantaged communities from the harms caused by environmental crimes, pollution, and climate change. The Budget further supports State and local efforts to promote equity and protect civil rights by including $10 million for a new initiative to modernize outdated criminal statutes with a discriminatory impact on HIV-positive individuals, $50 million in VAWA programs specifically focused on delivering equitable services, and $50 million for programs to combat hate crimes.

- **Reforms the Federal Criminal Justice System.** The Budget leverages the capacity of the Federal justice system to advance criminal justice reform and serve as a model that is comprehensive, evidence-based, and that enhances public safety and equity. The Budget supports key investments in First Step Act (FSA) implementation, including continuing the historic collaboration between the Bureau of Prisons and the Department of Labor to provide comprehensive, intensive, and market-driven workforce development and reentry services for people in the Federal prison system. In total, the Budget continues to invest $409 million in base resources for FSA implementation, to support rehabilitative programming, improve confinement conditions, and hire additional FSA-dedicated staff.

- **Addresses Emerging Cyber and Counterintelligence Threats.** The Budget expands DOJ's ability to pursue threats through investments in FBI's cyber and counterintelligence investigative capabilities. These investments sustain the FBI's cyber intelligence, counterintelligence, and analysis capabilities and include an additional $25 million to enhance those cyber response and counterintelligence capabilities. The Budget also includes $5 million to expand a new section within the DOJ's National Security Division to focus on cyber threats. These investments are in line with the National Cybersecurity Strategy that emphasizes a whole-of-Nation approach to addressing ongoing cyber threats. The Budget also provides $2 million for DOJ to support implementation of Executive Order 14110, "Safe, Secure, and Trustworthy Development and Use of Artificial Intelligence."

- **Bolsters Antitrust Enforcement.** The Budget proposes $288 million for the Antitrust Division, which is an increase of $63 million over the 2023 enacted level and $103 million over the 2021 enacted level, sustaining the significant investments made under this Administration. These resources would strengthen antitrust enforcement efforts to promote vigorous marketplace competition and reduce costs and raise wages for the American people.

- **Reiterates the Administration's Request for Immediate Funding to Secure the Border and Build Capacity to Enforce Immigration Law.** In addition to the EOIR investments included in the Budget, the Budget also reiterates the $1.7 billion for DOJ requested in the Administration's October 2023 border, immigration, and countering fentanyl supplement request. Of this amount, $1.3 billion is requested for EOIR to fund the hiring of 375 new immigration judge teams to help reduce the immigration case backlog.

DEPARTMENT OF LABOR

The Department of Labor (DOL) is responsible for protecting the health, safety, wages, and economic security of workers and retirees. The President's 2025 Budget for DOL supports: building the skills of America's workers; protecting workers' rights and benefits, health and safety, and wages; strengthening the integrity and accessibility of the Unemployment Insurance (UI) program; and creating good jobs that are safe and equitable, provide fair wages and benefits, empower workers, and offer opportunities for advancement and a pathway to the middle class.

The Budget requests $13.9 billion in discretionary budget authority for 2025, a $318 million or 2.3-percent increase from the 2023 level.

The President's 2025 Budget:

- **Empowers and Protects Workers.** Workers power America's economic prosperity, building the economy from the middle out and bottom up. To ensure workers are treated with dignity and respect in the workplace, the Budget invests $2 billion, an increase of $121 million above the 2023 enacted level, in the Department's worker protection agencies. These investments would build upon the nearly $100 million increase in base appropriations for these agencies since the beginning of the Administration, in addition to the $200 million in American Rescue Plan Act funding the Administration secured for the agencies to address the unprecedented COVID-19 emergency. The Budget would enable DOL to protect workers' wages and benefits, ensure that children are working only in conditions that are safe and legal, address the misclassification of workers as independent contractors, and improve workplace health and safety. Since 2019, DOL has seen an 88-percent increase in children being employed illegally by companies. The Administration is focused on preventing and addressing child labor exploitation, and has assessed more than $16 million in child labor penalties since taking office. The Budget includes funding to combat exploitative child labor, including among migrant children, who are particularly vulnerable. The Budget also includes funding to implement the significant reforms to employer-sponsored retirement plans enacted in the SECURE 2.0 Act of 2022, helping to ensure that workers' retirement plans are always protected.

- **Expands Access to Paid Family and Medical Leave and Proposes Paid Sick Days.** The vast majority of America's workers do not have access to employer-provided paid family leave, including 73 percent of private sector workers. Among the lowest-paid workers, who are disproportionately women and workers of color, 94 percent lack access to paid family leave through their employers. In addition, as many as one in five retirees leave the workforce earlier than planned to care for an ill family member, which negatively impacts families as well as the Nation's labor supply and productivity. The Budget proposes to establish a national, comprehensive paid family and medical leave program administered by the Social

Security Administration to ensure that all workers can take up to 12 weeks of leave to bond with a new child; care for a seriously ill loved one; heal from their own serious illness; address circumstances arising from a loved one's military deployment; find safety from domestic violence, dating violence, sexual assault, or stalking—otherwise known as "safe leave"; or up to three days to grieve the death of a loved one. The Budget also invests in a program at DOL's Women's Bureau to help States expand access to paid leave benefits, including through grants to support States in implementing new paid leave programs and through the creation of a Technical Assistance Hub to share best practices among States. Further, the President continues to call on the Congress to require employers to provide seven job-protected paid sick days each year to all workers, and ensure that employers cannot penalize workers for taking time off to address their health needs, or the health needs of their families, or for safe leave.

- **Expands Workforce Training and Provides Pathways to In-Demand Jobs for More Americans.** The President's historic legislative accomplishments are rebuilding U.S. infrastructure, supporting clean energy, boosting American manufacturing, and creating millions of high-quality jobs. The Administration has worked with States, localities, and community-based organizations to leverage American Rescue Plan Act, Bipartisan Infrastructure Law, Inflation Reduction Act, and CHIPS and Science Act resources to advance effective, evidence-based training models that ensure all workers, particularly women, workers of color, those living in rural areas, workers with disabilities, and others underrepresented in growing fields, have the skills they need to compete for and fill these and other jobs. The Budget makes major new investments in expanding these strategies, through an $8 billion mandatory Career Training Fund and a $50 million new Sectoral Employment through Career Training for Occupational Readiness program, both of which would support the development and expansion of public-private partnerships among employers, education and training providers, and community-based groups to equitably deliver evidence-based, high-quality training, focused on creating pathways into good jobs in growing, in-demand industries. The Career Training Fund would provide full funding for 750,000 individuals to enroll in evidence-based training programs, such as Registered Apprenticeships, that are proven to deliver sustained earnings increases. These new investments would supplement Workforce Innovation and Opportunity Act programs by providing the resources necessary to deliver high-quality training at scale.

- **Broadens Access to Registered Apprenticeships**. The Budget increases support for Registered Apprenticeships, an evidence-based earn-and-learn model that is a critical tool for training future workforces for good jobs in the clean energy, construction, semiconductor, transportation and logistics, education, health, and other growing and in-demand industries. The Budget invests $335 million, a $50 million increase above the 2023 enacted level, and supports expanding existing Registered Apprenticeship programs in clean energy-related occupations. This investment would also be used to increase the number of workers from historically underrepresented groups, including people of color, women, and people with disabilities, who participate in Registered Apprenticeships.

- **Centers Community Colleges in American Workforce Development**. The President recognizes the crucial role that community colleges play in making high-quality training accessible to all Americans. For this reason, the Budget invests $70 million, a $5 million increase above the 2023 enacted level, in the Strengthening Community College training program, which builds community colleges' capacity to work with the public workforce development system and employers to design and deliver high-quality, evidence-based training programs in communities across the Nation.

- **Expands Penalties when Employers Violate Workers' Rights to Organize, Receive Fair Wages, or Have a Safe and Healthy Workplace Free from Discrimination.** For too long, employers have only received a slap on the wrist—at most—when they fire or retaliate against workers for exercising their right to organize and collectively bargain, steal wages from workers, force workers to work in unsafe conditions, exploit children, or otherwise flagrantly violate the Nation's labor laws. To create meaningful deterrence for employers from violating workers' rights, ensure those who do violate their rights are held accountable, and level the playing field for responsible employers, the Budget proposes instituting and significantly increasing penalties at DOL, the Equal Employment Opportunity Commission, and the National Labor Relations Board for employers that violate workplace safety and, health, wage and hour, child labor, equal opportunity, and labor organizing rules.

- **Modernizes, Protects, and Strengthens UI.** The UI program provides a critical safety net for workers who have lost a job through no fault of their own and helps protect the economy as a whole from further damage during downturns. The Budget invests $3.5 billion, an increase of $313 million above the 2023 enacted level, to modernize, protect, and strengthen the UI program. This includes investments to tackle fraud and support more robust identity verification for UI applicants. Further, the Budget proposes a comprehensive legislative package designed to provide States with new tools and resources to combat UI fraud and improper payments while ensuring equity and accessibility for all claimants. The Budget also includes principles to guide future efforts to reform the UI system, including improving benefit levels and access, scaling UI benefits automatically during recessions, expanding eligibility to reflect the modern labor force, improving Federal and State solvency through more equitable and progressive financing, expanding reemployment services, and further safeguarding the program from fraud.

- **Strengthens Mental Health Parity Protections.** The Budget requires all health plans to cover mental health and substance use disorder benefits, ensures that plans have an adequate network of behavioral health providers, and improves DOL's ability to enforce the law. In addition, the Budget includes $275 million over 10 years to increase the Department's capacity to ensure that large group market health plans and issuers comply with mental health and substance use disorder requirements, and to take action against plans and issuers that do not comply.

- **Proposes to Reauthorize the Trade Adjustment Assistance (TAA) Program.** The TAA program provides employment services, job training, income support, job search allowances, and relocation allowances for workers who lose their jobs due to trade. Since the program's expiration in 2022, however, approximately 10,000 trade-affected workers per month have been deprived of these services. The Administration proposes to reauthorize the TAA program that expired in 2022, and looks forward to working with the Congress on a broader reauthorization to modernize the program to help trade-affected workers return to quality employment as quickly as possible.

- **Helps to Ensure Compliance with the Labor Provisions of the United States-Mexico -Canada Agreement (USMCA).** The Budget includes a $45 million increase for the Bureau of International Labor Affairs to allow it to continue Mexico-specific technical assistance in support of ongoing USMCA implementation by advancing labor protections, improving working conditions, stabilizing labor relations, and increasing public awareness and engagement.

- **Builds Capacity and Infrastructure for Responsible Artificial Intelligence (AI) Use and Innovation.** The Budget includes funding for a new AI policy office to oversee and manage AI-related work at the Department. The office, led by a new Chief AI Officer, would guide the effective use of AI, promote AI innovation in DOL programs, and help DOL agencies mitigate risk, as well as coordinate the AI-related activities already occurring across the Department.

DEPARTMENT OF STATE AND OTHER INTERNATIONAL PROGRAMS

The Department of State (State), U.S. Agency for International Development (USAID), and other international programs deliver on the President's vision of a more free, open, secure, and prosperous world in which all Americans and people everywhere have the opportunity to reach their full potential. The President's 2025 Budget strengthens U.S. national security to Out-Compete China and counter Russian aggression, revitalize long-standing U.S. alliances and partnerships, and galvanize a U.S. global response to shared challenges in nearly 200 countries.

The Budget requests $64.4 billion in discretionary budget authority for 2025 for State, USAID, and other international programs, a $0.7 billion or 1.1-percent increase from the estimated 2023 level which includes actual offsetting collections and fee revenue. Within this total, the Budget includes $58.8 billion for State and USAID, a $0.7 billion or 1.2-percent increase from the estimated 2023 level. The Budget also includes $2.5 billion for international programs at the Department of the Treasury, a $0.1 billion or 5-percent increase from the estimated 2023 level.

In addition, the Budget includes a request for unmet needs from the Administration's October 2023 supplemental request for urgent security needs through the end of 2024.

The President's 2025 Budget:

- **Drives Inclusive and Sustainable Economic Growth and Quality International Infrastructure through the Partnership for Global Infrastructure and Investment (PGI).** The Budget advances the President's goal of mobilizing $200 billion for infrastructure investment in low- and middle-income countries by 2027, building on the $30 billion in financing already mobilized by the Administration, which was announced by the President at the May 2023 G7 Summit. PGI aims to promote infrastructure development along critical economic corridors to drive inclusive and sustainable economic growth, secure energy supply chains, fortify trusted digital connectivity, advance gender equality and equity, and build more resilient food and health systems, as well as critical transport and logistics networks. The Budget includes approximately $50 billion for PGI across all departments and agencies, inclusive of private sector financing leveraged, including $250 million in flexible resources to support strategic, high-quality infrastructure to connect workers to good jobs, allow businesses to grow and thrive, and advance shared national security priorities. To further PGI goals, the Budget includes $2 billion in mandatory funding over five years to establish the International Infrastructure Fund to combat People's Republic of China (PRC) coercive financing, and spur U.S. economic growth. This includes development of the Port of Rades in Tunisia and includes $200 million for the Millennium Challenge Corporation with a focus on critical investments across Africa. The Budget also leverages U.S. Development Finance Corporation investments to strengthen U.S. global infrastructure.

- **Provides Lifesaving Humanitarian Assistance and Combats Global Food Insecurity.** The Budget provides $10.3 billion in lifesaving humanitarian and refugee assistance to support more than 330 million people in need in more than 70 countries, in addition to the October 2023 emergency supplemental request of $10 billion to address the unprecedented humanitarian need globally. The Budget also fully supports the President's commitment to resettle up to 125,000 refugees in the United States, as well as the Enduring Welcome and Safe Mobility Office initiatives. The Budget also provides more than $1 billion to support the President's pledge to alleviate global food insecurity, including $100 million for the Vision for Adapted Crops and Soils, as part of the overall U.S. Government's flagship food security initiative, Feed the Future, which works to build more resilient and sustainable food systems and nutritious food crops in underserved regions. State and USAID would have to reduce lifesaving assistance around the globe without the additional $10 billion in humanitarian assistance requested in the Administration's October 2023 national security supplemental request.

- **Unlocks New Lending to Address Global Challenges and Provides a Credible Alternative to the PRC's Coercive Lending.** The Budget builds on the Administration's October 2023 supplemental request and unlocks roughly $36 billion in new World Bank financing to address global challenges by leveraging $1 billion in contributions to the World Bank, largely for International Bank for Reconstruction and Development (IBRD) loan guarantees. This funding would provide an alternative to the PRC's coercive financing and address global challenges.

- **Disrupts the International Synthetic Drug Trade.** The Budget includes $169 million across State and USAID to counter fentanyl and other synthetic drug production and trafficking, which is 58 percent above 2023 levels. These resources would counter the worldwide flow of fentanyl and other synthetics that endanger public safety and health, and contribute to tens of thousands of drug-overdose deaths in the United States annually.

- **Galvanizes Action against Strategic Competitors.** The Budget builds on the Administration's October 2023 supplemental request and provides approximately $1.5 billion to counter Russian aggression across Europe, Eurasia, and Central Asia, including more than $300 million to support procurement of American equipment across the region and $482 million for Ukraine to continue its efforts to expel Russian forces from its territory, establish civilian security in newly liberated territories, and spur economic growth. The Budget also includes $400 million for the Countering PRC Influence Fund to support strategic opportunities to counter the PRC globally, and $241 million in military assistance to reaffirm American national security commitments in the Indo-Pacific. In addition, the Budget provides $25 million for a new Countering Russian Malign Actors in Africa Fund to suppress Russian or other malign actors in the region, and to improve security force responsiveness and democracy. The Budget also invests $50 million for a new capital increase to the European Bank for Reconstruction and Development to maintain support to Ukraine and deliver on multilateral development bank evolution reforms.

- **Secures American Presence and Commitment in the Indo-Pacific.** The Budget provides over $4 billion to realize a more free, open, secure, and connected Indo-Pacific that bolsters U.S. alliances and partnerships, nearly $600 million above the 2023 level. This includes $2.1 billion in bilateral and regional foreign assistance, including $100 million for a standalone request for Taiwan military assistance and $20 million for the Indo-Pacific Economic Framework. The

Budget includes over $62 million in support of the Association of Southeast Asian Nations (ASEAN), demonstrating America's continued commitment to ASEAN centrality. The Indo-Pacific Strategy total also includes $2 billion to support diplomatic presence and programs in the region, including new and planned U.S. diplomatic posts in the Pacific and Indian Oceans. The Budget reflects a substantial commitment to the Indo-Pacific and relies on the $2 billion investment that the Administration requested in the October 2023 national security supplemental request in security assistance to fully address urgent regional security needs and deter acts of aggression.

- **Achieves the Administration's Historic Climate Finance Pledge.** The Budget provides a path to achieving the President's $11 billion commitment for international climate finance, including $3 billion for the *President's Emergency Plan for Adaptation and Resilience (PREPARE)*. A signature initiative, PREPARE supports more than half a billion people in developing countries to adapt to and manage the impacts of climate change. The Budget also supports a $500 million contribution through mandatory funding to finance the Green Climate Fund, as part of the $3 billion multiyear pledge to expand climate adaptation and mitigation projects in developing countries, and $100 million for the Amazon Fund to combat deforestation and preserve the world's largest tropical rainforest. The Budget builds on historic international climate finance progress made over the course of the Administration, in which estimated 2023 levels of $9.5 billion represent a near-six-fold increase from 2021.

- **Protects Americans at Home and Abroad, and Strengthens Health Systems Globally.** The Budget provides nearly $10 billion for global health programs, which would increase support for global health programs, strengthening health systems, and pandemic preparedness. The Budget fulfills the President's commitment to the seventh replenishment of the Global Fund to Fight AIDS, Tuberculosis, and Malaria by providing $1.2 billion to match $1 for every $2 contributed by other donors. The Budget also provides more than $900 million for global health security, including $250 million for the Pandemic Fund. The Budget invests $30 million in new resources for the World Bank's Global Financing Facility for Women, Children, and Adolescents, a contribution anticipated to leverage at least $210 million to strengthen health systems, and $20 million for the Administration's Global Health Worker Initiative to better train, equip, and protect the health workforce. In addition, the Budget includes loan guarantees to the World Bank's IBRD to support investments in global challenges, including pandemic preparedness, which would bolster the impact of these global health activities.

- **Fulfills the President's Commitment to Central America and Strengthens America's Partnership in the Western Hemisphere.** The Budget provides approximately $1 billion for Central American programming to meet the President's commitment to invest $4 billion in Central America over four years to address the root causes of migration. The Budget also supports hemispheric programs to advance economic prosperity and regional security through key initiatives such as the Americas Partnership for Economic Prosperity, including $75 million for a capital increase to the Inter-American Investment Corporation—known as IDB Invest—to advance clean energy projects, modernize agriculture, strengthen transportation systems, and expand access to financing. The Budget also includes $35 million in additional targeted funding for regional migration management, including $25 million for the Inter-American Development Bank's Migration Grant Facility to support integration efforts for migrants and host communities, and address the root causes of irregular migration. The Budget also further strengthens America's diplomatic presence in the region with funding for posts in the Eastern Caribbean. The Budget continues robust support for Haiti to curb gang violence, improve security, and address drivers of migration, including $100 million for the Haiti Multinational

Security Support to address insecurity and create the necessary conditions for long-term stability and growth.

- **Invests in America's Workforce to Ensure U.S. Foreign Policy Delivers for the American people.** The Budget requests more than $8 billion for America's national security workforce to underpin America's global leadership, modernize diplomacy, and implement the President's *National Security Strategy*. The Budget includes pay increases for the U.S. workforce and locally employed and foreign service national staff at the 75th percentile of the median wage in their respective countries to retain and attract the local personnel critical to U.S. diplomatic and development efforts. The Budget also expands State and USAID's workforce by nearly 550, including 145 new positions in support of the Global Development Partnership Initiative at USAID and 58 new positions at State in support of the Indo-Pacific—including increased support for the Australia-United Kingdom-United States enhanced trilateral security partnership and Pacific Island posts. To equip the workforce with cutting-edge technology, the Budget also provides over $800 million in information technology and cybersecurity, a 17-percent increase above 2023 levels. These resources include substantial funding for zero trust architecture implementation to strengthen cybersecurity, and approximately $20 million in targeted artificial intelligence investments firmly aligned with the goals laid out in the Executive Order 14110, "Safe, Secure, and Trustworthy Development and Use of Artificial Intelligence."

- **Bolsters Sustainable, Inclusive, and Democratic Global Development.** The Budget supports the President's goal to strengthen American development efforts through local expertise and by deploying a more expansive set of development tools. The Budget provides over $3 billion for bolstering global democracy, human rights, and governance, including $345 million for the President's Initiative for Democratic Renewal to foster transparent and accountable governance. The Budget provides more than $3 billion to advance gender equity and equality worldwide, including $200 million for the Gender Equity and Equality Action Fund. The Budget also includes $110 million in support of internet freedom, including $50 million for the U.S. Agency for Global Media Open Technology Fund. The Budget also provides $594 million, an increase of $37 million above 2023 levels, for USAID-directed high-impact and lifesaving voluntary family planning and reproductive health programs and America's voluntary contribution to the United Nations Population Fund. The Budget also continues America's commitment to contributions for the United Nations, including $25 million for United Nations Educational, Scientific, and Cultural Organization back payments incurred since 2011, restoring America's seat at the table on scientific cooperation, freedom of expression, and media independence.

- **Advances International Digital Connectivity and Security.** The Budget provides $500 million to further the *National Security Strategy's* commitment to American leadership to ensure an open and secure technological ecosystem. This includes $91 million for USAID's whole-of-Government *Digital Strategy*, which expands secure internet access, increases adoption of open and secure digital technology policies, and supports the American economy through export of U.S. information technology goods and services. The Budget also includes $65 million for the Administration's signature Digital Transformation with Africa initiative to promote the African digital economy.

- **Promotes Stability and Security in the Middle East.** The Budget builds on the Administration's October 2023 supplemental request and sustains core investments in the stability of the Middle East and the security of key partners. The Budget maintains support for Israel with $3.3 billion in security assistance, consistent with the U.S.-Israel Memorandum of Understanding, as well as sustains assistance for the Palestinian people in the West Bank and Gaza and continues investments in peacebuilding as a foundation for a sustainable, two-state solution with Israel. The Budget also demonstrates enduring commitments to other U.S. partners in the region, including nearly $1.5 billion for Jordan and $1.4 billion to support the U.S. strategic partnership with Egypt. U.S. assistance in the Middle East and North Africa continues efforts to combat terrorism and Iran-backed malign actors and helps mitigate the economic shocks and instability worsened by the Israel-Hamas conflict.

- **Complements the Urgent National Security Supplemental.** In October 2023, the Administration submitted an emergency national security supplemental request to the Congress to fund key national security priorities through the end of 2024. This request included $34 billion to provide security and economic assistance to Ukraine, critical support for Israel, lifesaving humanitarian assistance, including for the Palestinian people, foreign military financing to support America's partners in the Indo-Pacific, and to address irregular migration and other national security priorities. Absent congressional action on this emergency request, the United States would not be able to provide the necessary support to Ukraine, and State and USAID would have to reduce lifesaving assistance around the globe. The Administration appreciates the bipartisan supplemental legislation that passed the Senate and would address these urgent needs.

DEPARTMENT OF TRANSPORTATION

The Department of Transportation (DOT) is responsible for delivering the world's leading transportation system, serving the American people and economy through the safe, efficient, sustainable, and equitable movement of goods and people. The President's 2025 Budget for DOT continues to complement the President's historic Bipartisan Infrastructure Law by: continuing to rebuild and modernizing America's roads, bridges, rail, transit systems, and airports; and prioritizing significant investments in the Federal Aviation Administration (FAA) to ensure the agency has the people, facilities, and equipment necessary for a safe and efficient National Airspace System (NAS).

The Budget requests $25.4 billion in discretionary budget authority for 2025. The Budget also includes $81.7 billion in obligation limitations and $1.9 billion in mandatory resources, as well as $36.8 billion in emergency-designated advance budget authority, for transportation infrastructure and safety investments in 2025. In total, the Budget represents an increase of $58 billion or a 67-percent increase above the enacted level for 2021, the year prior to enactment of the Bipartisan Infrastructure Law, demonstrating the Administration's commitment to rebuilding and modernizing America's infrastructure.

The President's 2025 Budget:

- **Continues Implementation of the President's Historic Bipartisan Infrastructure Law.** The Budget provides a total of $78.4 billion for highway, highway safety, and transit formula programs, supporting the amounts authorized for year four of the Bipartisan Infrastructure Law. This includes $62.1 billion in obligation limitation funding for the Federal-aid Highways program, an increase of $3.3 billion above the 2023 enacted level and $15.7 billion above the enacted level for 2021, the year prior to enactment of the Bipartisan Infrastructure Law. This funding would support construction and safety projects of highways and bridges across the United States. The Budget also includes $14.3 billion for Transit Formula Grants, a $645 million increase above the 2023 enacted level, to support core capital and planning programs for transit agencies across the Nation, as well as transit research, technical assistance, and data collection. The Budget also reflects an additional $9.5 billion in advance appropriations provided by the Bipartisan Infrastructure Law for bridge replacement and rehabilitation, electric vehicle charging infrastructure, and other programs to improve the safety, sustainability, and resilience of America's transportation network.

- **Prioritizes Investment in the FAA.** The Budget provides $17.5 billion in discretionary budget authority for the FAA, an increase of $2.1 billion above the 2023 enacted level, less Congressional Directed Spending. This funding supports robust hiring and training of air traffic controllers started in 2023 to rebuild the pipeline of new controllers needed to safely meet projected air traffic demands. The Budget also continues FAA's multiyear effort of reforming aircraft certification as well as increasing its safety oversight capabilities. In addition, the Budget increases investment in the facilities and systems that comprise the NAS by over $650 million for a total investment of $3.6 billion, to ensure the NAS continues to safely accommodate the growth in traditional commercial aviation traffic alongside new entrants from the commercial space, unmanned aircraft, and advanced air mobility industries. The Administration also proposes to increase the fuel tax for high-end business jets, to better align the costs of the services provided to those users on the system.

- **Modernizes FAA Facilities**. The Administration supports a long-term FAA authorization that: improves safety; enables access to the system by current and emerging users; reduces emissions and improves resiliency; and expands consumer protections and access. However, it would be difficult to achieve these important goals if FAA does not have the modern facilities and systems necessary to operate the NAS. Over the last decade, FAA capital spending has not kept up with the Agency's needs. Therefore, the Budget proposes a five-year, $8 billion mandatory program to significantly modernize FAA's major facilities and radars. This effort would ensure that the American people and all travelers can continue to depend on a safe, modern, and efficient aviation system.

- **Builds on Investments for a Safe and Efficient Passenger and Freight Rail Network.** The Budget expands on the Bipartisan Infrastructure Law's already significant investments toward improving the safety and efficiency of the Nation's rail network. This includes $2.5 billion for grants to Amtrak, along with $250 million for the Consolidated Rail Infrastructure and Safety Improvements program, a flexible and oversubscribed competitive grant program that advances the Justice40 Initiative. These amounts are in addition to the $13.2 billion in rail funding directly provided by the Bipartisan Infrastructure Law. In addition, the Budget increases funding for critical safety programs, such as $8 million for the Confidential Close Call Reporting System, doubling the 2023 enacted level. This program, which all Class I railroads have agreed to join, allows railroads and their employees to report unsafe events and conditions without fear of reprisal.

- **Supports the Nation's Transit Systems**. The Nation's transit systems play a critical role in: ensuring riders can access jobs, school, healthcare, and opportunity; spurring sustainable economic development; reducing highway congestion; and lowering greenhouse gas emissions. The Budget includes $2.4 billion for the Capital Investment Grant program, which provides essential funding for transit expansion projects. At the same time, the Budget recognizes that many transit systems face an uncertain future as ridership and fare revenue have still not fully rebounded to pre-COVID-19 pandemic levels. To ensure transit continues to be a vital and viable transportation option, the Budget includes language to temporarily allow larger transit systems to use existing formula funds for operating expenses, and also encourages States to support their transit systems.

- **Makes Supply Chains More Resilient and Moves Goods More Quickly through the Nation's Ports and Waterways.** The Budget continues support for modernizing America's port and waterway infrastructure initiated under the Bipartisan Infrastructure Law. The Budget includes $80 million for the Port Infrastructure Development Program to strengthen maritime freight capacity on top of the $450 million in the Bipartisan Infrastructure Law for 2025. In addition to keeping the Nation's supply chain moving by improving efficiency, DOT would prioritize projects that also lower emissions—reducing environmental impact in and around the Nation's ports.

- **Supports Competitive Programs for Multimodal Projects.** The Budget provides $800 million for the Rebuilding American Infrastructure with Sustainability and Equity (RAISE) and National Infrastructure Project Assistance—also known as the Mega grant program—competitive grant programs, matching the 2023 enacted level for National Infrastructure Investments, by redirecting balances from the Transportation Infrastructure Finance and Innovation Act program. The RAISE and Mega grant programs support innovative highway, transit, passenger rail, freight, port and other transportation projects across the Nation, and advance the Justice40 Initiative. The RAISE program invests in locally- or regionally-significant projects such as complete streets projects that improve transportation options and protect all transportation system users, infrastructure to support healthier and more sustainable means of travel, and projects that provide significant benefits to disadvantaged communities. The Mega program accelerates delivery of larger projects that can transform and better connect regions and strengthen major supply chain networks, such as the Brent Spence Bridge Project connecting Kentucky and Ohio, and the I-5 Bridge Replacement Project connecting Oregon and Washington.

- **Addresses the Roadway and Pedestrian Safety Crisis**. Despite improvements in vehicle safety technologies, the National Highway Traffic Safety Administration (NHTSA) estimates that 42,795 people died in motor vehicle traffic crashes in 2022. While this is a very small decrease from 2021, the Nation continues to face a national crisis of traffic deaths on America's roadways. The Budget provides $1.3 billion for NHTSA, which is $83 million above the 2023 enacted level, to conduct critical research to reduce roadway fatalities and injuries on the Nation's highways. The Budget also includes increased funding for the newly formed Office of Automation Safety which would lead NHTSA's efforts to safely and securely integrate autonomous vehicles onto the Nation's roadways. The Office of Automation Safety, in coordination with NHTSA research, would address vehicle cyber security risks as well as risks related to artificial intelligence, in alignment with the implementation of Executive Order 14110, "Safe, Secure, and Trustworthy Development and Use of Artificial Intelligence." The Budget also provides almost $965 million to the Federal Motor Carrier Safety Administration to continue its essential safety activities, including its Large Truck and Medium-Duty Truck Crash Causal Factors Studies.

- **Invests in Merchant Mariner Training**. The Budget provides $191 million for the United States Merchant Marine Academy (USMMA) to support an exemplary standard of excellence in education and training opportunities for the next generation of diverse seagoing officers and maritime leaders to serve the Nation. This includes funding for sexual assault and sexual harassment prevention and response activities, newly created subject matter expert Advisory Council positions, and expanded measures to support survivors of sexual assault. The Budget also proposes $86 million in priority maintenance and improvement projects at the USMMA campus.

DEPARTMENT OF THE TREASURY

> The Department of the Treasury (Treasury) is responsible for maintaining a strong economy, promoting economic conditions that enable inclusive growth and stability, protecting the integrity of the financial system, combating global financial crime and corruption, and managing the U.S. Government's finances and resources effectively. The President's 2025 Budget for Treasury: supports a fair and robust tax system that ensures the wealthy and large corporations pay the taxes they owe; maintains improved taxpayer experience and service; combats terrorism and financial crime; promotes community development and access to credit in disadvantaged communities; strengthens corporate transparency; and builds institutional capacity to address emerging issues and advance equity across all Treasury programs.
>
> The Budget requests $14.4 billion in discretionary budget authority for 2025, a $0.2 billion or a 1.2-percent increase from the 2023 level.

The President's 2025 Budget:

- **Protects Improvements to Taxpayer Experience and Supports Ensuring the Wealthy and Big Corporations Pay the Taxes They Owe.** The Inflation Reduction Act addressed long-standing Internal Revenue Service (IRS) funding deficiencies by providing stable, multi-year funding to improve tax compliance by finally cracking down on high-income individuals and corporations who have too often avoided paying their lawfully owed taxes, and improving service for the millions of Americans who do pay their taxes. The IRS is using Inflation Reduction Act funding to modernize its information technology infrastructure, administer new clean energy tax credits, rebuild the administrative capacity of the Agency to better assist taxpayers, and crack down on tax evasion by the wealthy and big corporations. These goals can only be realized if annual discretionary appropriations are provided to maintain and protect current services. To ensure that taxpayers continue to receive high-quality customer service and that all Americans are treated fairly by the U.S. tax system, the Budget maintains annual funding at the 2023 level for all IRS activities and provides a total of $12.3 billion for the Agency. In addition to annual discretionary funding, the Budget proposes to restore the full Inflation Reduction Act investment and provide new funding over the long-term to maintain progress on service enhancements and deficit-reducing tax compliance initiatives. This proposal reflects a robust research base demonstrating that program integrity investments to enforce existing tax laws increase revenues in a progressive way and, in doing so, shrink the tax gap—the difference between taxes owed and taxes paid.

- **Promotes Access to Capital to Underserved Communities.** The Budget provides $325 million for the Community Development Financial Institutions (CDFI) Fund, an increase of $1 million above the 2023 level, and $55 million, or a 20-percent increase above the 2021 level, to provide access to credit and technical assistance to historically underserved and often low-income communities. To address the shortage of long-term affordable credit for development projects in disadvantaged communities, the Budget also includes a $10 million subsidy for the CDFI Fund's Bond Guarantee Program and proposes changes to broaden participation while still minimizing the risk of loss to the Federal Government. The Budget would also broaden access to the Small Dollar Loan Program, allowing more organizations to participate in the program that supports individuals seeking affordable credit building loans and alternatives to costly payday loans.

- **Combats Terrorism and Corruption and Increases Corporate Transparency.** Treasury plays a leading role in monitoring and disrupting corruption, money laundering, terrorist financing, the use of the financial system by malicious actors domestically and abroad, and combatting the trafficking of illicit substances such as fentanyl in American communities. The Budget provides $231 million to the Office of Terrorism and Financial Intelligence, $15 million above the 2023 level, to expand Treasury's capacity to provide financial intelligence and conduct sanctions-related economic analysis while continuing to modernize the sanctions process. These investments would expand Treasury's ability to craft, implement, and enforce sanctions, including the historic sanctions program targeting Russia's illegal war in Ukraine, and sanctions on key Hamas terrorist group members and financial facilitators in Gaza. The Budget also provides $216 million for the Financial Crimes Enforcement Network, $26 million above the 2023 level, to support Beneficial Ownership Information reporting which will be required for existing covered companies beginning in 2025. This reporting will provide investigative tools making it harder for bad actors to hide or benefit from their ill-gotten gains through shell companies or other opaque ownership structures.

- **Builds Critical Agency Capacity to Address Emerging Threats.** The Budget provides $312 million for Treasury's Departmental Offices, an increase of $38 million, or a 14-percent increase above the 2023 level, to continue to rebuild staffing levels for Treasury's core policy offices and support Treasury's role in promoting investment security in sensitive technologies and products critical to the national security of the United States. The increase in funding would also allow Treasury to support a Chief Artificial Intelligence Officer to ensure responsible use and development of artificial intelligence capabilities. The Budget builds institutional capacity to support Treasury-wide coordination of program evaluation and expand engagement with historically underrepresented and underserved groups to advance equity across all Treasury programs.

- **Strengthens Enterprise Cybersecurity.** The Budget provides $150 million for the Cybersecurity Enhancement Account, an increase of $50 million above the 2023 level, to protect and defend sensitive agency systems and information, including those designated as high-value assets. The Budget increases centralized funding to strengthen Treasury's overall cybersecurity efforts and to continue the implementation of a Zero Trust Architecture. These investments would protect Treasury's systems, and the American public's sensitive data safeguarded within these systems, from future attacks. The Budget also provides $396 million for the Bureau of the Fiscal Service, $24 million above the 2023 level. This includes funding to enhance the security posture of core Government financial systems by modernizing and transitioning all mainframe applications to the secure cloud.

DEPARTMENT OF VETERANS AFFAIRS

The Department of Veterans Affairs (VA) is responsible for providing military veterans and their families, caregivers, and survivors with the benefits, care, and support they have earned through sacrifice and service to the Nation. The President's 2025 Budget for VA honors the Nation's sacred obligation to veterans by: investing in world-class healthcare, including enhancing veterans' general well-being and mental health; prioritizing veteran mental health services and suicide prevention programs; increasing support for family caregivers; improving delivery of benefits, including disability claims processing; supporting efforts to end veteran homelessness; and bolstering other benefits to enhance veterans' prosperity.

The Budget requests $153.7 billion for VA, which is a 10-percent increase over the 2023 level, including $129.3 billion in discretionary budget authority and $24.5 billion in mandatory budget authority provided by the Fiscal Responsibility Act of 2023 (FRA) for the Cost of War Toxic Exposures Fund (TEF) in 2025. The Budget also includes advance appropriations of $131.4 billion in discretionary budget authority and $22.8 billion in mandatory budget authority for TEF for VA medical care programs in 2026.

The President's 2025 Budget:

- **Expands Healthcare, Benefits, and Services for Environmental Exposures.** The Sergeant First Class Heath Robinson Honoring our Promise to Address Comprehensive Toxics Act of 2022 (PACT Act) represented the most significant expansion of VA healthcare and disability compensation benefits for veterans exposed to burn pits and other environmental exposures in 30 years. As part of the PACT Act, the Congress authorized TEF to fund increased costs above 2021 funding levels for healthcare and benefits delivery for veterans exposed to certain environmental hazards—and ensure there is sufficient funding available to cover these costs without shortchanging other elements of veteran medical care and benefits delivery. The Budget continues this commitment and includes $24.5 billion for TEF in 2025, through funds appropriated by the FRA, which is $19.5 billion above the 2023 enacted level.

- **Strengthens VA Medical Care.** The Budget provides a total of $112.6 billion in discretionary medical care funding in 2025, equal to the 2025 advance appropriation request. In addition, the Budget, through funds appropriated by FRA, includes $21.5 billion in TEF for medical care, bringing the medical care total to $134 billion in 2025, an $11.5 billion increase over the 2023 enacted level. In addition to fully funding inpatient, outpatient, mental health, and long-term care services, the Budget supports programs that enhance VA healthcare quality and delivery, including a $2 billion investment for non-recurring maintenance to improve medical facility infrastructure, and continued efforts to address the opioid and drug overdose epidemic. In addition, to provide VA with a committed cadre of veteran-oriented, mission-focused physicians, the Budget implements a joint VA-Public Health Services Health Professions Scholarship Program for medical students enrolled in the F. Edward Hébert School of Medicine at the Uniformed Services University of the Health Sciences.

- **Advances the Biden Cancer Moonshot.** The Budget invests $45 million within VA research programs, together with $215 million within the VA Medical Care program, for precision oncology and to provide access to the best possible cancer care for veterans. Funds also support research and programs that address cancer care, rare cancers, and cancers in women, as well as genetic counseling and consultation that advance tele-oncology and precision oncology care to improve veterans' health outcomes.

- **Prioritizes Veterans' Mental Health Services and Suicide Prevention.** The Budget invests $135 million within VA research programs, together with $17.1 billion within the VA Medical Care program, to increase access to quality mental healthcare with the goal of helping veterans take charge of their treatment and live full, meaningful lives. VA will also expand and strengthen the future mental health provider pipeline in innovative ways through strategic engagement, planning, interagency collaboration, and academic expansion. In addition, the Budget provides $583 million to further advance the Administration's veteran suicide prevention initiatives, including continued support of the Veterans Crisis Line's 988 and additional support for VA's National Strategy for Preventing Veteran Suicide.

- **Supports Women Veterans' Healthcare.** The Budget invests $13.7 billion for women veterans' healthcare, including $1.1 billion toward women's gender-specific care. More women are choosing VA healthcare than ever before, with women accounting for over 30 percent of the increase in enrolled veterans over the past five years. These investments support comprehensive specialty medical and surgical services for women veterans, improve maternal health outcomes, increase access to infertility counseling and assisted reproductive technology, and eliminate copayments for contraceptive coverage. The Budget also improves the safety of women veterans seeking healthcare at VA facilities by supporting implementation of the zero-tolerance policy for sexual harassment and assault.

- **Bolsters Efforts to End Veteran Homelessness.** The President believes that every veteran should have permanent, safe, and sustainable housing with access to healthcare and other supportive services. The Budget invests $3.2 billion to end current veteran homelessness and prevent veterans from becoming homeless in the future. In addition to investments made in VA programs, the Budget for the Department of Housing and Urban Development provides $13 billion in mandatory funding to expand the Housing Choice Voucher Program to reach an additional 400,000 extremely low-income veteran families, paving a path to guaranteed assistance for all who have served the Nation and are in need.

- **Invests in Caregivers Support Programs.** Recognizing the critical role family caregivers play in supporting the health and wellness of veterans, the Budget provides critical funding for the Program of General Caregivers Support Services. The Budget also specifically provides $2.9 billion for the Program of Comprehensive Assistance for Family Caregivers, which includes stipend payments and support services to help empower family caregivers of eligible veterans.

- **Invests in Overdose Prevention and Treatment Programs.** The Budget invests $713 million toward opioid use disorder prevention and treatment programs, including using predictive analytics to stratify a patient's risk of overdose, provide augmented care as appropriate, and to support programs authorized in the Jason Simcakoski PROMISE Act. In addition, investments contribute to distribution of naloxone to veterans, which, according to researchers with the VA Palo Alto Health Care System, has demonstrated success in effective utilization of the lifesaving opioid overdose reversal medication, and development of an opioid safety toolkit that provides clinicians materials that aid in decisions related to safe opioid prescribing and non-opioid pain management options.

- **Honors the Memory of All Veterans.** The Budget includes $495 million to ensure veterans and their families have access to exceptional memorial benefits. These funds maintain national shrine standards at the 158 VA-managed cemeteries and support the operations and maintenance of Mare Island Cemetery transferred in 2023 from the City of Vallejo, California.

- **Invests in Veteran Medical and Other Facilities.** The Budget includes $2.8 billion in budgetary resources for construction and expansion of critical infrastructure and facilities, in addition to the $2 billion investment for non-recurring maintenance to improve medical facility infrastructure. The Budget also provides $141 million for grants for construction of State extended care facilities to deliver high-quality healthcare, benefits, and services for veterans.

- **Modernizes VA Information Technology.** The Budget provides $6.2 billion in total budgetary resources for VA's Office of Information Technology to continue upgrades to information technology systems to enable faster benefits delivery and easier access to medical care services. In addition, VA will continue its investments in expanding the safe use of artificial intelligence to improve veteran care.

- **Supports Claims Processing and Benefits Delivery.** The Budget provides $4 billion to the General Operating Expenses, Veterans Benefits Administration account, notably to support the timely processing of claims. This is an increase $172 million over the 2023 enacted level and would enable VA to continue to focus on delivering timely benefits and services to veterans.

- **Invests in Housing.** The Budget provides $326 million in discretionary housing loan program administration resources aiding veterans in buying, building, improving, or refinancing a home. The Budget supports program modernization, loss mitigation efforts to keep veterans in their homes, and the Administration's Justice40 and Property Appraisal Valuation Equity initiatives.

CORPS OF ENGINEERS—CIVIL WORKS

> The Army Corps of Engineers—Civil Works program (Corps) is responsible for: developing, managing, restoring, and protecting water resources primarily through the construction, operation, maintenance, and study of water-related infrastructure projects; regulating development in waters of the United States; and working with Federal agencies to help communities respond to and recover from floods and other natural disasters. The President's 2025 Budget for the Corps invests in high return projects, improves the supply chain at the Nation's coastal ports and on the inland waterways, increases climate resilience, and promotes environmental justice.
>
> The Budget requests $7.2 billion in discretionary budget authority for 2025, including Harbor Maintenance Trust Fund appropriations that are exempted from budget enforcement, building on the $17 billion in the Bipartisan Infrastructure Law for the Corps.

The President's 2025 Budget:

- **Invests in Projects with High Economic, Environmental, and Public Safety Returns.** The Budget invests in projects and programs in the main mission areas of the Corps, which are commercial navigation, flood and storm damage reduction, and aquatic ecosystem restoration, which provide a high economic or environmental return, increase resilience to climate change, promote environmental justice, or address a significant risk to public safety. For example, the Budget improves the safety of Corps' dams by investing in projects that the Corps has identified as among the highest potential risks to public safety nationwide.

- **Increases Climate Resilience.** The Budget protects and maintains funding for programs that help communities identify and address their flood risks and improve the operation of reservoirs to strengthen ecosystems consistent with other project purposes. For example, the Budget includes $20 million for the Floodplain Management Services Program, $9 million for Planning Assistance to States, and $5 million for the Sustainable Rivers Program. The Budget also provides: $51.5 million for emergency preparedness, which is $11 million above the 2023 enacted level; and $16.5 million to dredge the Lower Mississippi River Main Stem project's navigation channel, including funds the Corps can use in the event of future low water levels such as those experienced over the last two years.

- **Strengthens Supply Chains at Coastal Ports and on the Inland Waterways.** The Budget facilitates safe and efficient navigation at the Nation's coastal ports and along the highest use inland waterways. The Budget includes $930 million for operation and maintenance work on the inland waterways, with an emphasis on investments that would improve the condition of locks and dams and help keep supply chains flowing. The Budget also provides over $1.7 billion in spending from the Harbor Maintenance Trust Fund to support navigation in Federal channels that serve the Nation's coastal ports. The Budget continues construction of the Soo Locks replacement lock in Sault Ste. Marie, Michigan, funded in part through the Bipartisan Infrastructure Law.

- **Promotes Environmental Justice.** The Budget continues to invest in projects and programs that help disadvantaged and tribal communities address their water resources challenges in line with the President's Justice40 Initiative. For example, the Budget includes funding for the Tribal Partnership Program, for technical and planning assistance for communities, and to continue construction of the Pajaro River at Watsonville, California project initiated with funding from the Bipartisan Infrastructure Law.

- **Restores Aquatic Ecosystems.** The Budget invests in restoration of some of the Nation's most unique aquatic ecosystems, such as the Chesapeake Bay, the Upper Mississippi River, the Missouri River, and the Louisiana Coast. The Budget includes $444 million for Florida's Everglades restoration program, a $195 million or 77.6-percent increase above the 2021 enacted level, and $145 million, a $80 million or 123-percent increase above the 2023 enacted level, to support salmon recovery efforts in the Columbia River Basin. The Budget includes $13 million for small aquatic ecosystem restoration projects to help protect wetlands that may be negatively impacted by the Supreme Court's Sackett v. Environmental Protection Agency decision on the Administration's Waters of the United States rule.

- **Invests in Research and Development.** The Budget builds on the investments proposed in prior budgets for research and development that would benefit the civil works program. The Budget includes $79 million for this research and development, with a focus on innovative solutions that would help achieve significant cost savings in the Civil Works program or would address emerging water resources challenges, including climate change. For example, this continued investment would help reduce the cost to maintain existing water resources infrastructure and improve its reliability, safety, and environmental sustainability—including through more effective water management at certain dams and innovative methods to identify risks to existing infrastructure.

ENVIRONMENTAL PROTECTION AGENCY

The Environmental Protection Agency (EPA) is responsible for protecting human health and the environment. The President's 2025 Budget for EPA continues the historic progress and investments made by the Administration and supports the continuing restoration of the Agency's capacity to carry out its vital mission to ensure clean air and water, tackle the climate crisis, return contaminated land to productive use, safeguard chemicals in commerce, and advance environmental justice.

The Budget requests $11 billion in discretionary budget authority for 2025, an $858 million or 8.4-percent increase from the 2023 level.

The President's 2025 Budget:

- **Tackles the Climate Crisis.** The Budget prioritizes tackling climate change with the urgency that science demands. Resources in the Budget support efforts to mitigate and adapt to the impacts of the climate crisis while spurring economic progress and creating good-paying jobs. The Budget builds on the historic climate investments made in the Inflation Reduction Act and Bipartisan Infrastructure Law and includes $2.9 billion in EPA climate-related programs to address the climate crisis by: reducing greenhouse gas (GHG) emissions; expanding upon the GHG Reporting Program and Sinks inventory; implementing provisions in the American Innovation and Manufacturing Act of 2020 to continue phasing down the production and consumption of hydrofluorocarbons; advancing equitable implementation of EPA authorities and directives in Indian Country; and engaging with the global community to respond to the shared challenge of building resilience in the face of climate impacts.

- **Invests in Clean Air.** The Budget provides a total of $1.5 billion for the Office of Air and Radiation, an increase of $690 million since the beginning of the Administration, to continue the development of national programs, policies, and regulations that control indoor and outdoor air pollution and radiation exposure. This funding includes a historic $187 million for the Atmospheric Protection Program to support implementation and compliance with GHG emission standards and to tackle the climate crisis at home and abroad. The Budget also includes $100 million for the Diesel Emissions Reduction Act Program, which funds grants and rebates to reduce harmful emissions from diesel engines, and $70 million for the Targeted Airshed Grants program, which helps reduce air pollution in the most polluted nonattainment areas. The Administration continues to support investment in EPA's work of limiting emissions of harmful air pollutants, such as air toxics that are especially harmful to frontline communities and greenhouse gases that are contributing to the climate crisis.

- **Supports the Administration's Goal of Replacing All Lead Pipes.** The Budget provides a total of $101 million for two EPA grant programs dedicated to remediating lead contamination in drinking water—the Reducing Lead in Drinking Water grant program and the Voluntary School and Child Care Lead Testing and Reduction Grant Program—an increase of $53 million over the 2021 enacted level. This investment, along with other programs at EPA that can be used for lead projects, like the Drinking Water State Revolving Fund, builds on the historic $15 billion in direct funding for lead pipe replacement through the Bipartisan Infrastructure Law and underscores the Administration's commitment to ensuring access to safe drinking water and creating good-paying jobs in the process.

- **Advances Environmental Justice.** The Administration continues to take bold steps and prioritize efforts to deliver environmental justice in communities across the United States, including implementing the President's Justice40 Initiative and keeping up the momentum of the historic Bipartisan Infrastructure Law and Inflation Reduction Act environmental justice investments. The Budget bolsters these efforts by providing robust funding for EPA's newly established Office of Environmental Justice and External Civil Rights and investing nearly $1.5 billion across numerous programs throughout the Agency in support of environmental justice efforts, including investments that would support cleaner air and cleaner water in frontline communities. This includes a new $25 million categorical grant program to develop Direct Implementation Tribal Cooperative Agreements to carry out crucial environmental programs in Indian Country that would include a focus on addressing the impacts of climate change.

- **Invests in Critical Water Infrastructure.** The Budget provides a total of $2.4 billion for the State Revolving Funds (SRFs) for drinking water and wastewater infrastructure, an increase of more than $1 billion over the 2023 enacted level for those programs. The SRFs allow States to fund high priority projects that improve human health and environmental conditions. These funds and other water infrastructure programs within EPA, such as the Water Infrastructure Finance and Innovation Act credit program, investments in lead pipe replacement, and funding grants authorized in the Drinking Water and Wastewater Infrastructure Act of 2021, complement significant resources provided for water infrastructure in the Bipartisan Infrastructure Law. The Budget also includes $30 million for a new program that addresses gaps in resources to help improve the Federal response to water-related emergencies.

- **Safeguards against Dangerous Chemicals and Protects Public Health and the Environment.** The Budget continues to build core capacity under the Toxic Substances Control Act (TSCA) and modernize information technology and data software for the TSCA program with an investment of $132 million, which is $49 million above the 2023 enacted level. The Superfund and Brownfields Programs support efforts to clean up and revitalize sites contaminated by hazardous waste releases to the environment. The Budget includes $661 million for Superfund and would be complemented by an estimated $2.2 billion in Superfund tax revenue that is expected to be available in 2025, for a total of approximately $2.9 billion. In addition, the Budget includes $208 million for Brownfields, an increase of $34 million over the 2023 enacted level. The Budget proposes approximately $170 million for EPA to continue addressing per- and polyfluoroalkyl substances (PFAS) through actions highlighted in the Agency's PFAS Strategic Roadmap.

- **Continues to Build Back Critical Capacity to Carry Out EPA's Core Mission.** The Budget adds more than 2,000 full-time equivalents (FTEs) relative to 2023 levels, for a total of more than 17,000 FTEs, working on protective regulations, oversight of delegated programs, enforcement and compliance, land clean-up, grant deployment, public communication and engagement, and scientific research in support of all offices at EPA. In addition, the Budget includes necessary resources for EPA to begin addressing Executive Order 14110, "Safe, Secure, and Trustworthy Development and Use of Artificial Intelligence." These staffing investments would enable EPA to better serve the American people and protect the Nation's public and environmental health.

- **Ensures Compliance with and Enforcement of the Nation's Environmental Laws.** The Budget provides $260 million for civil enforcement efforts, which is $50 million above the 2023 enacted level and $88 million above the 2021 enacted level, including funding to prevent the illegal importation and use of hydrofluorocarbons in the United States. The Budget also includes: $172 million for compliance monitoring efforts, $57 million above the 2023 enacted level, including funds to conduct inspections in underserved, disadvantaged, and overburdened communities, and funds to rebuild the inspector corps; and $77 million for criminal enforcement efforts, an increase of $6 million over the 2023 enacted level. The Agency would also implement the National Enforcement and Compliance Initiatives to target these investments on the most serious environmental violations.

NATIONAL AERONAUTICS AND SPACE ADMINISTRATION

The National Aeronautics and Space Administration (NASA) is responsible for sending astronauts and robotic missions to explore the solar system, advancing the Nation's understanding of the Earth and space, and developing new technologies and approaches to improve aviation and space activities. The President's 2025 Budget for NASA enables progress toward priority goals including: exploring the Moon with U.S. and international partner astronauts; understanding the Earth system; conducting a broad space science program consisting of multiple exciting missions; and transitioning from a Government-led to commercially-led space stations.

The Budget requests $25.4 billion in discretionary budget authority for 2025, a 9.1-percent increase since the start of the Administration, to advance space exploration, improve understanding of the Earth and space, develop and test new aviation and space technologies, and to do this all with increased efficiency, including through the use of tools such as artificial intelligence.

The President's 2025 Budget:

- **Invests in the U.S.-led Artemis Program of Lunar Exploration.** The Budget includes $7.8 billion for the Artemis program, which would bring astronauts—including the first women, first people of color, and first international astronauts—to the lunar surface as part of a long-term journey of science and exploration. The Budget invests in new systems to assist lunar surface science and exploration activities, including a small lunar rover and a large cargo lander that would be used to deliver larger rovers and habitats to the surface in the 2030s.

- **Supports Highly-Efficient and Greener Commercial Airliners.** The Budget invests $966 million in NASA's Aeronautics program. Within this topline, the Budget provides a 12-percent increase above the 2023 enacted level for green aviation projects, which would develop hybrid-electric jet engines, lightweight aircraft structures, and a major new flight demonstrator to pave the way for new commercial airliners that would be cheaper to operate and produce less pollution.

- **Enhances Climate Science and Information.** The Budget invests $2.4 billion, $184 million above the 2023 enacted level, in the Earth Science program for missions and activities that advance Earth systems science and also increase accessibility to information to mitigate natural hazards, support climate action, and manage natural resources. This includes $150 million for the next generation of Landsat satellites, ensuring continuity of data that is used for water resource management and climate science. This also includes development of applications and tools to support wildland fire management, provide farmers with information they can use, and better understand greenhouse gas emissions from natural and human-caused sources through the U.S. Greenhouse Gas Center, a multi-agency collaboration to improve data sets and analysis tools.

- **Advances Exploration of the Solar System and Universe.** The Budget provides $5.2 billion for space science, enabling a broad portfolio of missions to explore the solar system and universe. The Budget supports: continued operations of the James Webb Space Telescope; increasing space weather research and applications; and expanding technology maturation efforts at NASA Goddard Space Flight Center to find habitable planets beyond the solar system. Given that the Mars Sample Return mission is a major part of part of NASA's planetary science budget, the Budget enables NASA's internal assessment of mission architecture options to be completed to address mission cost overruns before providing more details for the $2.7 billion in planetary science budget.

- **Increases Science, Technology, Engineering, and Mathematics (STEM) Opportunities at Minority-Serving Institutions.** The Budget provides $46 million to the Minority University Research and Education Project, to increase competitive awards to Historically Black Colleges and Universities, Tribal Colleges and Universities, and other Minority-Serving Institutions, and recruit and retain underrepresented and underserved students in STEM fields.

- **Advances U.S. Space Industry Technology Development.** The Budget provides $1.2 billion for NASA's Space Technology portfolio to foster innovative technology research and development to meet the needs of NASA, support the expanding U.S. space industry which is creating a growing number of good jobs, and keep America ahead of competitors at the forefront of space innovation. The Budget funds the close-out of the On-orbit Servicing, Assembly, and Manufacturing mission, freeing up funding to grow early-stage space technology research and development programs, fund additional technology collaboration opportunities between NASA and industry, and fully-fund the Demonstration Rocket for Agile Cislunar Operations nuclear propulsion demonstration project, a cooperative program with the Defense Advanced Research Projects Agency.

- **Continues the Transition to Commercial Space Stations.** The Budget funds continued operation of the International Space Station (ISS), a vehicle to safely de-orbit the space station after it is retired in 2030, and the commercial space stations that NASA would use as soon as they become available. The Budget gradually reduces research and other activities on board the ISS in order to provide the funding necessary for the de-orbit vehicle and commercial space stations. The Administration continues to strongly support the transition to commercial space stations in 2030, which would maintain U.S. leadership in low earth orbit and free up resources to allow NASA to make greater investments in cutting-edge science and exploration activities.

NATIONAL SCIENCE FOUNDATION

The National Science Foundation (NSF) is responsible for promoting the progress of science and innovation, including advancing science education. The President's 2025 Budget for NSF builds on previous years' investments and furthers the goals of the CHIPS and Science Act, including: strengthening U.S. leadership in artificial intelligence (AI) and other critical emerging technologies; boosting research and development, including for combating the climate crisis; supporting the Nation's research infrastructure; advancing equity while promoting education and workforce development in science, technology, engineering, and mathematics (STEM); and increasing research security and oversight.

The Budget requests $10.2 billion in discretionary budget authority for 2025, a $644 million or 6.8-percent increase from the 2023 level.

The President's 2025 Budget:

- **Accelerates Regional Innovation across the Nation.** In support of a major priority of the CHIPS and Science Act, the Budget increases investments to translate the results of basic research into practical applications and processes that can benefit the Nation, including $900 million for the Directorate for Technology, Innovation, and Partnerships, an increase of $236 million from the 2023 enacted level. The Budget also includes $205 million for the Regional Innovation Engines program, which facilitates the creation of regional innovation ecosystems, particularly in areas of the Nation that do not already have strong technology ecosystems, bringing good-paying jobs in in-demand industries to more areas.

- **Strengthens U.S. Leadership in AI and Emerging Technologies.** The Budget provides more than $2 billion for research and development (R&D) in critical emerging technology areas in alignment with CHIPS and Science Act priorities of boosting U.S. competitiveness in science and technology, including AI, advanced manufacturing, advanced wireless, biotechnologies, microelectronics and semiconductors, and quantum information science. The Budget also includes $30 million for the second year for a pilot of the National AI Research Resource, as highlighted in Executive Order 14110, "Safe, Secure, and Trustworthy Development and Use of Artificial Intelligence," which aims to democratize access to resources to support the research and innovation needed to build the next generation of safe and trustworthy AI.

- **Advances Climate Research and Development.** The Budget includes $1.4 billion for R&D on climate and clean energy technologies, an increase of $80 million from the 2023 enacted level. This investment supports a broad portfolio of research that includes: atmospheric composition; water and carbon cycles; renewable energy technologies; climate resilience technologies for communities heavily affected by climate change; and social, behavioral, and economic research on human responses to climate change, among other topics.

- **Bolsters the Nation's Research Infrastructure.** The Budget includes $300 million for research infrastructure at NSF to support the construction and procurement of research facilities and instrumentation across the Nation to enable scientific and technological advances. The Budget provides support for: upgrades to the Large Hadron Collider, the world's largest particle accelerator; construction of the Leadership-Class Computing Facility to support science and engineering research that requires the largest and most computationally intensive capabilities; and long-term upgrades of NSF's major Antarctic infrastructure. The Budget also includes support for continued design and development work for a single extremely large telescope, which has the potential to advance ground-based astronomy observing capabilities for U.S. researchers.

- **Promotes Equity in STEM Education and Workforce Training.** In support of the CHIPS and Science Act's priority of building a diverse, STEM-capable workforce, the Budget provides $1.4 billion for STEM education and workforce development programs at NSF that have an emphasis on diversity, equity, inclusion, and accessibility. Within this amount, the Budget includes $592 million, an increase of $51 million from the 2023 enacted level, for programs focused on increasing the participation of groups historically underrepresented in science and engineering fields, including women and girls and people of color, by supporting: curriculum design; research on successful recruitment and retention methods; development of outreach or mentorship programs; fellowships; and building science and engineering research and education capacity at Historically Black Colleges and Universities, Tribally Controlled Colleges and Universities, and Minority-Serving Institutions.

- **Increases Research Security and Oversight.** The Budget includes $18 million for research security activities at NSF, an increase of $6 million from the 2023 enacted level, to identify risks to the U.S. research enterprise and to develop policies and best practices to mitigate against those risks. The Budget also includes support for the expanded role of the Office of the Inspector General to conduct oversight and prosecution cases of sexual assault and harassment in the United States Antarctic Program.

SMALL BUSINESS ADMINISTRATION

The Small Business Administration (SBA) is responsible for ensuring that small businesses, entrepreneurs, innovative startups, and disaster-impacted communities have access to the tools and resources they need to start, recover, build, and grow. The President's 2025 Budget for SBA supports comprehensive and equitable access to business technical assistance services, affordable capital, and Government contracting opportunities.

The Budget requests $971 million in discretionary budget authority for 2025, a 25-percent increase over the 2021 enacted level at the beginning of the Administration. The Budget continues to build on the historic small business growth achieved under this Administration by expanding access to capital, counseling services, contracting opportunities, and disaster recovery assistance.

The President's 2025 Budget:

- **Expands Access to Capital for Small Businesses.** Building on the historic growth in small business applications under the President and Vice President's leadership, the Budget supports historic lending levels across SBA's business lending programs, including: the 7(a) business loan guarantee; capital for major fixed assets, otherwise known as a 504 loan guarantee; the Small Business Investment Company (SBIC) program; and Microloan programs. The over $58 billion in lending provided in the Budget would address the need for greater access to affordable capital, particularly in underserved communities. The Budget proposes a new direct 7(a) lending program, which would further enable SBA to address gaps in access to small dollar lending. In addition, increasing the authorized lending level for the SBIC program by 16 percent to $7 billion would significantly expand the availability of venture capital funding for small businesses.

- **Supports Disaster Mitigation and Recovery.** As communities across the Nation face increased risks from natural disasters, the Budget continues to support SBA's Disaster Loan Program, a program that is vital to ensuring SBA can continue to administer low-interest disaster loans that provide a financial lifeline for homeowners and businesses recovering from natural disasters.

- **Delivers Equitable Access to Counseling and Training Resources.** The Budget provides $20 million for the Community Navigator Pilot Program, which works with community organizations to provide and amplify awareness of free and low-cost business counseling and training resources. Community Navigators are reducing resource and access barriers in underserved communities, including veterans, women, rural communities, and communities of color.

- **Invests in Innovators.** The Budget provides $30 million to support SBA's Growth Accelerator Fund Competition, Regional Innovation Clusters, and the Federal and State Technology Partnership Program to provide entrepreneurs at various technical readiness levels with a network of technical assistance providers including accelerators, State and local economic development agencies, colleges and universities, and other technology-based economic development entities. This technical assistance provides small business entrepreneurs access to the tools, networks, and services they need to commercialize cutting-edge innovation and bring solutions to the market.

- **Invests in Veteran-Owned Small Businesses.** In January 2023, SBA began accepting applications for the Veteran Small Business Certification program to expand small business contracting opportunities for veterans. The Budget provides $16 million to support this important program, including the cost to review certification and recertification applications for veteran and service-disabled veteran-owned small businesses.

SOCIAL SECURITY ADMINISTRATION

The Social Security Administration (SSA) is responsible for providing essential benefits to retirees, survivors, individuals with disabilities, and older Americans with limited income and resources, helping Americans retire with dignity. The President's 2025 Budget for SSA supports investments in improving service delivery and advancing equity and proposes a national paid family and medical leave program that would give workers the time they need to care for themselves or a loved one or to bond with a new child.

The Budget requests $15.4 billion in discretionary budget authority for 2025, a $1.3 billion or 8.9-percent increase from the 2023 level, including cap adjustment funding.

The President's 2025 Budget:

- **Protects the Benefits that Americans Have Earned.** The Administration is committed to protecting and strengthening Social Security and opposes any attempt to cut Social Security benefits as well as proposals to privatize Social Security. The Administration believes that protecting Social Security should start with asking the highest-income Americans to pay their fair share. In addition, the Administration supports efforts to improve Social Security benefits, as well as Supplemental Security Income benefits, for seniors and people with disabilities, especially for those who face the greatest challenges making ends meet.

- **Improves Service Delivery.** The Administration is committed to improving service delivery for the more than six million retirement, survivor, and Medicare claimants, as well as the more than two million individuals applying for disability and Supplemental Security Income every year. The Budget provides an increase of $1.3 billion, nine percent over the 2023 enacted level, to improve customer service at SSA's field offices, State disability determination services, and teleservice centers for retirees, individuals with disabilities, and their families. The Budget also improves access to SSA's services by reducing wait times.

- **Provides National, Comprehensive Paid Family and Medical Leave.** The vast majority of America's workers do not have access to employer-provided paid family leave, including 73 percent of private sector workers. Among the lowest-paid workers, who are disproportionately women and workers of color, 94 percent lack access to paid family leave through their employers. In addition, as many as one in five retirees leave the workforce earlier than planned to care for an ill family member, which negatively impacts families, as well as the Nation's labor supply and productivity. The Budget proposes to establish a national, comprehensive paid family and medical leave program administered by SSA. The program would: provide workers with progressive, partial wage replacement to take time off for family and medical reasons; include robust administrative funding; and use an inclusive family definition. The Budget would provide up to 12 weeks of leave to allow eligible workers to take time off to: care for and bond with a new child; care for a seriously ill loved one; heal from their own serious illness; address circumstances arising from a loved one's military deployment; or find safety from domestic violence, dating violence, sexual assault, or stalking—otherwise known as "safe leave." The Budget would also provide up to three days to grieve the death of a loved one. The Administration looks forward to continuing to work with the Congress to make this critical investment and strengthen America's economy.

- **Advances Equity and Accessibility.** The Administration is committed to making it easier for people to access the services they rely on, including individuals experiencing homelessness, children with disabilities, and people with mental health and intellectual disabilities. The Budget makes investments to decrease customer wait times, to simplify Supplemental Security Income application processes, and to expand access to Agency programs and services, particularly for underserved communities. SSA will also continue to modernize its information technology systems to make more services available online and improve 800 Number access for those who call. The Budget also prioritizes actions to prevent overpayments and to allow customers to navigate the recovery and waiver processes more easily.

Summary Tables

Table S–1.　Budget Totals

(In billions of dollars and as a percent of GDP)

	2023	2024	2025	2026	2027	2028	2029	2030	2031	2032	2033	2034	Totals 2025–2029	Totals 2025–2034
Budget totals in billions of dollars:														
Receipts	4,441	5,082	5,485	5,873	6,186	6,510	6,830	7,164	7,509	7,873	8,258	8,639	30,883	70,328
Outlays	6,135	6,941	7,266	7,419	7,697	8,083	8,313	8,805	9,123	9,544	10,060	10,316	38,777	86,625
Deficit[1]	1,694	1,859	1,781	1,547	1,510	1,573	1,483	1,640	1,614	1,671	1,801	1,677	7,894	16,297
Debt held by the public	26,236	28,156	29,984	31,639	33,250	34,892	36,441	38,139	39,795	41,502	43,339	45,056		
Debt held by the public net of financial assets	23,728	25,587	27,370	28,917	30,428	32,001	33,485	35,129	36,748	38,419	40,220	41,897		
Gross domestic product (GDP)	26,977	28,255	29,340	30,553	31,816	33,129	34,511	35,984	37,546	39,176	40,877	42,654		
Budget totals as a percent of GDP:														
Receipts	16.5%	18.0%	18.7%	19.2%	19.4%	19.6%	19.8%	19.9%	20.0%	20.1%	20.2%	20.3%	19.4%	19.7%
Outlays	22.7%	24.6%	24.8%	24.3%	24.2%	24.4%	24.1%	24.5%	24.3%	24.4%	24.6%	24.2%	24.3%	24.4%
Deficit	6.3%	6.6%	6.1%	5.1%	4.7%	4.7%	4.3%	4.6%	4.3%	4.3%	4.4%	3.9%	5.0%	4.6%
Debt held by the public	97.3%	99.6%	102.2%	103.6%	104.5%	105.3%	105.6%	106.0%	106.0%	105.9%	106.0%	105.6%		
Debt held by the public net of financial assets	88.0%	90.6%	93.3%	94.6%	95.6%	96.6%	97.0%	97.6%	97.9%	98.1%	98.4%	98.2%		
Memorandum, real net interest:														
Real net interest in billions of dollars	–453	187	349	389	410	441	461	480	502	533	558	574	2,051	4,699
Real net interest as a percent of GDP	–1.7%	0.7%	1.2%	1.3%	1.3%	1.3%	1.3%	1.3%	1.3%	1.4%	1.4%	1.3%	1.3%	1.3%

[1] The estimated deficit for 2024 is based on partial year actual data and generally incorporates actuals through November.

Table S–2. Effect of Budget Proposals on Projected Deficits

(Deficit increases (+) or decreases (–) in billions of dollars)

	2023	2024	2025	2026	2027	2028	2029	2030	2031	2032	2033	2034	Totals 2025–2029	Totals 2025–2034
Projected deficits in the baseline	1,694	1,909	1,865	1,784	1,752	1,815	1,763	1,933	1,985	2,080	2,313	2,233	8,980	19,524
Percent of GDP	6.3%	6.8%	6.4%	5.8%	5.5%	5.5%	5.1%	5.4%	5.3%	5.3%	5.7%	5.2%		
Proposals in the 2025 Budget:														
Lowering everyday costs for the American people:														
Expand access to child care and early learning			15	23	40	56	65	73	75	81	85	87	199	600
Reduce the cost of health care			9	37	46	48	50	52	53	55	59	61	190	470
Reduce the cost of prescription drugs			*	–1	–7	–19	–20	–26	–26	–32	–38	–38	–46	–205
Reduce the cost of and expand access to postsecondary education and training			3	8	21	32	39	39	37	37	37	37	103	290
Reduce the cost of housing for home owners and renters		1	31	19	14	13	15	17	17	19	19	20	91	183
Offset by tax reforms to ensure the wealthiest Americans and big corporations pay their fair share:														
Impose a minimum income tax on the wealthiest taxpayers				–50	–56	–59	–60	–60	–59	–53	–50	–54	–227	–503
Increase the top marginal income tax rate for high-income earners		–10	–75	–31	–14	–15	–16	–17	–18	–19	–20	–21	–151	–246
Reform the taxation of capital income			–18	–24	–25	–26	–28	–29	–31	–32	–34	–42	–121	–289
Close loopholes in the estate and gift taxes and related reforms			–2	–4	–6	–8	–10	–12	–12	–13	–14	–16	–30	–97
Expand limitation on deductibility of excessive employee remuneration			–37	–19	–30	–35	–31	–28	–22	–21	–22	–26	–153	–272
Subtotal, tax reforms to ensure the wealthiest Americans and big corporations pay their fair share		–10	–132	–128	–132	–144	–145	–146	–142	–138	–141	–158	–681	–1,406
Total, lowering everyday costs for the American people		–9	–75	–41	–18	–13	3	10	14	23	21	8	–144	–68
Invest in working families and improve healthcare:														
Provide national, comprehensive paid family and medical leave			2	10	18	20	25	50	50	50	50	50	75	325
Restore and make permanent the American Rescue Plan expansion of the earned income tax credit for workers without qualifying children		*	15	16	16	16	16	16	17	17	17	17	80	163
Expand the child credit, and make permanent full refundability and advanceability		5	210	11	8	11	12	12	12	12	13	9	252	310
Improve home care			3	4	6	8	10	13	17	23	30	40	30	154
Strengthen public health and improve health outcomes		2	11	31	42	42	42	46	44	45	48	51	167	402
Total, invest in working families and improve healthcare		8	241	72	90	97	105	137	140	147	158	168	604	1,354
Tax reforms to make big corporations pay their fair share:														
Raise the corporate income tax rate to 28 percent		–75	–122	–125	–128	–129	–128	–129	–138	–145	–150	–155	–633	–1,350
Increase the corporate alternative minimum tax rate to 21 percent		–10	–14	–12	–13	–13	–14	–14	–15	–15	–16	–16	–63	–137
Revise the global minimum tax regime, limit inversions, and make related reforms		–9	–28	–36	–35	–35	–36	–38	–39	–41	–42	–44	–169	–374

Table S–2. Effect of Budget Proposals on Projected Deficits—Continued

(Deficit increases (+) or decreases (–) in billions of dollars)

	2023	2024	2025	2026	2027	2028	2029	2030	2031	2032	2033	2034	Totals 2025–2029	Totals 2025–2034
Adopt the undertaxed profits rule	....	....	–10	–15	–14	–14	–14	–14	–14	–14	–14	–14	–67	–136
Increase the excise tax rate on repurchase of corporate stock and close loopholes	....	–4	–15	–15	–15	–15	–16	–16	–17	–18	–19	–20	–76	–166
Total, tax reforms to make big corporations pay their fair share	....	–97	–189	–202	–204	–206	–208	–211	–222	–232	–240	–249	–1,008	–2,164
Close Medicare tax loopholes and increase Medicare tax for people making over $400,000	....	–17	–81	–61	–64	–70	–75	–80	–85	–89	–94	–99	–351	–797
Additional investments and reforms	....	67	24	4	–29	–27	–76	–111	–171	–199	–284	–296	–103	–1,165
Debt service and other interest effects	....	–1	–4	–9	–16	–23	–30	–38	–47	–59	–72	–88	–83	–388
Total proposals in the 2025 Budget	....	**–50**	**–84**	**–238**	**–242**	**–242**	**–281**	**–292**	**–371**	**–409**	**–512**	**–556**	**–1,086**	**–3,227**
Resulting deficits in the 2025 Budget	**1,694**	**1,859**	**1,781**	**1,547**	**1,510**	**1,573**	**1,483**	**1,640**	**1,614**	**1,671**	**1,801**	**1,677**	**7,894**	**16,297**
Percent of GDP	6.3%	6.6%	6.1%	5.1%	4.7%	4.7%	4.3%	4.6%	4.3%	4.3%	4.4%	3.9%		

* $500 million or less.

Table S-3. Baseline by Category [1]

(In billions of dollars)

	2023	2024	2025	2026	2027	2028	2029	2030	2031	2032	2033	2034	Totals 2025–2029	Totals 2025–2034
Outlays:														
Discretionary programs:														
Defense	806	852	884	902	923	938	958	972	998	1,022	1,046	1,070	4,604	9,712
Non-defense	912	965	995	993	1,003	1,009	1,019	1,033	1,054	1,087	1,112	1,136	5,019	10,441
Subtotal, discretionary programs	1,718	1,818	1,879	1,894	1,926	1,947	1,977	2,005	2,052	2,109	2,158	2,206	9,624	20,153
Mandatory programs:														
Social Security	1,348	1,452	1,543	1,637	1,730	1,824	1,919	2,018	2,118	2,221	2,325	2,432	8,653	19,767
Medicare	839	839	936	997	1,075	1,219	1,176	1,335	1,423	1,534	1,789	1,766	5,402	13,249
Medicaid	616	567	587	622	662	701	742	785	833	885	940	996	3,314	7,752
Other mandatory programs	955	1,308	1,038	1,038	1,037	1,041	1,106	1,174	1,191	1,230	1,285	1,291	5,260	11,431
Subtotal, mandatory programs	3,758	4,165	4,104	4,294	4,503	4,786	4,943	5,311	5,565	5,870	6,339	6,484	22,629	52,199
Net interest	658	890	969	1,022	1,088	1,158	1,220	1,278	1,347	1,425	1,500	1,572	5,457	12,579
Total outlays	6,135	6,873	6,952	7,211	7,517	7,891	8,140	8,594	8,964	9,404	9,997	10,262	37,710	84,931
Receipts:														
Individual income taxes	2,176	2,510	2,639	2,915	3,145	3,325	3,496	3,658	3,848	4,055	4,265	4,486	15,520	35,834
Corporation income taxes	420	520	467	453	440	454	483	494	512	550	559	570	2,297	4,982
Social insurance and retirement receipts:														
Social Security payroll taxes	1,194	1,240	1,285	1,343	1,399	1,469	1,528	1,592	1,658	1,725	1,817	1,887	7,023	15,702
Medicare payroll taxes	358	384	399	415	433	456	475	496	518	540	570	593	2,178	4,894
Unemployment insurance	49	54	56	59	62	64	64	67	70	71	73	78	306	664
Other retirement	14	14	14	15	16	16	17	18	18	19	20	21	78	175
Excise taxes	76	97	97	100	100	99	101	103	103	104	105	105	497	1,016
Estate and gift taxes	34	29	31	33	49	51	53	56	60	65	70	75	218	543
Customs duties	80	81	61	53	53	55	57	59	61	53	56	58	277	564
Deposits of earnings, Federal Reserve System	1	......	......	......	25	40	51	62	71	79	85	90	116	503
Other miscellaneous receipts	40	35	37	40	43	47	51	56	60	63	66	68	218	530
Total receipts	4,441	4,964	5,087	5,426	5,765	6,076	6,376	6,661	6,979	7,324	7,684	8,029	28,730	65,407
Deficit	1,694	1,909	1,865	1,784	1,752	1,815	1,763	1,933	1,985	2,080	2,313	2,233	8,980	19,524
Net interest	658	890	969	1,022	1,088	1,158	1,220	1,278	1,347	1,425	1,500	1,572	5,457	12,579
Primary deficit	1,035	1,019	896	762	664	657	544	655	638	655	814	661	3,523	6,945
On-budget deficit	1,666	1,837	1,753	1,648	1,590	1,637	1,550	1,692	1,712	1,770	1,990	1,872	8,179	17,214
Off-budget deficit	27	72	112	136	162	178	213	241	273	310	323	361	801	2,310

[1] Baseline estimates are on the basis of the economic assumptions shown in Table S–9, which incorporate the effects of the Administration's fiscal policies.

Table S–4. Proposed Budget by Category

(In billions of dollars)

	2023	2024	2025	2026	2027	2028	2029	2030	2031	2032	2033	2034	Totals 2025–2029	Totals 2025–2034
Outlays:														
Discretionary programs:														
Defense	806	884	900	906	920	940	961	967	981	990	998	1,005	4,626	9,566
Non-defense	912	1,001	1,029	1,021	1,014	993	986	986	993	1,018	1,038	1,057	5,042	10,134
Subtotal, discretionary programs	1,718	1,885	1,929	1,927	1,934	1,933	1,946	1,952	1,974	2,008	2,036	2,062	9,669	19,700
Mandatory programs:														
Social Security	1,348	1,452	1,543	1,637	1,730	1,824	1,919	2,018	2,118	2,221	2,325	2,432	8,653	19,767
Medicare	839	839	936	997	1,069	1,202	1,158	1,311	1,398	1,504	1,721	1,693	5,362	12,989
Medicaid	616	567	589	625	666	707	749	797	850	907	969	1,035	3,335	7,893
Other mandatory programs	955	1,310	1,303	1,221	1,225	1,281	1,350	1,487	1,483	1,538	1,580	1,609	6,381	14,077
Subtotal, mandatory programs	3,758	4,167	4,372	4,479	4,690	5,014	5,176	5,612	5,849	6,169	6,595	6,769	23,731	54,725
Net interest	658	889	965	1,013	1,072	1,136	1,190	1,241	1,301	1,367	1,428	1,485	5,377	12,199
Total outlays	6,135	6,941	7,266	7,419	7,697	8,083	8,313	8,805	9,123	9,544	10,060	10,316	38,777	86,625
Receipts:														
Individual income taxes	2,176	2,503	2,679	2,976	3,178	3,369	3,549	3,734	3,925	4,129	4,341	4,574	15,751	36,455
Corporation income taxes	420	613	668	721	703	710	741	770	806	859	882	905	3,544	7,766
Social insurance and retirement receipts:														
Social Security payroll taxes	1,194	1,240	1,284	1,342	1,397	1,467	1,526	1,591	1,656	1,723	1,814	1,885	7,016	15,685
Medicare payroll taxes	358	413	542	519	543	572	597	625	653	682	720	752	2,772	6,203
Unemployment insurance	49	54	56	59	62	64	64	67	70	71	73	78	306	664
Other retirement	14	14	14	15	16	16	17	18	18	19	20	21	78	175
Excise taxes	76	100	110	112	113	113	115	118	118	120	122	122	563	1,163
Estate and gift taxes	34	29	33	35	53	57	61	65	69	75	80	87	238	614
Customs duties	80	81	61	53	53	55	57	59	61	53	56	58	277	564
Deposits of earnings, Federal Reserve System	1	......	......	......	25	40	51	62	71	79	85	90	116	503
Other miscellaneous receipts	40	35	38	41	43	47	52	56	60	64	66	69	221	537
Total receipts	4,441	5,082	5,485	5,873	6,186	6,510	6,830	7,164	7,509	7,873	8,258	8,639	30,883	70,328
Deficit	1,694	1,859	1,781	1,547	1,510	1,573	1,483	1,640	1,614	1,671	1,801	1,677	7,894	16,297
Net interest	658	889	965	1,013	1,072	1,136	1,190	1,241	1,301	1,367	1,428	1,485	5,377	12,199
Primary deficit	1,035	971	816	533	438	437	293	400	313	304	373	192	2,516	4,098
On-budget deficit	1,666	1,788	1,669	1,410	1,346	1,392	1,268	1,398	1,338	1,359	1,476	1,313	7,086	13,970
Off-budget deficit	27	72	112	137	164	180	215	243	275	312	326	364	807	2,327

Table S–5.　Proposed Budget by Category as a Percent of GDP

(As a percent of GDP)

	2023	2024	2025	2026	2027	2028	2029	2030	2031	2032	2033	2034	Averages 2025–2029	Averages 2025–2034
Outlays:														
Discretionary programs:														
Defense	3.0	3.1	3.1	3.0	2.9	2.8	2.8	2.7	2.6	2.5	2.4	2.4	2.9	2.7
Non-defense	3.4	3.5	3.5	3.3	3.2	3.0	2.9	2.7	2.6	2.6	2.5	2.5	3.2	2.9
Subtotal, discretionary programs	6.4	6.7	6.6	6.3	6.1	5.8	5.6	5.4	5.3	5.1	5.0	4.8	6.1	5.6
Mandatory programs:														
Social Security	5.0	5.1	5.3	5.4	5.4	5.5	5.6	5.6	5.6	5.7	5.7	5.7	5.4	5.5
Medicare	3.1	3.0	3.2	3.3	3.4	3.6	3.4	3.6	3.7	3.8	4.2	4.0	3.4	3.6
Medicaid	2.3	2.0	2.0	2.0	2.1	2.1	2.2	2.2	2.3	2.3	2.4	2.4	2.1	2.2
Other mandatory programs	3.5	4.6	4.4	4.0	3.9	3.9	3.9	4.1	3.9	3.9	3.9	3.8	4.0	4.0
Subtotal, mandatory programs	13.9	14.7	14.9	14.7	14.7	15.1	15.0	15.6	15.6	15.7	16.1	15.9	14.9	15.3
Net interest	2.4	3.1	3.3	3.3	3.4	3.4	3.4	3.4	3.5	3.5	3.5	3.5	3.4	3.4
Total outlays	22.7	24.6	24.8	24.3	24.2	24.4	24.1	24.5	24.3	24.4	24.6	24.2	24.3	24.4
Receipts:														
Individual income taxes	8.1	8.9	9.1	9.7	10.0	10.2	10.3	10.4	10.5	10.5	10.6	10.7	9.9	10.2
Corporation income taxes	1.6	2.2	2.3	2.4	2.2	2.1	2.1	2.1	2.1	2.2	2.2	2.1	2.2	2.2
Social insurance and retirement receipts:														
Social Security payroll taxes	4.4	4.4	4.4	4.4	4.4	4.4	4.4	4.4	4.4	4.4	4.4	4.4	4.4	4.4
Medicare payroll taxes	1.3	1.5	1.8	1.7	1.7	1.7	1.7	1.7	1.7	1.7	1.8	1.8	1.7	1.7
Unemployment insurance	0.2	0.2	0.2	0.2	0.2	0.2	0.2	0.2	0.2	0.2	0.2	0.2	0.2	0.2
Other retirement	0.1	*	*	*	*	*	*	*	*	*	*	*	*	*
Excise taxes	0.3	0.4	0.4	0.4	0.4	0.3	0.3	0.3	0.3	0.3	0.3	0.3	0.4	0.3
Estate and gift taxes	0.1	0.1	0.1	0.1	0.2	0.2	0.2	0.2	0.2	0.2	0.2	0.2	0.1	0.2
Customs duties	0.3	0.3	0.2	0.2	0.2	0.2	0.2	0.2	0.2	0.1	0.1	0.1	0.2	0.2
Deposits of earnings, Federal Reserve System	*	......	......	0.1	0.1	0.1	0.1	0.2	0.2	0.2	0.2	0.2	0.1	0.1
Other miscellaneous receipts	0.1	0.1	0.1	0.1	0.1	0.1	0.2	0.2	0.2	0.2	0.2	0.2	0.1	0.2
Total receipts	16.5	18.0	18.7	19.2	19.4	19.6	19.8	19.9	20.0	20.1	20.2	20.3	19.4	19.7
Deficit	**6.3**	**6.6**	**6.1**	**5.1**	**4.7**	**4.7**	**4.3**	**4.6**	**4.3**	**4.3**	**4.4**	**3.9**	**5.0**	**4.6**
Net interest	2.4	3.1	3.3	3.3	3.4	3.4	3.4	3.4	3.5	3.5	3.5	3.5	3.4	3.4
Primary deficit	3.8	3.4	2.8	1.7	1.4	1.3	0.8	1.1	0.8	0.8	0.9	0.4	1.6	1.2
On-budget deficit	6.2	6.3	5.7	4.6	4.2	4.2	3.7	3.9	3.6	3.5	3.6	3.1	4.5	4.0
Off-budget deficit	0.1	0.3	0.4	0.4	0.5	0.5	0.6	0.7	0.7	0.8	0.8	0.9	0.5	0.6

* 0.05 percent of GDP or less.

Table S–6. Mandatory and Receipt Proposals

(In millions of dollars)

	2024	2025	2026	2027	2028	2029	2030	2031	2032	2033	2034	Totals 2025–2029	Totals 2025–2034
Lower everyday costs for the American people:													
Expand access to child care and early learning:													
Department of Health and Human Services:													
Expand access to affordable, quality child care for low- and middle-income families	....	9,900	16,400	32,200	43,800	47,600	52,000	53,100	54,800	56,600	57,900	149,900	424,300
Expand access to free, universal preschool	....	5,000	7,000	8,000	15,000	20,000	25,000	25,000	30,000	32,500	32,500	55,000	200,000
Account for child care and preschool interaction	....	....	....		–2,600	–3,100	–3,600	–3,600	–3,700	–3,800	–3,900	–5,700	–24,300
Subtotal, expand access to child care and early learning	....	14,900	23,400	40,200	56,200	64,500	73,400	74,500	81,100	85,300	86,500	199,200	600,000
Reduce the cost of health care:													
Crosscutting reforms:													
Permanently extend enhanced premium tax credits[1]	....	....	18,408	25,980	27,783	29,326	31,171	32,051	33,715	35,967	38,302	101,497	272,703
Permanently extend coverage to low-income individuals in States that have not expanded Medicaid	....	8,500	19,000	20,000	20,500	21,000	21,500	21,500	22,000	23,000	23,000	89,000	200,000
Replenish and extend No Surprises Act implementation fund	....	103	115	118	122	42	....	....	....	....	....	500	500
Extend surprise billing protections to ground ambulances[1]	....	....	–74	–101	–104	–113	–117	–121	–128	–133	–140	–392	–1,031
Ban "facility fees" for telehealth and certain outpatient services in commercial insurance	....	....	–190	–190	–190	–280	–280	–280	–280	–280	–280	–850	–2,250
Subtotal, reduce the cost of health care	....	8,603	37,259	45,807	48,111	49,975	52,274	53,150	55,307	58,554	60,882	189,755	469,922
Reduce the cost of prescription drugs:													
Department of Health and Human Services:													
Expand Medicare drug negotiation, extend inflation rebates and out-of-pocket cost caps to the commercial market, and other steps to build on the Inflation Reduction Act (IRA) drug provisions	....	....	–1,000	–7,000	–18,000	–19,000	–25,000	–25,000	–31,000	–37,000	–37,000	–45,000	–200,000
Limit Medicare Part D cost-sharing on certain generic drugs to $2	....	....	....	129	173	173	173	174	174	173	173	475	1,342
Modify the Medicaid Drug Rebate Program in the Territories	....	....	....	....	....	....	....	....	....	....	....	....	....
Permit biosimilar substitution without Food and Drug Administration (FDA) determination of interchangeability	....	....	....	....	....	....	....	....	....	....	....	....	....
Authorize the Department of Health and Human Services (HHS) to negotiate Medicaid supplemental rebates on behalf of States	....	....	....	....	....	....	....	....	....	....	....	....	....
Apply Medicaid drug rebates to separate Children's Health Insurance Programs (CHIP)	....	....	....	....	–670	–690	–710	–740	–770	–790	–810	–1,360	–5,180
Crosscutting reforms:	....	–220	–230	–240	–260	–280	–290	–230	–180	–180	–180	–1,230	–2,290

Table S-6. Mandatory and Receipt Proposals—Continued

(In millions of dollars)

	2024	2025	2026	2027	2028	2029	2030	2031	2032	2033	2034	Totals 2025-2029	Totals 2025-2034
Reduce insulin cost-sharing in commercial plans[1]	......	580	473	108	24	25	27	22	25	27	27	1,210	1,338
Subtotal, reduce the cost of prescription drugs	......	360	−757	−7,003	−18,733	−19,772	−25,800	−25,774	−31,751	−37,770	−37,790	−45,905	−204,790
Reduce the cost of and expand access to postsecondary education and training:													
Department of Education:													
Double Pell Grants for students at public and non-profit institutions	......	906	3,922	6,974	10,354	14,151	16,777	17,040	17,315	17,584	17,891	36,307	122,914
Create the Reducing the Costs of College Fund	......	240	600	840	960	1,200	1,320	1,320	1,560	1,680	2,280	3,840	12,000
Fund free community college	......	......	531	7,190	13,752	16,590	13,294	10,443	9,579	9,278	9,343	38,063	90,000
Fund Advancing Affordability for Students (Historically Black Colleges and Universities (HBCU)/Tribally Controlled Colleges and Universities (TCCU)/Minority Serving Institution (MSI) Tuition Subsidies)	......	1,278	85	2,662	3,477	3,596	3,925	4,050	4,138	4,228	3,839	9,820	30,000
Eliminate student loan origination fees	......	......	1,910	1,939	1,966	2,000	2,040	2,079	2,052	2,048	2,099	9,093	19,411
Department of Labor:													
Create a Classroom to Career Training Fund to support high-quality training	......	89	585	884	1,000	1,078	1,091	1,091	1,091	1,091	......	3,636	8,000
Corporation for National and Community Service:													
Expand the American Climate Corps	......	125	250	430	600	860	990	1,180	1,180	1,190	1,195	2,265	8,000
Subtotal, reduce the cost of and expand access to postsecondary education and training	......	2,638	7,883	20,919	32,109	39,475	39,437	37,203	36,915	37,099	36,647	103,024	290,325
Reduce the cost of housing for home owners and renters:													
Department of Housing and Urban Development:													
Create an Innovation Fund for Housing Expansion	......	10	310	910	1,680	2,500	3,190	3,370	3,090	2,320	1,500	5,410	18,880
Fund new units for extremely low-income households	......	610	638	666	696	728	761	795	831	868	907	3,338	7,500
Modernize the public housing stock	......	......	75	375	1,125	1,125	1,275	1,275	1,950	300	......	2,700	7,500
Create a housing voucher program for youth aging out of foster care	......	......	215	422	720	951	1,124	1,254	1,372	1,487	1,606	2,308	9,151
Create a housing voucher program for extremely low-income veterans	......	......	241	507	711	868	1,037	1,211	1,682	2,748	4,120	2,327	13,125
Provide down payment assistance to first generation homebuyers	......	243	755	1,523	2,386	2,338	1,768	558	237	192	......	7,245	10,000
Fund efforts to support and sustain eviction prevention	......	500	1,000	750	750	......	......	......	......	......	......	3,000	3,000
Fund new assistance for homelessness	......	2	67	329	603	871	1,108	1,278	1,175	915	685	1,872	7,033
Provide emergency rental assistance for older adults at risk of homelessness	......	300	300	300	300	300	300	300	300	300	300	1,500	3,000
Department of the Treasury:													

Table S–6. Mandatory and Receipt Proposals—Continued

(In millions of dollars)

	2024	2025	2026	2027	2028	2029	2030	2031	2032	2033	2034	Totals 2025–2029	Totals 2025–2034
Provide Mortgage Relief Credit[1]	710	28,517	14,066	5,005	–218	–69	....	....	....	....	....	47,301	47,301
Provide a neighborhood homes credit[1]	....	270	1,145	1,829	1,963	2,099	2,183	2,253	2,304	2,371	2,428	7,306	18,845
Expand and enhance the low-income housing credit[1]	....	84	354	980	1,918	2,961	4,010	5,054	6,090	7,118	8,077	6,297	36,646
Affordable Housing Program:													
Increase Federal Home Loan Banks' contribution to the Affordable Housing Program[1,2]	....	95	95	95	95	95	95	95	95	95	95	475	950
Subtotal, reduce the cost of housing for home owners and renters	710	30,631	19,261	13,691	12,729	14,767	16,851	17,443	19,126	18,714	19,718	91,079	182,931
Offset by tax reforms to ensure the wealthiest Americans and big corporations pay their fair share:													
Impose a minimum income tax on the wealthiest taxpayers[1]	....	....	–50,310	–56,387	–59,430	–60,451	–59,974	–59,331	–53,057	–50,215	–53,513	–226,578	–502,668
Increase the top marginal income tax rate for high-income earners[1]	–9,871	–75,419	–31,189	–13,798	–14,939	–15,859	–16,818	–17,833	–18,885	–19,997	–21,187	–151,204	–245,924
Reform the taxation of capital income[1]	....	–18,031	–23,713	–25,164	–26,417	–27,624	–29,050	–30,727	–32,158	–33,758	–41,941	–120,949	–288,583
Close loopholes in the estate and gift taxes and related reforms:													
Improve tax administration for trusts and decedents' estates[1]	....	–9	–79	–83	–96	–112	–130	–150	–174	–199	–227	–379	–1,259
Limit duration of generation-skipping transfer tax exemption[1]	....	....	....	....	....	....	....	....	....	....	....	....	....
Modify income, estate, gift, and generation-skipping transfer tax rules for certain trusts[1]	....	–1,290	–2,625	–5,032	–6,855	–8,871	–10,566	–10,749	–11,608	–12,587	–13,567	–24,673	–83,750
Revise rules for valuation of certain property[1]	....	–331	–955	–1,025	–1,139	–1,225	–1,296	–1,390	–1,493	–1,613	–1,745	–4,675	–12,212
Subtotal, close loopholes in the estate and gift taxes and related reforms	....	–1,630	–3,659	–6,140	–8,090	–10,208	–11,992	–12,289	–13,275	–14,399	–15,539	–29,727	–97,221
Expand limitation on deductibility of excessive employee remuneration[1,2]	....	–37,169	–19,015	–30,421	–34,951	–31,354	–28,057	–22,148	–20,594	–22,385	–25,760	–152,910	–271,854
Subtotal, tax reforms to ensure the wealthiest Americans and big corporations pay their fair share	–9,871	–132,249	–127,886	–131,910	–143,827	–145,496	–145,891	–142,328	–137,969	–140,754	–157,940	–681,368	–1,406,250
Subtotal, lower everyday costs for the American people	–9,161	–75,117	–40,840	–18,296	–13,411	3,449	10,271	14,194	22,728	21,143	8,017	–144,215	–67,862
Invest in working families and improve healthcare:													
Provide national, comprehensive paid family and medical leave:													
Social Security Administration:													
Provide national, comprehensive paid family and medical leave	....	2,000	10,000	18,000	20,000	25,000	50,000	50,000	50,000	50,000	50,000	75,000	325,000
Subtotal, provide national, comprehensive paid family and medical leave	....	2,000	10,000	18,000	20,000	25,000	50,000	50,000	50,000	50,000	50,000	75,000	325,000

Table S-6. Mandatory and Receipt Proposals—Continued

(In millions of dollars)

	2024	2025	2026	2027	2028	2029	2030	2031	2032	2033	2034	Totals 2025–2029	Totals 2025–2034
Restore and make permanent the American Rescue Plan expansion of the earned income tax credit for workers without qualifying children[1]	388	15,330	15,770	15,998	16,126	16,310	16,451	16,503	16,587	16,695	16,783	79,534	162,553
Expand the child credit, and make permanent full refundability and advanceability[1]	5,409	209,890	11,210	7,769	11,376	11,586	11,827	12,157	12,372	12,717	9,120	251,831	310,024
Improve home care:													
Department of Health and Human Services:													
Improve Medicaid home and community-based services		3,000	4,000	5,250	7,050	9,400	12,550	16,750	22,350	29,850	39,800	28,700	150,000
Reclassify discretionary nursing home Survey and Certification activities as mandatory			218	352	448	458	469	480	490	501	513	1,476	3,929
Discretionary effects (non-add)			*–200*	*–325*	*–413*	*–422*	*–431*	*–441*	*–451*	*–462*	*–472*	*–1,360*	*–3,617*
Require Medicaid adult and home and community-based services quality reporting		25	26	27	28	29	30	32	33	34	35	135	299
Increase private equity and real estate investment trust ownership transparency in long-term care (LTC) facilities		....	....	....	....	....	....	....	....	....	....	....	....
Reduce survey frequency for high-performing LTC facilities		....	....	....	....	....	....	....	....	....	....	....	....
Provide authority for the Secretary to collect and expend re-survey fees from LTC facilities within the Survey and Certification Program that require a revisit survey		....	....	....	....	....	....	....	....	....	....	....	....
Increase per instance civil monetary penalty authority for LTC facilities		....	....	....	....	....	....	....	....	....	....	....	....
Hold LTC facility owners accountable for noncompliant closures and substandard care		....	....	....	....	....	....	....	....	....	....	....	....
Improve the accuracy and reliability of Nursing Home Care Compare data		....	....	....	....	....	....	....	....	....	....	....	....
Extend to the United States Public Health Service Commissioned Corps (USPHS) Commissioned Corps benefits available to other uniformed services		....	....	....	....	....	....	....	....	....	....	....	....
Align USPHS Commissioned Corps authorities with select Armed Forces authorities and the Military Department Exemption to the Uniformed Services Employment and Reemployment Rights Act (USERRA)		....	....	....	....	....	....	....	....	....	....	....	....
Subtotal, improve home care		3,025	4,244	5,629	7,526	9,887	13,049	17,262	22,873	30,385	40,348	30,311	154,228
Strengthen public health and improve health outcomes:													
Guarantee stable and adequate funding for the Indian Health Service (IHS):													
Department of Health and Human Services:													
Shift the IHS to mandatory spending (gross)		....	11,078	19,769	25,719	31,219	37,259	35,390	36,494	38,924	41,401	87,785	277,253

Table S–6. Mandatory and Receipt Proposals—Continued

(In millions of dollars)

	2024	2025	2026	2027	2028	2029	2030	2031	2032	2033	2034	Totals 2025–2029	Totals 2025–2034
Reduction in discretionary spending (non-add)	......	......	–5,127	–6,906	–8,422	–8,616	–8,814	–9,019	–9,224	–9,438	–9,653	–29,071	–75,219
Subtotal, guarantee adequate and stable funding for the IHS	......	......	11,078	19,769	25,719	31,219	37,259	35,390	36,494	38,924	41,401	87,785	277,253
Transform behavioral health:													
Department of Health and Human Services:													
Modernize inpatient psychiatric and behavioral health facilities' health information technology			400	300	300	......	......	......	......	......	......	1,000	1,000
Apply the Mental Health Parity and Addiction Equity Act to Medicare[3]			......	......	......	......	......	......	......	......	......	......	......
Eliminate the 190-day lifetime limit on inpatient psychiatric facility services		140	175	180	200	205	220	235	240	260	265	900	2,120
Require Medicare to cover three behavioral health visits without cost-sharing[1]			110	140	150	160	170	170	180	190	200	560	1,470
Revise criteria for psychiatric hospital terminations from Medicare			......	......	......	......	......	......	......	......	......	......	......
Modernize Medicare mental health benefits[3]			......	......	......	......	......	......	......	......	......	......	......
Broaden the Health Professional Shortage Area (HPSA) Incentive Program to include additional non-physician and behavioral health practitioners			......	......	......	......	......	......	......	......	......	......	......
Provide mandatory funding for State enforcement of mental health parity requirements		10	40	25	25	25	......	......	......	......	......	125	125
Create a Mental Health Transformation Fund		400	400	400	400	400	......	......	......	......	......	2,000	2,000
Provide grants to Community Mental Health Centers		124	289	372	413	413	413	413	413	413	413	1,611	3,676
Convert Medicaid demonstration to improve community mental health services into a permanent program				......	223	641	1,033	2,160	2,304	2,453	2,604	864	11,418
Department of Labor:													
Authorize the Department of Labor (DOL) to pursue parity violations by entities that provide administrative services to Employee Retirement Income Security Act (ERISA) group health plans			......	......	......	......	......	......	......	......	......	......	......
Authorize DOL to impose civil monetary penalties for Mental Health Parity and Addiction Equity Act (MHPAEA) noncompliance			–3	–4	–4	–4	–4	–4	–4	–4	–4	–15	–35
Provide mandatory funding for DOL to perform additional Non-Quantitative Treatment Limitations (NQTL) audits		2	5	25	25	34	35	36	37	38	38	91	275
Crosscutting reforms:													

Table S-6. Mandatory and Receipt Proposals—Continued

(In millions of dollars)

	2024	2025	2026	2027	2028	2029	2030	2031	2032	2033	2034	Totals 2025–2029	Totals 2025–2034
Improve access to behavioral healthcare in the private insurance market[1]	....	....	....	2,549	3,532	3,701	3,884	4,055	4,283	4,496	4,724	9,782	31,224
Require coverage of three behavioral health visits and three primary care visits without cost-sharing[1]	....	....	....	5,011	4,756	1,966	1,286	1,301	1,384	1,462	1,548	11,733	18,714
Subtotal, transform mental health	....	676	1,416	8,998	10,020	7,541	7,037	8,366	8,837	9,308	9,788	28,651	71,987
Strengthen public health and combat disease:													
Department of Health and Human Services:													
Expand access to maternal health supports in Medicaid	....	6	10	15	19	24	23	22	27	27	31	74	204
Require 12 months of Medicaid postpartum coverage[1]	....	–55	–58	–62	–65	–68	–70	–71	–79	–86	–93	–308	–707
Expand and enhance access to Medicare coverage of nutrition and obesity counseling	....	4	71	123	181	213	224	236	248	264	277	592	1,841
Conduct a subnational Medicare medically-tailored meal demonstration[3]	....	....	....	....	....	....	....	....	....	....	....	....	....
Increase access to Pre-Exposure Prophylaxis (PrEP):													
Establish PrEP delivery program to end the HIV epidemic in the United States	....	213	371	526	687	853	1,027	1,206	1,394	1,587	1,789	2,650	9,653
Eliminate barriers to PrEP under Medicaid	....	–730	–790	–850	–920	–990	–1,070	–1,160	–1,250	–1,340	–1,450	–4,280	–10,550
Establish the National Hepatitis C Elimination Program	....	435	1,280	1,496	1,617	–168	–1,327	–1,648	–1,798	–1,878	–2,038	4,660	–4,029
National Hepatitis C Elimination Program Costs (non-add)	....	*940*	*1,880*	*2,350*	*2,820*	*1,410*	....	....	....	....	....	*9,400*	*9,400*
Medicaid prescription drug and medical savings (non-add)	....	*–700*	*–890*	*–1,120*	*–1,390*	*–1,690*	*–1,120*	*–1,320*	*–1,480*	*–1,600*	*–1,830*	*–5,790*	*–13,140*
Medicare zero cost sharing on drugs and medical savings (non-add)	....	*195*	*290*	*266*	*187*	*112*	*–207*	*–328*	*–318*	*–278*	*–208*	*1,050*	*–289*
Establish the Vaccines for Adults program	....	823	1,036	1,077	1,118	1,162	1,208	1,255	1,304	1,354	1,408	5,216	11,745
Expand Vaccines for Children (VFC) program to all CHIP children and make program improvements	....	174	175	186	209	210	221	197	184	185	195	954	1,936
Encourage development of innovative antimicrobial drugs[3,4]	....	....	....	....	....	....	....	....	....	....	....	....	....
Enable the Secretary to temporarily modify or waive the application of specific requirements of the Clinical Laboratory Improvement Amendments of 1988 (CLIA) Act[3]	....	....	....	....	....	....	....	....	....	....	....	....	....
Extend Teaching Health Center Graduate Medical Education (GME)	61	212	292	115	68	36	....	....	....	....	....	784	784
Reauthorize the Special Diabetes Program for Type 1 Diabetes Research (National Institutes of Health, NIH)	10	33	65	102	139	157	124	62	17	3	1	506	713

Table S–6. Mandatory and Receipt Proposals—Continued

(In millions of dollars)

	2024	2025	2026	2027	2028	2029	2030	2031	2032	2033	2034	Totals 2025–2029	Totals 2025–2034
Reauthorize the Special Diabetes Program for Indians (IHS)	177	257	269	11								714	714
Increase funding for the National Health Service Corps (NHSC) program	144	553	730	596	155	32	8					2,210	2,218
Extend Family-to-Family Health Information Centers		3	10	12	12	12	9	2				49	60
Extend the 21st Century Cures Act Cancer Moonshot:[5]													
Extend mandatory spending for the Cancer Moonshot		361	1,066	996	348	77	34	14				2,848	2,896
Discretionary budget authority (BA) (non-add)		716										716	716
Total Cancer Moonshot request (non-add)		1,077	1,066	996	348	77	34	14				3,564	7,176
Expand cancer care quality measurement in Medicare[3]													
Provide a pathway to double funding for the Health Center Program													
Subtotal, strengthen public health and combat disease		1,538	4,664	6,774	4,078	138	75					17,267	17,267
Strengthen biodefense:													
Department of Health and Human Services:													
Strengthen biodefense to protect against 21st Century biothreats	1,930	6,953	11,301	8,421	3,706	1,625	411	115	47	116	120	32,006	32,815
Authorize coverage for specific products and services, including unapproved drugs, vaccines, and devices authorized for emergency use[3]		3,000	7,000	5,000	2,400	1,400	1,200					18,800	20,000
Create Federal public health data reporting authority[3]													
Subtotal, strengthen biodefense		3,000	7,000	5,000	2,400	1,400	1,200					18,800	20,000
Subtotal, invest in working families and improve healthcare	1,930	10,629	30,795	42,188	41,845	41,785	45,907	43,871	45,378	48,348	51,309	167,242	402,055
	7,727	240,874	72,019	89,584	96,873	104,568	137,234	139,793	147,210	158,145	167,560	603,918	1,353,860
Tax reforms to make big corporations pay their fair share:													
Raise the corporate income tax rate to 28 percent[1]	−74,646	−122,474	−125,105	−128,114	−128,353	−128,624	−129,396	−137,888	−144,919	−150,028	−155,040	−632,670	−1,349,941
Increase the corporate alternative minimum tax rate to 21 percent[1]	−10,050	−13,543	−11,759	−12,264	−12,675	−13,119	−13,672	−14,238	−14,800	−15,379	−15,980	−63,360	−137,429
Revise the global minimum tax regime, limit inversions, and make related reforms[1]	−8,875	−27,920	−35,889	−34,589	−34,819	−36,215	−37,719	−39,261	−40,846	−42,483	−44,178	−169,432	−373,919
Adopt the undertaxed profits rule[1]		−9,596	−14,541	−14,065	−14,389	−14,181	−14,088	−13,837	−13,752	−13,916	−13,948	−66,772	−136,313
Increase the excise tax rate on repurchase of corporate stock and close loopholes[1]	−3,863	−15,344	−14,980	−14,936	−15,184	−15,792	−16,458	−17,167	−17,912	−18,691	−19,502	−76,236	−165,966
Subtotal, tax reforms to make big corporations pay their fair share	−97,434	−188,877	−202,274	−203,968	−205,691	−207,660	−211,333	−222,391	−232,229	−240,497	−248,648	−1,008,470	−2,163,568

Table S-6. Mandatory and Receipt Proposals—Continued

(In millions of dollars)

	2024	2025	2026	2027	2028	2029	2030	2031	2032	2033	2034	Totals 2025–2029	Totals 2025–2034
Close Medicare tax loopholes and increase Medicare tax for people making over $400,000:													
Apply the net investment income tax to pass-through business income of high-income taxpayers[1] ...	–8,496	–38,302	–29,950	–31,931	–34,819	–37,435	–39,950	–42,143	–43,986	–46,126	–48,579	–172,437	–393,221
Increase the net investment income tax rate and additional Medicare tax rate for high-income taxpayers[1] ...	–8,394	–42,920	–31,327	–32,285	–34,710	–37,224	–39,822	–42,450	–44,963	–47,602	–50,487	–178,466	–403,790
Subtotal, close Medicare tax loopholes and increase Medicare tax for people making over $400,000 ...	–16,890	–81,222	–61,277	–64,216	–69,529	–74,659	–79,772	–84,593	–88,949	–93,728	–99,066	–350,903	–797,011
Reduce crime and protect victims:													
Department of Health and Human Services:													
Support Centers for Disease Control and Prevention (CDC) Community Violence Intervention (CVI) initiative ...	....	150	150	150	150	150	150	150	150	150	150	750	1,500
Department of Justice:													
Invest in Community Oriented Policing Services...	....	870	1,305	1,740	2,023	2,175	1,305	870	435	152	....	8,113	10,875
Establish Gun Crime Prevention Strategic Fund ...	....	194	530	839	884	884	690	354	44	....	....	3,331	4,419
Support the Accelerating Justice System Reform (AJSR) Program ...	....	66	279	654	1,064	1,358	1,540	1,705	1,888	1,988	2,000	3,421	12,542
Restore the Crime Victims Fund ...	....	....	187	377	516	623	650	650	619	630	635	1,703	4,887
Establish the Violent Crime Reduction and Prevention Fund ...	....	158	195	223	239	247	89	52	24	8	....	1,062	1,235
Expand Community Violence Intervention Programs ...	....	33	90	143	150	150	150	150	150	150	150	566	1,316
Subtotal, reduce crime and protect victims ...	....	1,471	2,736	4,126	5,026	5,587	4,574	3,931	3,310	3,078	2,935	18,946	36,774
Outcompete China:													
Department of the Interior:													
Renew Compacts of Free Association ...	32	1,443	343	248	154	150	147	149	155	164	165	2,370	3,150
International Assistance Programs:													
Advance the Indo-Pacific Strategy ...	....	200	300	350	375	400	200	100	50	25	....	1,625	2,000
Invest in International Infrastructure Fund ...	....	220	510	475	355	265	100	43	22	10	....	1,825	2,000
Subtotal, outcompete China ...	32	1,863	1,153	1,073	884	815	447	292	227	199	165	5,788	7,118
Additional investments and reforms:													
Department of Agriculture:													
End subsidy recapture for Single Family Housing Direct Loans ...	....	1,120	....	....	....	....	....	....	....	....	....	1,120	1,120
Extend crop insurance for Pandemic Cover Crop Program ...	....	60	65	70	75	80	85	90	95	100	105	350	825
Improve The Emergency Food Assistance Program (TEFAP) infrastructure in underserved communities ...	....	25	25	25	25	25	25	25	25	25	25	125	250
Waive the Summer Electronic Benefit Transfer (EBT) administrative match requirement ...	....	101	131	94	69	56	43	22	26	....	....	451	542

Table S–6. Mandatory and Receipt Proposals—Continued

(In millions of dollars)

	2024	2025	2026	2027	2028	2029	2030	2031	2032	2033	2034	Totals 2025–2029	Totals 2025–2034
Provide Summer EBT implementation grants	....	40	50	50	10	....	....	....	....	....	....	150	150
Expand Community Eligibility Provision (CEP) for school meals	....	187	1,233	1,522	1,569	1,614	1,658	1,705	1,753	1,808	1,823	6,125	14,872
Improve utilization of USDA Foods	....	....	....	....	....	....	....	....	....	....	....	....	....
Subtotal, Department of Agriculture	....	1,533	1,504	1,761	1,748	1,775	1,811	1,842	1,899	1,933	1,953	8,321	17,759
Department of Commerce:													
Fund the Regional Technology and Innovation Hub Program	....	225	270	675	810	800	645	500	75	....	....	2,780	4,000
Subtotal, Department of Commerce	....	225	270	675	810	800	645	500	75	....	....	2,780	4,000
Department of Defense......Military Programs:													
Permanently increase Department of Defense (DOD) Voluntary Separation Incentive Payment ceiling	....	1	2	3	4	5	6	7	7	8	8	15	51
Fund Survivor Benefit Plan	....	....	....	....	....	....	....	....	....	....	....	....	....
Fund State Active Duty Reimbursement	....	44	46	46	47	48	49	50	51	52	53	231	486
Post–9/11 Educational Assistance for Dependent Victims of Domestic Violence	....	4	7	8	8	8	9	9	10	10	11	35	84
Subtotal, Department of Defense......Military Programs	....	49	55	57	59	61	64	66	68	70	72	281	621
Department of Education:													
Fund Academic Acceleration and Achievement Grants	....	480	2,160	2,160	2,800	400	....	....	....	....	....	8,000	8,000
Academic Acceleration and Achievement Grants (Budget authority) (non-add)	....	8,000	....	....	....	....	....	....	....	....	....	8,000	8,000
Fund Vocational Rehabilitation State Grants without an inflationary increase	....	....	–66	–126	–136	–140	–142	–146	–153	–161	–165	–468	–1,235
Subtotal, Department of Education	....	480	2,094	2,034	2,664	260	–142	–146	–153	–161	–165	7,532	6,765
Department of Health and Human Services:													
Increase mandatory Health Care Fraud and Abuse Control (HCFAC) funding	....	–260	–390	–510	–510	–530	–540	–560	–560	–580	–600	–2,200	–5,040
Provide cybersecurity support for hospitals	....	....	....	412	412	262	262	....	....	....	....	1,086	1,348
Medicare Enhancements:													
Add Medicare coverage of services furnished by community health workers[3]	....	....	....	....	....	....	....	....	....	....	....	....	....
Enhance Medicaid managed care enforcement	....	–120	–130	–140	–150	–160	–170	–180	–200	–210	–220	–700	–1,680
Require remittance of medical loss ratios in Medicaid and CHIP managed care	....	....	–900	–1,000	–1,000	–1,100	–1,100	–1,200	–1,200	–1,300	–1,300	–4,000	–10,100
Continuous Medicaid and CHIP coverage for children:													
Allow States to provide 36-month continuous eligibility for all children in Medicaid and CHIP	....	109	243	525	539	579	607	643	675	719	760	1,995	5,399
Allow States to provide continuous eligibility up to age 6 in Medicaid and CHIP[1]	....	30	89	282	380	490	519	546	588	616	657	1,271	4,197

Table S-6. Mandatory and Receipt Proposals—Continued

(In millions of dollars)

	2024	2025	2026	2027	2028	2029	2030	2031	2032	2033	2034	Totals 2025–2029	Totals 2025–2034
Prohibit CHIP enrollment fees and premiums[1] .	......	112	125	133	144	143	154	–1	2	2	2	657	816
Good Governance and other technical proposals:													
Implement targeted risk-adjustment pre-payment review in Medicare Advantage[3]	......	......	......	......	......	......	......	......	......	......	......	......	......
Ensure providers that violate Medicare safety requirements and have harmed patients cannot quickly reenter the program	......	......	......	......	......	......	......	......	......	......	......	......	......
Standardize data collection to improve quality and promote equitable care	......	......	......	......	......	......	......	......	......	......	......	......	......
Refine the Quality Payment Program (QPP); measure development funding for QPP	......	10	10	10	10	10	......	......	......	......	......	50	50
Allow collection of demographic and social determinants of health data through Center for Medicaid and Medicare Services (CMS) quality reporting and payment programs	......	......	......	......	......	......	......	......	......	......	......	......	......
Create a consolidated Medicare hospital quality payment program	......	......	......	......	......	......	......	......	......	......	......	......	......
Implement value-based purchasing and quality programs for Medicare facilities[3]	......	......	......	......	......	......	......	......	......	......	......	......	......
Create a permanent Medicare Home Health Value-Based Purchasing program	......	......	......	......	......	......	......	......	......	......	......	......	......
Create a permanent Medicare Diabetes Prevention Program benefit	......	......	......	......	......	......	......	......	......	......	......	......	......
Reauthorize Medicare Improvements for Patients and Providers Act (MIPPA)	......	50	50	50	50	50	......	......	......	......	......	250	250
Change the Medicare Appeal Council's standard of review to appellate-level to expedite adjudication procedures and timelines	......	......	......	......	......	......	......	......	......	......	......	......	......
Provide CMS Program Management implementation funding	......	50	150	100	......	......	......	......	......	......	......	300	300
Strengthen Medicare Advantage by establishing new Medical Loss Ratio requirements for supplemental benefits[3]	......	......	......	......	......	......	......	......	......	......	......	......	......
Prohibit unsolicited Medicare beneficiary contacts[3]	......	......	......	......	......	......	......	......	......	......	......	......	......
Expand tools to identify and investigate fraud in the Medicare Advantage program	......	......	......	......	......	......	......	......	......	......	......	......	......
Increase transparency by disclosing accreditation surveys	......	......	......	......	......	......	......	......	......	......	......	......	......
Require Average Sales Price (ASP) reporting for oral Methadone[3]	......	......	......	......	......	......	......	......	......	......	......	......	......
Remove restrictions on the certification of new entities as Organ Procurement Organizations and increase enforcement flexibility	......	......	......	......	......	......	......	......	......	......	......	......	......
Establish meaningful measures for the End-Stage Renal Disease Quality Incentive Program	......	......	......	......	......	......	......	......	......	......	......	......	......

Table S–6. Mandatory and Receipt Proposals—Continued

(In millions of dollars)

	2024	2025	2026	2027	2028	2029	2030	2031	2032	2033	2034	Totals 2025–2029	Totals 2025–2034
Extend Post-9/11 GI Bill educational benefits and Montgomery GI Bill Selected Reserve Program to USPHS Commissioned Corps	......	1	1	1	1	1	1	1	1	2	2	5	12
Authorize Tribal health programs to pay Medicare Part B premiums directly on behalf of Tribal members	......	......	......	......	......	......	......	......	......	......	......	......	......
Prohibit billing of beneficiaries after Medicare bad debt payments	......	......	......	......	......	......	......	......	......	......	......	......	......
Fully cover costs for all living organ donors for Medicare	......	......	......	......	......	......	......	......	......	......	......	......	......
Improve access and coverage for beneficiaries dually eligible for Medicare and Medicaid:													
Align Qualified Medicare Beneficiary renewal period with other Medicaid groups	......	......	......	......	......	......	......	......	......	......	......	......	......
Unify Medicare and Medicaid appeals procedures[3]	......	......	......	......	......	......	......	......	......	......	......	......	......
Align Medicare Savings Program and Part D Low Income Subsidy eligibility methodologies[3]	......	320	340	360	380	410	440	470	500	540	580	1,810	4,340
Allow retroactive coverage of Medicare Part B premiums for Qualified Medicare Beneficiary applicants	......	50	60	70	80	80	90	100	110	120	130	340	890
Administration for Children and Families:													
Provide comprehensive tribal child welfare funding	......	42	49	55	62	69	75	82	88	95	102	277	719
Increase support for kinship foster care placements and guardianships	......	88	88	88	88	90	91	92	94	98	103	442	920
Reauthorize Personal Responsibility Education Program (PREP)	......	3	17	35	11	6	3	......	......	......	......	72	75
Reauthorize, increase funding for, and amend Promoting Safe and Stable Families program	......	84	240	294	297	300	300	300	300	300	300	1,215	2,715
Prevent and combat religious, sexual orientation, gender identity, gender expression, or sex discrimination in the child welfare system	......	......	......	......	......	......	......	......	......	......	......	......	......
Treat certain populations as refugees for public benefit purposes	......	57	88	101	109	111	113	59	25	11	6	466	680
Authorize program integrity data collection for Temporary Assistance for Needy Families	......	......	......	......	......	......	......	......	......	......	......	......	......
Improve Internal Revenue Service (IRS) data disclosure to tribal child support services and child support services contractors	......	–165	–185	–206	–83	–85	–87	–89	–91	–93	–95	–724	–1,179
Reduce reimbursement rates for foster care congregate care placements	......	–27	–24	–21	–18	–17	–16	–15	–14	–14	–14	–107	–180

Table S–6. Mandatory and Receipt Proposals—Continued

(In millions of dollars)

	2024	2025	2026	2027	2028	2029	2030	2031	2032	2033	2034	Totals 2025–2029	Totals 2025–2034
Create new flexibilities and support in the Chafee program for youth who experienced foster care, including a Post-Foster Care Healthy Transition Assistance Demonstration.	....	126	182	197	234	241	245	249	251	252	249	980	2,226
Allow Tribes that do not currently receive IV-E funding to be eligible for IV-E Prevention funding	....	1	1	2	3	4	6	7	9	12	15	11	60
Expand and encourage participation in the title IV-E Prevention Services and Kinship Navigator programs	....	279	318	376	445	389	457	539	628	701	767	1,807	4,899
Increase the repatriation ceiling		1	1	1	1	1	1	1	1	1	1	5	10
Private health insurance interactions		......	......	1	1	1	1	1	1	1	1	3	8
Medicare interactions		......	......	......	–8	–3	......	8	12	3	......	–11	12
Medicaid interactions		–27	–59	–127	–132	–141	–149	–181	–189	–200	–211	–486	–1,416
CHIP interactions		–3	–6	–11	–10	–12	–12	......	......	......	......	–42	–54
Subtotal, Department of Health and Human Services		811	358	1,078	1,336	1,189	1,291	872	1,031	1,076	1,235	4,772	10,277
Department of Homeland Security:													
Extend expiring Customs and Border Patrol (CBP) user fees		......	......	......	......	......	......	......	–5,628	–5,115	–5,276	......	–16,019
Expand Expand CBP user fee facilities costs		–7	–7	–7	–7	–8	–8	–8	–8	–8	–9	–36	–77
End deficit reduction contributions from Passenger Security Fee		1,600	1,640	1,680	......	......	......	......	......	......	......	4,920	4,920
Establish an affordability program for the National Flood Insurance Program (NFIP)		220	426	467	512	556	598	638	674	706	734	2,181	5,531
Reauthorize the NFIP		......	......	......	......	......	......	......	......	......	......	......	......
Establish Electronic Visa Update System (EVUS) user fee[1]		......	......	......	......	......	......	......	......	......	......	......	......
Subtotal, Department of Homeland Security		1,813	2,059	2,140	505	548	590	630	–4,962	–4,417	–4,551	7,065	–5,645
Department of the Interior:													
Reclassify Tribal lease payments		......	122	124	126	129	132	135	138	141	144	501	1,191
Discretionary effects (non-add)			–122	–124	–126	–129	–132	–135	–138	–141	–144	–501	–1,191
Reclassify Contract Support Costs (CSC)		......	252	423	436	449	462	475	485	495	505	1,560	3,982
Discretionary effects (non-add)			–252	–423	–436	–449	–462	–475	–485	–495	–505	–1,560	–3,982
Provide mandatory funding for previously enacted Tribal Water Settlements Operations and Maintenance		34	34	34	34	34	34	34	34	34	34	170	340
Provide mandatory funding for current and future Indian Water Rights Settlements		250	250	250	250	250	250	250	250	250	250	1,250	2,500
Subtotal, Department of the Interior		284	658	831	846	862	878	894	907	920	933	3,481	8,013
Department of Labor:													
Extend Trade Adjustment Assistance		232	288	299	247	273	283	300	320	338	364	1,339	2,944

Table S–6. Mandatory and Receipt Proposals—Continued

(In millions of dollars)

	2024	2025	2026	2027	2028	2029	2030	2031	2032	2033	2034	Totals 2025–2029	Totals 2025–2034
Shift timing of Pension Benefit Guaranty Corporation (PBGC) Single Employer premiums ...	......	3,020	–3,022	......	......	......	......	......	......	......	–1	–2	–3
Provide authority to keep and spend H–2A labor certification fees	......	3	4	6	6	6	7	7	7	8	8	25	62
Eliminate funding cliff for Federal Employees' Compensation Act (FECA) benefits	......	......	......	......	......	......	......	21	20	19	18	......	78
Improve Unemployment Insurance (UI) program integrity[1]	......	–139	–289	–322	–312	–328	–339	–351	–367	–375	–392	–1,390	–3,214
Subtotal, Department of Labor	......	2,884	–3,307	–316	–306	–316	–332	–323	–340	–348	–366	–1,367	–3,077
Department of Transportation:													
Increase business aviation kerosene jet fuel tax rate[1]	......	–44	–106	–169	–235	–300	–322	–325	–329	–332	–336	–854	–2,498
Fund facility replacements and radar modernizations	......	136	226	551	900	1,246	1,348	1,289	961	572	362	3,059	7,591
Subtotal, Department of Transportation	......	92	120	382	665	946	1,026	964	632	240	26	2,205	5,093
Department of the Treasury:													
Extend investments in Internal Revenue Service (IRS)[1,6]	......	......	2,673	2,822	2,177	648	–27,973	–42,108	–51,231	–60,198	–63,520	8,320	–236,710
Expand Treasury's authority to require bank account verification	......	......	......	......	......	......	......	......	......	......	......	......	......
Simplify Debt Management Services (DMS) fees ...	......	......	......	......	......	......	......	......	......	......	......	......	......
Retain Surety Bond Program Fees	......	2	2	2	2	2	2	2	2	2	2	10	20
Enhance Participation in the Small Dollar Loan Program	......	......	......	......	......	......	......	......	......	......	......	......	......
Ensure the Treasury Do Not Pay Business Center (DNP) has full access to complete State death data	......	......	......	......	......	......	......	......	......	......	......	......	......
Allow DNP to use Fair Credit Reporting Act (FCRA) data for improper payment purposes ...	......	......	......	......	......	......	......	......	......	......	......	......	......
Expand Treasury's access to the National Directory of New Hires (NDNH) for improper payments	......	......	......	......	......	......	......	......	......	......	......	......	......
Reauthorize and reform the Community Development Financial Institutions (CDFI) Fund Bond Guarantee Program	......	......	......	......	......	......	......	......	......	......	......	......	......
Increase access to the Capital Magnet Fund ...	......	......	......	......	......	......	......	......	......	......	......	......	......
Enable alternative metal compositions for circulating coins	......	......	......	......	......	......	......	......	......	......	......	......	......
Make technical corrections regarding calculation of Current Value of Fund rate	......	......	......	......	......	......	......	......	......	......	......	......	......
Subtotal, Department of the Treasury	......	2	2,675	2,824	2,179	650	–27,971	–42,106	–51,229	–60,196	–63,518	8,330	–236,690
Department of Veterans Affairs:													
Expand eligibility for government-furnished headstone, marker, or medallion for Medal of Honor recipients	......	......	......	......	......	......	......	......	......	......	......	......	......

Table S–6. Mandatory and Receipt Proposals—Continued

(In millions of dollars)

	2024	2025	2026	2027	2028	2029	2030	2031	2032	2033	2034	Totals 2025–2029	Totals 2025–2034
Expand plot allowance for certain individuals eligible for interment in a national cemetery	....	16	15	16	16	17	17	17	18	18	19	80	169
Amend the miscellaneous receipts statute for retention of parking receipts from the Department of Veterans Affairs Central Office (VACO) parking facilities	....	....	....	....	....	....	....	....	....	....	....	....	....
Enhance veterans health care programs	....	4	3	4	4	5	5	6	7	8	9	20	55
Subtotal, Department of Veterans Affairs	....	20	18	20	20	22	22	23	25	26	28	100	224
General Services Administration:													
Invest in Acquisition Workforce Training Fund	....	....	....	....	....	....	....	....	....	....	....	....	....
Establish and capitalize the Federal Capital Revolving Fund	....	–128	25	493	1,238	1,622	1,395	832	343	–38	–260	3,250	5,522
Expand Disposal Fund authority	....	1	1	1	1	1	1	1	1	1	1	5	10
Subtotal, General Services Administration	....	–127	26	494	1,239	1,623	1,396	833	344	–37	–259	3,255	5,532
International Assistance Programs:													
Contribute to the Green Climate Fund	....	500	750	750	1,000	....	....	....	....	....	....	3,000	3,000
Subtotal, International Assistance Programs	....	500	750	750	1,000	....	....	....	....	....	....	3,000	3,000
National Aeronautics and Space Administration:													
Eliminate the Science, Space, and Technology Education Trust Fund	....	14	–1	–1	–1	–1	–1	–1	–1	–1	–1	10	5
Subtotal, National Aeronautics and Space Administration	....	14	–1	–1	–1	–1	–1	–1	–1	–1	–1	10	5
Office of Personnel Management:													
Improve financial management of Tribal Federal Employees Health Benefits (FEHB) admin fee by treating as mandatory authority	....	2	2	2	2	2	2	2	2	2	2	10	20
Expand family member eligibility under Federal Employee Dental and Vision Insurance Program (FEDVIP)	....	....	....	....	....	....	....	....	....	....	....	....	....
Expand FEDVIP to certain tribal employers	....	....	....	....	....	....	....	....	....	....	....	....	....
Expand FEHB to tribal colleges and universities	....	....	....	....	....	....	....	....	....	....	....	....	....
Preempt State/local taxation of FEDVIP carriers to align with FEHB carriers	....	....	....	....	....	....	....	....	....	....	....	....	....
Shorten FEDVIP contract terms to allow flexibility for new carriers	....	....	....	....	....	....	....	....	....	....	....	....	....
Establish OPM trust fund authority for Postal Service Health Benefits (PSHB) and FEHB enrollment systems	....	....	37	45	51	54	55	56	57	59	60	187	474
Provide permanent authority to collect reimbursement for Voluntary Early Retirement Authority (VERA) and Voluntary Separation Incentive Payment (VSIP) processing costs	....	....	....	....	....	....	....	....	....	....	....	1	2
Subtotal, Office of Personnel Management	....	2	39	47	53	56	57	58	59	61	62	197	494

Table S–6. Mandatory and Receipt Proposals—Continued

(In millions of dollars)

	2024	2025	2026	2027	2028	2029	2030	2031	2032	2033	2034	Totals 2025–2029	Totals 2025–2034
Social Security Administration:													
Authorize Social Security Administration (SSA) to refer Social Security Disability Insurance (SSDI) and Supplemental Security Income (SSI) beneficiaries to State vocational rehabilitation services													
Subtotal, Social Security Administration													
Consumer Product Safety Commission:													
Remove barriers to establishing mandatory consumer safety rules[3]													
Strengthen mandatory recall authorities[3]													
Streamline the release of consumer safety information to the public[3]													
Increase civil penalties for violations of consumer product safety laws[3]													
Subtotal, Consumer Product Safety Commission													
Corporation for National and Community Service:													
Authorize the expenditure of interest earnings in the National Service Trust		46	67	68	60	55	52	50	48	47	46	296	539
Subtotal, Corporation for National and Community Service		46	67	68	60	55	52	50	48	47	46	296	539
Delta Regional Authority:													
Outyear effects of Delta Regional Authority user fee proposal												2	4
Subtotal, Delta Regional Authority												2	4
Election Assistance Commission:													
Fund election grants		1,625	375	375	375	375	375	375	375	375	375	3,125	5,000
Subtotal, Election Assistance Commission		1,625	375	375	375	375	375	375	375	375	375	3,125	5,000
Federal Communications Commission:													
Extend radio frequency spectrum general auction authority for 10 years				–17,050	3,450	–17,050	3,450	–17,050	3,450	–17,050	3,450	–30,650	–54,400
Subtotal, Federal Communications Commission				–17,050	3,450	–17,050	3,450	–17,050	3,450	–17,050	3,450	–30,650	–54,400
Japan-United States Friendship Commission:													
Fund Japan-U.S. Trust Fund Endowment			1	1	1	1	1	1	1	1	1	4	9
Subtotal, Japan-United States Friendship Commission			1	1	1	1	1	1	1	1	1	4	9
Postal Service:													
Pay United States Postal Service (USPS)[7] past losses													
Subtotal, Postal Service													
Crosscutting reforms:													

Table S–6. Mandatory and Receipt Proposals—Continued

(In millions of dollars)

	2024	2025	2026	2027	2028	2029	2030	2031	2032	2033	2034	Totals 2025–2029	Totals 2025–2034
Increase Afghan Special Immigrant Visas (SIVs) by 20,000	......	130	262	342	277	236	225	215	201	205	206	1,247	2,299
Extend Balanced Budget and Emergency Deficit Control Act (BBEDCA) Section 251A sequestration	......	......	......	......	......	......	......	......	−7,698	−39,427	−42,478	......	−89,603
Provide for the safe, secure, and trustworthy development and use of artificial intelligence (AI)	......	63	138	63	21	15	......	......	......	......	......	300	300
Increase civil monetary penalties for labor law violations[1]	......	−150	−200	−250	−250	−250	−250	−250	−300	−300	−300	−1,100	−2,500
Support pandemic fraud prevention and enforcement	......	320	320	320	320	320	......	......	......	......	......	1,600	1,600
Subtotal, crosscutting reforms	......	363	520	475	368	321	−25	−35	−7,797	−39,522	−42,572	2,047	−87,904
Subtotal, additional investments and reforms	......	10,848	8,569	−3,056	17,318	−7,556	−16,530	−52,253	−55,248	−116,645	−102,888	26,123	−317,441
Subtotal, mandatory initiatives and savings	**−115,726**	**−90,160**	**−219,914**	**−194,753**	**−168,530**	**−175,456**	**−155,109**	**−201,027**	**−202,951**	**−268,305**	**−271,925**	**−848,813**	**−1,948,130**
Additional receipt proposals:													
Reform business taxation:													
Tax corporate distributions as dividends	......	−110	−160	−170	−180	−190	−200	−210	−230	−240	−250	−810	−1,940
Limit tax avoidance through inappropriate leveraging of parties to divisive reorganizations	......	−279	−826	−1,614	−2,550	−3,569	−4,645	−5,769	−6,937	−8,150	−9,408	−8,838	−43,747
Limit losses recognized in liquidation transactions	......	−30	−50	−52	−54	−56	−57	−59	−61	−63	−65	−242	−547
Prevent basis shifting by related parties through partnerships	......	−3,851	−5,537	−3,999	−2,325	−563	177	215	275	341	402	−16,275	−14,865
Conform definition of "control" with corporate affiliation test	......	−447	−651	−667	−681	−695	−709	−719	−727	−733	−736	−3,141	−6,765
Strengthen limitation on losses for noncorporate taxpayers	......	−1,185	−2,241	−2,519	−2,666	−12,901	−14,735	−10,543	−9,789	−9,621	−9,526	−21,512	−75,726
Prevent prison facility rent payments from contributing to qualification as a REIT	......	......	......	......	......	......	......	......	......	......	......	......	......
Subtotal, reform business taxation	......	−5,902	−9,465	−9,021	−8,456	−17,974	−20,169	−17,085	−17,469	−18,466	−19,583	−50,818	−143,590
Reform international taxation:													
Repeal the deduction for foreign-derived intangible income:													
Repeal the deduction for foreign-derived intangible income	......	−13,938	−17,669	−14,213	−14,639	−15,078	−15,531	−15,997	−16,477	−16,971	−17,480	−75,537	−157,993
Provide additional support for research and experimentation expenditures	......	13,938	17,669	14,213	14,639	15,078	15,531	15,997	16,477	16,971	17,480	75,537	157,993
Subtotal, repeal the deduction for foreign-derived intangible income	......	......	......	......	......	......	......	......	......	......	......	......	......
Revise the rules that allocate Subpart F income and GILTI between taxpayers to ensure that Subpart F income and GILTI are fully taxed	......	−106	−196	−225	−250	−272	−294	−313	−332	−349	−366	−1,049	−2,703

Table S–6. Mandatory and Receipt Proposals—Continued

(In millions of dollars)

	2024	2025	2026	2027	2028	2029	2030	2031	2032	2033	2034	Totals 2025–2029	Totals 2025–2034
Require a controlled foreign corporation's taxable year to match that of its majority U.S. shareholder	....	....	....	....	....	....	....	....	....	....	....	....	....
Limit foreign tax credits from sales of hybrid entities	....	....	....	....	....	....	....	....	....	....	....	....	....
Restrict deductions of excessive interest of members of financial reporting groups	....	–343	–535	–484	–446	–418	–397	–381	–370	–362	–357	–2,226	–4,093
Conform scope of portfolio interest exclusion for 10-percent shareholders to other tax rules	....	–2,691	–4,281	–4,038	–3,918	–3,910	–4,002	–4,113	–4,219	–4,341	–4,481	–18,838	–39,994
Treat payments substituting for partnership effectively connected income as U.S. source dividends	....	–64	–54	–39	–22	–5	....	....	....	....	....	–184	–184
Expand access to retroactive qualified electing fund elections	....	–1	–2	–4	–5	–6	–6	–7	–8	–8	–9	–18	–56
Reform taxation of foreign fossil fuel income:													
Modify foreign oil and gas extraction income and foreign oil related income rules	....	–184	–310	–318	–329	–340	–352	–363	–377	–393	–409	–1,481	–3,375
Modify tax rule for dual capacity taxpayers	....	–3,908	–6,582	–6,735	–6,966	–7,214	–7,458	–7,703	–7,994	–8,332	–8,671	–31,405	–71,563
Subtotal, reform taxation of foreign fossil fuel income	....	–4,092	–6,892	–7,053	–7,295	–7,554	–7,810	–8,066	–8,371	–8,725	–9,080	–32,886	–74,938
Provide tax incentives for locating jobs and business activity in the United States and remove tax deductions for shipping jobs overseas:													
Provide tax credit for inshoring jobs to the United States	....	3	6	6	7	7	8	8	8	9	9	29	71
Remove tax deductions for shipping jobs overseas	....	–3	–6	–6	–7	–7	–8	–8	–8	–9	–9	–29	–71
Subtotal, provide tax incentives for locating jobs and business activity in the United States and remove tax deductions for shipping jobs overseas	....	....	....	....	....	....	....	....	....	....	....	....	....
Subtotal, reform international taxation	....	–7,297	–11,960	–11,843	–11,936	–12,165	–12,509	–12,880	–13,300	–13,785	–14,293	–55,201	–121,968
Support housing and urban development:													
Make permanent the new markets tax credit and formalize allocation incentives for investing in areas of higher distress	....	....	97	278	483	716	990	1,290	1,602	1,796	1,866	1,574	9,118
Subtotal, support housing and urban development	....	....	97	278	483	716	990	1,290	1,602	1,796	1,866	1,574	9,118
Modify energy taxes:													
Eliminate fossil fuel tax preferences:													
Repeal the enhanced oil recovery credit	....	....	....	....	....	....	....	....	....	....	....	....	....
Repeal the credit for oil and natural gas produced from marginal wells	....	–19	–34	–26	–14	–4	....	....	....	....	....	–97	–97
Repeal expensing of intangible drilling costs	....	–1,790	–2,652	–1,971	–1,234	–478	–204	–265	–334	–406	–448	–8,125	–9,782

Table S-6. Mandatory and Receipt Proposals—Continued

(In millions of dollars)

	2024	2025	2026	2027	2028	2029	2030	2031	2032	2033	2034	Totals 2025–2029	Totals 2025–2034
Repeal the deduction for costs paid or incurred for any qualified tertiary injectant used as part of tertiary recovery method	....	–6	–8	–9	–9	–9	–9	–9	–9	–9	–9	–41	–86
Repeal the exception to passive loss limitations provided to working interests in oil and natural gas properties	....	–5	–9	–8	–8	–8	–8	–7	–7	–7	–7	–38	–74
Repeal the use of percentage depletion with respect to oil and natural gas wells	....	–880	–1,476	–1,493	–1,521	–1,562	–1,611	–1,671	–1,741	–1,820	–1,900	–6,932	–15,675
Increase geological and geophysical amortization period for independent producers	....	–65	–251	–414	–455	–448	–439	–432	–419	–395	–360	–1,633	–3,678
Repeal expensing of mine exploration and development costs	....	–148	–220	–164	–102	–39	–17	–22	–28	–34	–38	–673	–812
Repeal percentage depletion for hard mineral fossil fuels	....	–57	–103	–112	–122	–128	–136	–145	–148	–148	–153	–522	–1,252
Repeal capital gains treatment for royalties	....	–26	–54	–56	–54	–53	–52	–53	–50	–49	–48	–243	–495
Repeal the exemption from the corporate income tax for fossil fuel publicly traded partnerships	....	......	......	......	......	......	–75	–148	–186	–220	–251	......	–880
Repeal the Oil Spill Liability Trust Fund and Superfund excise tax exemption for crude oil derived from bitumen and kerogen-rich rock[2]	....	–115	–160	–166	–172	–179	–183	–186	–192	–198	–200	–792	–1,751
Repeal accelerated amortization of air pollution control equipment	....	–12	–30	–47	–62	–77	–91	–103	–101	–90	–79	–228	–692
Subtotal, eliminate fossil fuel tax preferences	....	–3,123	–4,997	–4,466	–3,753	–2,985	–2,825	–3,041	–3,215	–3,376	–3,493	–19,324	–35,274
Eliminate drawbacks on petroleum taxes that finance the Oil Spill Liability Trust Fund and Superfund[2]	....	–149	–202	–206	–210	–213	–216	–218	–222	–224	–227	–980	–2,087
Impose digital asset mining energy excise tax[2]	....	–107	–302	–533	–670	–744	–832	–935	–1,052	–1,197	–1,361	–2,356	–7,733
Subtotal, modify energy taxes	....	–3,379	–5,501	–5,205	–4,633	–3,942	–3,873	–4,194	–4,489	–4,797	–5,081	–22,660	–45,094
Modify rules relating to retirement plans:													
Prevent excessive accumulations by high-income taxpayers in tax-favored retirement accounts and make other reforms	....	–6,926	–6,142	–3,402	–1,992	–1,278	–931	–776	–724	–726	–759	–19,740	–23,656
Subtotal, modify rules relating to retirement plans	....	–6,926	–6,142	–3,402	–1,992	–1,278	–931	–776	–724	–726	–759	–19,740	–23,656
Support workers, families, and economic security:													
Make the adoption tax credit refundable and allow certain guardianship arrangements to qualify[8]	....	2	2,642	1,420	1,186	1,183	1,180	1,186	1,187	1,173	1,182	6,433	12,341
Make permanent the income exclusion for forgiven student debt[8]	....	......	2	17	37	234	252	270	290	311	333	290	1,746
Extend tax-preferred treatment to certain Federal and tribal scholarship and education loan programs	....	62	104	114	120	123	127	130	133	134	136	523	1,183

Table S–6. Mandatory and Receipt Proposals—Continued

(In millions of dollars)

	2024	2025	2026	2027	2028	2029	2030	2031	2032	2033	2034	Totals 2025–2029	Totals 2025–2034
Increase the employer-provided childcare tax credit for businesses	……	19	37	38	40	41	43	43	44	44	44	175	393
Improve the design of the work opportunity tax credit to promote longer-term employment	……	−85	−93	−22	−12	−9	−7	−5	−4	−3	−2	−221	−242
Subtotal, support workers, families, and economic security	……	−2	2,692	1,567	1,371	1,572	1,595	1,624	1,650	1,659	1,693	7,200	15,421
Close loopholes:													
Tax carried (profits) interests as ordinary income	……	−397	−661	−659	−657	−664	−677	−691	−705	−719	−733	−3,038	−6,563
Repeal deferral of gain from like-kind exchanges	……	−680	−1,870	−1,926	−1,984	−2,044	−2,104	−2,169	−2,232	−2,300	−2,369	−8,504	−19,678
Require 100 percent recapture of depreciation deductions as ordinary income for certain depreciable real property	……	−41	−128	−267	−417	−579	−755	−946	−1,151	−1,373	−1,611	−1,432	−7,268
Modify depreciation rules for purchases of general aviation passenger aircraft	……	−46	−141	−206	−217	−207	−175	−142	−125	−117	−116	−817	−1,492
Limit use of donor advised funds to avoid a private foundation payout requirement	……	−65	−61	−42	−27	−14	−11	−12	−12	−13	−13	−209	−270
Exclude payments to disqualified persons from counting toward private foundation payout requirement	……	−1	−2	−1	−1	−1	−1	……	……	……	……	−6	−7
Extend the period for assessment of tax for certain Qualified Opportunity Fund investors	−11	−26	−19	−15	−11	−10	−9	−6	−2	……	……	−81	−98
Impose ownership diversification requirement for small insurance company election	……	−272	−908	−1,023	−1,097	−1,165	−1,235	−1,310	−1,395	−1,497	−1,587	−4,465	−11,489
Expand pro rata interest expense disallowance for business-owned life insurance	……	−609	−618	−646	−668	−691	−717	−748	−780	−813	−850	−3,232	−7,140
Modify rules for insurance products that fail the statutory definition of a life insurance contract	……	−3	−10	−12	−14	−17	−19	−22	−26	−29	−33	−56	−185
Limit tax benefits for private placement life insurance and similar contracts	……	−140	−208	−288	−387	−505	−651	−825	−1,032	−1,276	−1,567	−1,528	−6,879
Correct drafting errors in the taxation of insurance companies under the Tax Cuts and Jobs Act of 2017	……	−77	−105	−111	−107	−73	−56	−47	−39	−35	−32	−473	−682
Define the term "ultimate purchaser" for purposes of diesel fuel exportation[2]	……	−7	−9	−11	−13	−15	−19	−21	−23	−26	−28	−55	−172
Limit the deduction for the transfer of property to the value of property actually included in income	……	−85	−128	−130	−136	−141	−147	−154	−159	−167	−173	−620	−1,420
Subtotal, close loopholes	−11	−2,449	−4,868	−5,337	−5,736	−6,126	−6,576	−7,093	−7,681	−8,365	−9,112	−24,516	−63,343
Improve tax administration:													
Enhance accuracy of tax information:													
Expand the Secretary's authority to require electronic filing for forms and returns	……	……	……	……	……	……	……	……	……	……	……	……	……
Improve information reporting for reportable payments subject to backup withholding	……	−41	−95	−161	−221	−231	−241	−252	−263	−275	−301	−749	−2,081
Subtotal, enhance accuracy of tax information	……	−41	−95	−161	−221	−231	−241	−252	−263	−275	−301	−749	−2,081

Table S-6. Mandatory and Receipt Proposals—Continued

(In millions of dollars)

	2024	2025	2026	2027	2028	2029	2030	2031	2032	2033	2034	Totals 2025–2029	Totals 2025–2034
Amend the centralized partnership audit regime to permit the carryover of a reduction in tax that exceeds a partner's tax liability		5	5	5	6	6	7	7	7	8	8	29	66
Incorporate chapters 2/2A in centralized partnership audit regime proceedings													
Allow partnerships to resolve audits earlier		–127	–49	–8	–8	–9	–9	–10	–10	–10	–10	–201	–250
Modify requisite supervisory approval of penalty included in notice		–148	–152	–154	–160	–162	–175	–171	–178	–185	–194	–776	–1,679
Modify the requirement that general counsel review certain offers in compromise		–6	–15	–10	–2	–2	–2	–2	–2	–2	–2	–35	–45
Simplify foreign exchange gain or loss rules and exchange rate rules for individuals		1	2	3	3	3	3	3	4	4	4	12	29
Modernize reporting with respect to foreign tax credits to reduce burden and increase compliance		10	31	34	34	34	35	35	36	39	40	143	328
Authorize limited sharing of business tax return information to measure the economy more accurately													
Expand TIN matching and improve child support enforcement													
Clarify that information previously disclosed in a judicial or administrative proceeding is not return information		–2	–2	–2	–2	–2	–2	–2	–2	–2	–2	–10	–20
Require earlier electronic filing deadlines for certain information returns		–175	–153	–129	–118	–106	–75	–59	–41	–43	–45	–681	–944
Allow the Tax Court to review all evidence in innocent spouse relief cases													
Permit electronically provided notices													
Reform Federal grants to low-income taxpayer clinics													
Subtotal, improve tax administration		–483	–428	–421	–468	–468	–459	–451	–450	–466	–502	–2,268	–4,596
Improve tax compliance:													
Address taxpayer noncompliance with listed transactions:													
Extend statute of limitations for listed transactions		–23	–51	–64	–78	–76	–74	–73	–72	–70	–69	–292	–650
Impose liability on shareholders to collect unpaid income taxes of applicable corporations		–492	–513	–534	–556	–579	–604	–630	–658	–686	–716	–2,674	–5,968
Subtotal, address taxpayer noncompliance with listed transactions		–515	–564	–598	–634	–655	–678	–703	–730	–756	–785	–2,966	–6,618
Impose an affirmative requirement to disclose a position contrary to a regulation		–9	–11	–11	–12	–14	–14	–15	–16	–18	–18	–57	–135
Require employers to withhold tax on failed nonqualified deferred compensation plans		–206	–215	–225	–235	–245	–256	–267	–279	–291	–304	–1,126	–2,523

Table S–6. Mandatory and Receipt Proposals—Continued

(In millions of dollars)

	2024	2025	2026	2027	2028	2029	2030	2031	2032	2033	2034	Totals 2025–2029	Totals 2025–2034
Extend to six years the statute of limitations for certain tax assessments													
Increase the statute of limitations on assessment of the COVID-related paid leave and employee retention tax credits[8]	–42	–557	–1,624	–1,327	–218							–3,726	–3,726
Impose penalties for inaccurate or fraudulent employment tax returns[8]		–1,704	–95	–45	–11							–1,855	–1,855
Expand and increase penalties for noncompliant return preparation and e-filing and authorize IRS oversight of paid preparers:													
Expand and increase penalties for noncompliant return preparation and e-filing[8]		–40	–53	–49	–50	–55	–60	–66	–72	–78	–85	–247	–608
Grant authority to IRS for oversight of all paid preparers[8]		–28	–51	–70	–87	–98	–100	–100	–99	–98	–97	–334	–828
Subtotal, expand and increase penalties and oversight for return preparation and e-filing		–68	–104	–119	–137	–153	–160	–166	–171	–176	–182	–581	–1,436
Make repeated willful failure to file a tax return a felony for those with significant tax liability													
Expand IRS summons authority for large partnerships													
Address compliance in connection with tax responsibilities of expatriates		–143	–244	–255	–265	–276	–288	–300	–313	–326	–340	–1,183	–2,750
Define control of the payment of wage			–1	–2	–3	–4	–5	–5	–4	–4	–4	–10	–32
Subtotal, improve tax compliance	–42	–3,202	–2,858	–2,582	–1,515	–1,347	–1,401	–1,456	–1,512	–1,569	–1,633	–11,504	–19,075
Modernize rules, including those for digital assets:													
Apply the wash sale rules to digital assets and address related party transactions		–1,034	–1,774	–2,151	–2,313	–2,515	–2,776	–2,979	–3,201	–3,433	–3,650	–9,787	–25,826
Modernize rules treating loans of securities as tax-free to include other asset classes and address income inclusion													
Provide for information reporting by certain financial institutions and digital asset brokers for purposes of exchange of information		–239	–279	–297	–316	–334	–357	–382	–403	–427	–451	–1,465	–3,485
Require reporting by certain taxpayers of foreign digital asset accounts		–375	–439	–466	–497	–526	–561	–600	–634	–671	–708	–2,303	–5,477
Amend the mark-to-market rules to include digital assets		–8,047	58	64	70	77	85	94	103	113	125	–7,778	–7,258
Subtotal, modernize rules, including for digital assets		–9,695	–2,434	–2,850	–3,056	–3,298	–3,609	–3,867	–4,135	–4,418	–4,684	–21,333	–42,046
Improve benefits tax administration:													
Rationalize funding for post-retirement medical and life insurance benefits													
Clarify tax treatment of on-demand pay arrangements													

Table S-6. Mandatory and Receipt Proposals—Continued

(In millions of dollars)

	2024	2025	2026	2027	2028	2029	2030	2031	2032	2033	2034	Totals 2025–2029	Totals 2025–2034
Amend the excise tax on an employment-based group health plans ...													
Subtotal, improve benefits tax administration ...	-53	-39,335	-40,867	-38,816	-35,938	-44,310	-46,942	-44,888	-46,508	-49,137	-52,088	-199,266	-438,829
Subtotal, additional receipt proposals		-129,495	-260,781	-233,569	-204,468	-219,766	-202,051	-245,915	-249,459	-317,442	-324,013	-1,048,079	-2,386,959
Grand total, mandatory and receipt proposals..	-115,779	-129,495	-260,781	-233,569	-204,468	-219,766	-202,051	-245,915	-249,459	-317,442	-324,013	-1,048,079	-2,386,959

Note: Detail in this table may not add to the totals due to rounding. For receipt effects, positive figures indicate lower receipts. For outlay effects, positive figures indicate higher outlays. For net costs, positive figures indicate higher deficits.

[1] This proposal affects both outlays and receipts. The net effect is shown above. The receipt effects included in these estimates are as follows:

	2024	2025	2026	2027	2028	2029	2030	2031	2032	2033	2034	Totals 2025–2029	Totals 2025–2034
Permanently extend enhanced premium tax credits .			5,551	7,977	8,581	9,128	9,839	10,068	10,700	11,616	12,587	31,237	86,047
Extend surprise billing protections to ground ambulances			-57	-78	-81	-86	-90	-94	-100	-104	-110	-302	-800
Reduce insulin cost-sharing in commercial plans		409	335	66	69	-69						810	810
Provide Mortgage Relief Credit	710	17,230	7,820	2,062								26,825	26,825
Provide a neighborhood homes credit		270	1,145	1,829	1,963	2,099	2,183	2,253	2,304	2,371	2,428	7,306	18,845
Expand and enhance the low-income housing credit		84	354	980	1,918	2,961	4,010	5,054	6,090	7,118	8,077	6,297	36,646
Increase Federal Home Loan Banks' contribution to the Affordable Housing Program		-284	-284	-284	-284	-284	-284	-284	-284	-284	-284	-1,420	-2,840
Impose a minimum income tax on the wealthiest taxpayers			-50,310	-56,387	-59,430	-60,451	-59,974	-59,331	-53,057	-50,215	-53,513	-226,578	-502,668
Increase the top marginal income tax rate for high-income earners	-9,871	-75,419	-31,189	-13,798	-14,939	-15,859	-16,818	-17,833	-18,885	-19,997	-21,187	-151,204	-245,924
Reform the taxation of capital income		-18,031	-23,713	-25,164	-26,417	-27,624	-29,050	-30,727	-32,158	-33,758	-41,941	-120,949	-288,583
Improve tax administration for trusts and decedents' estates		-9	-79	-83	-96	-112	-130	-150	-174	-199	-227	-379	-1,259
Limit duration of generation-skipping transfer tax exemption													
Modify income, estate, gift, and generation-skipping transfer tax rules for certain trusts		-1,290	-2,625	-5,032	-6,855	-8,871	-10,566	-10,749	-11,608	-12,587	-13,567	-24,673	-83,750
Revise rules for valuation of certain property		-331	-955	-1,025	-1,139	-1,225	-1,296	-1,390	-1,493	-1,613	-1,745	-4,675	-12,212
Expand limitation on deductibility of excessive employee remuneration		-37,169	-19,015	-30,421	-34,951	-31,354	-28,057	-22,148	-20,594	-22,385	-25,760	-152,910	-271,854
Restore and make permanent the American Rescue Plan expansion of the earned income tax credit for workers without qualifying children	386	1,551	1,702	2,043	2,029	2,022	2,012	1,999	1,977	1,973	1,968	9,347	19,276
Expand the child credit, and make permanent full refundability and advanceability	5,329	23,570	-28,289	-854	3,189	3,398	3,627	3,896	4,196	4,522	4,262	1,014	21,517
Require Medicare to cover three behavioral health visits without cost-sharing				3,740	3,483	1,346	834	877	925	977	1,035	8,569	13,217
Improve access to behavioral healthcare in the private insurance market				1,836	2,555	2,669	2,804	2,945	3,101	3,272	3,442	7,060	22,624
Require 12 months of Medicaid postpartum coverage...					-1	-2	-3	-4	-5	-7	-8	-3	-30

Table S–6. Mandatory and Receipt Proposals—Continued

(In millions of dollars)

	2024	2025	2026	2027	2028	2029	2030	2031	2032	2033	2034	Totals 2025–2029	Totals 2025–2034
Raise the corporate income tax rate to 28 percent	−74,646	−122,474	−125,105	−128,114	−128,624	−128,353	−129,396	−137,888	−144,919	−150,028	−155,040	−632,670	−1,349,941
Increase the corporate alternative minimum tax rate to 21 percent	−10,050	−13,543	−11,759	−12,264	−12,675	−13,119	−13,672	−14,238	−14,800	−15,379	−15,980	−63,360	−137,429
Revise the global minimum tax regime, limit inversions, and make related reforms	−8,875	−27,920	−35,889	−34,589	−34,819	−36,215	−37,719	−39,261	−40,846	−42,483	−44,178	−169,432	−373,919
Adopt the undertaxed profits rule	....	−9,596	−14,541	−14,065	−14,389	−14,181	−14,088	−13,837	−13,752	−13,916	−13,948	−66,772	−136,313
Increase the excise tax rate on repurchase of corporate stock and close loopholes	−3,863	−15,344	−14,980	−14,936	−15,184	−15,792	−16,458	−17,167	−17,912	−18,691	−19,502	−76,236	−165,966
Apply the net investment income tax to pass-through business income of high-income taxpayers	−8,496	−38,302	−29,950	−31,931	−34,819	−37,435	−39,950	−42,143	−43,986	−46,126	−48,579	−172,437	−393,221
Increase the net investment income tax rate and additional Medicare tax rate for high-income taxpayers	−8,394	−42,920	−31,327	−32,285	−34,710	−37,224	−39,822	−42,450	−44,963	−47,602	−50,487	−178,466	−403,790
Allow States to provide continuous eligibility up to age 6 in Medicaid and CHIP	....	....	....	1	....	1	....	1	1	....	1	2	5
Prohibit CHIP enrollment fees and premiums	....	....	1	....	1	....	1	....	1	1	1	2	6
Establish Electronic Visa Update System (EVUS) user fee	....	−7	−7	−8	−8	−8	−8	−8	−8	−8	−8	−38	−78
Improve Unemployment Insurance (UI) program integrity	....	....	....	....	6	5	10	11	11	18	16	11	77
Increase business aviation kerosene jet fuel tax rate	....	−44	−106	−169	−235	−300	−322	−325	−329	−332	−336	−854	−2,498
Extend investments in Internal Revenue Service (IRS)	....	....	....	....	....	−3,046	−42,691	−60,911	−70,716	−80,001	−83,648	−3,046	−341,013
Increase civil monetary penalties for labor law violations	....	−150	−200	−250	−250	−250	−250	−250	−300	−300	−300	−1,100	−2,500
Total, receipt effect of mandatory proposals	−117,770	−359,719	−403,472	−381,203	−396,399	−408,231	−455,324	−484,084	−501,583	−524,147	−556,531	−1,949,024	−4,470,693

2 Net of income offsets.

3 Estimates were not available at the time of Budget publication.

4 This proposal represents a $9 billion dollar investment; potential savings could not be estimated, so the net effect of the proposal on spending is not available.

5 The Cancer Moonshot authorization expires in 2023. The Budget prioritizes the reauthorization of the Cancer Moonshot by requesting $716 million in discretionary resources within NIH in 2024 in discretionary resources and by proposing a mandatory reauthorization through 2026. The total Budget request for NIH Cancer Moonshot is $3.6 billion through 2026.

6 The current approach to revenue estimation does not consider many activities that are likely to influence revenue. A comprehensive approach would potentially yield an additional $353 billion from the IRS's investment and this proposal over the 10-year window. See the "Budget Process" chapter in the Analytical Perspectives volume for further discussion.

7 The Budget proposes to support the USPS through an intragovernmental transaction that increases the balances in the Postal Service Fund but results in no net deficit effect in the 10-year budget window. The General Fund appropriation of $494 million in 2025 can be found in the transmit 4 for the Payment to the Postal Service account and is offset in the receiving account, the Postal Service Fund.

8 This proposal affects both receipts and outlays. The net effect is shown above. The outlay effects included in these estimates are as follows:

	2024	2025	2026	2027	2028	2029	2030	2031	2032	2033	2034	Totals 2025–2029	Totals 2025–2034
Make the adoption tax credit refundable and allow certain guardianship arrangements to qualify	....	....	2,653	1,481	1,252	1,253	1,254	1,265	1,273	1,268	1,282	6,639	12,981
Make permanent the income exclusion for forgiven student debt	....	....	....	2	2	23	27	29	30	32	35	27	180

Table S-6. Mandatory and Receipt Proposals—Continued

(In millions of dollars)

| | 2024 | 2025 | 2026 | 2027 | 2028 | 2029 | 2030 | 2031 | 2032 | 2033 | 2034 | Totals | |
												2025–2029	2025–2034
Increase the statute of limitations on assessment of the COVID-related paid leave and employee retention tax credits	–10	–144	–434	–372	–72	....	....	....	....	....	....	–1,022	–1,022
Impose penalties for inaccurate or fraudulent employment tax returns	....	–596	–10	....	....	....	....	....	....	....	....	–606	–606
Expand and increase penalties for noncompliant return preparation and e-filing	....	–24	–29	–21	–19	–20	–22	–24	–26	–28	–30	–113	–243
Grant authority to IRS for oversight of all paid preparers	....	–10	–17	–18	–21	–24	–24	–24	–23	–21	–21	–90	–203
Total, outlay effect of receipt proposals	–10	–774	2,163	1,072	1,142	1,232	1,235	1,246	1,254	1,251	1,266	4,835	11,087

Table S–7. Funding Levels for Appropriated ("Discretionary") Programs by Category

(Budget authority in billions of dollars)

	Actual[1] 2023	CR/ Likely[2] 2024	Request 2025	2026	2027	2028	2029	Outyears 2030	2031	2032	2033	2034	Totals 2025-2029	2025-2034
Base Discretionary Funding[3]	1,618	1,603	1,629	1,691	1,728	1,766	1,805	1,830	1,856	1,883	1,911	1,938	8,619	18,038
Non-Defense Shifts to Mandatory[4]	......	......		-9	-9	-10	-10	-10	-10	-10	-11	-11	-38	-90
Bureau of Indian Affairs	......	......		-1	-1	-1	-1	-1	-1	-1	-1	-1	-2	-5
Indian Health Service	......	......		-8	-8	-9	-9	-9	-9	-9	-10	-10	-34	-80
CMS Survey and Certification	......	......		-*	-*	-*	-*	-*	-*	-*	-*	-*	-2	-4
Non-Base Discretionary Funding (not included above):[5]														
Enacted and Proposed Emergency Funding	88	148	8	4	4	4	4	4	4	4	4	4	24	45
Program Integrity	2	2	3	3	3	3	3	3	3	3	4	4	15	32
Disaster Relief	20	20	23	14	14	14	14	14	14	14	14	14	78	146
Wildfire Suppression	3	3	3	3	3	3	3	3	3	3	3	3	14	28
FRA Appropriations	14	......	......	......	......	......	......	......	......	......	......	......	......	......
Exempted from Budget Enforcement	4	5	5	5	4	4	4	4	4	5	5	5	22	45
Total, Non-Base Funding	132	178	42	28	27	27	28	28	28	29	29	29	152	295
Grand Total, Discretionary Budget Authority	1,750	1,780	1,671	1,710	1,746	1,784	1,823	1,848	1,875	1,901	1,929	1,957	8,733	18,243
Memorandum: Presentation of base discretionary by defense and non-defense[6]														
Defense Allocation[7]	858	886	895	924	944	963	983	990	997	1,004	1,011	1,018	4,709	9,730
Non-Defense Allocation	641	581	621	636	650	665	680	696	712	729	745	762	3,253	6,897
Veterans Affairs Medical Care Program	119	136	113	131	134	138	141	144	147	151	154	158	657	1,410
Memorandum: Presentation of base discretionary by security and nonsecurity[6]														
Security Allocation	980	1,007	1,017	1,050	1,072	1,097	1,120	1,131	1,141	1,152	1,163	1,173	5,357	11,117
Nonsecurity Allocation	519	460	499	510	521	531	543	556	568	581	594	607	2,605	5,510
Veterans Affairs Medical Care Program	119	136	113	131	134	138	141	144	147	151	154	158	657	1,410
Memorandum: Discretionary appropriations provided in the Infrastructure, Investment, and Jobs Act[8]	70	67	66	64	......	......	......	......	......	......	......	......	130	130

Table S–7. Funding Levels for Appropriated ("Discretionary") Programs by Category—Continued

(Budget authority in billions of dollars)

* Less than $500 million.

[1] The 2023 actual level includes changes that occur after appropriations are enacted that are part of budget execution such as transfers, reestimates, and the rebasing as mandatory any changes in mandatory programs (CHIMPs) enacted in appropriations bills. The 2023 levels are adjusted to add back OMB's scoring of CHIMPs enacted in 2023 appropriations acts for a better illustrative comparison with the 2025 request.

[2] At the time the 2025 Budget was prepared, 2024 appropriations remained incomplete and the 2024 column reflects at the account level enacted full-year and annualized continuing appropriations provided under the Continuing Appropriations Act, 2024 (Division A of Public Law 118–15, as amended) ("the 2024 CR"). The 2024 levels are further adjusted through allowances to illustratively reflect a "likely enacted" level to account for the appropriations topline deal reached by Congressional Leadership in January 2024.

[3] Base funding includes certain amounts designated as emergency requirements that are for base activities. These amounts are described as "shifted base" in numerous budget materials.

[4] The 2025 Budget proposes to shift the Indian Health Service (IHS) and the CMS Survey and Certification Program in HHS, as well as contract support costs and 105(l) leases within the Bureau of Indian Programs (BIA) in the Department of the Interior to the mandatory side of the Budget starting in 2026. See the "Budget Process" chapter of the *Analytical Perspectives* volume of the Budget for more information on these proposals.

[5] The 2025 Budget presents enacted and proposed cap adjustments such as emergency requirements, program integrity, disaster relief, wildfire suppression, and other appropriations exempted from budget enforcement outside of base allocations.

[6] The section presents base discretionary funding by both defense and non-defense and by security and nonsecurity allocations. The definition of security and nonsecurity is the same as the definition specified in the Budget Control Act of 2011 with security including the Departments of Defense, Homeland Security, Veterans Affairs, the National Nuclear Security Administration, the International Budget Function (150), and the Intelligence Community Management Account and with all other discretionary programs in the nonsecurity category. This presentation of discretionary excludes the proposed shifts to mandatory. After 2025, the Administration proposes that the Veterans Affairs Medical Care Program be budgeted for separately from the rest of non-defense programs given its anomalous growth pattern. See the "Budget Process" chapter of the *Analytical Perspectives* volume of the Budget for more information on this proposal.

[7] The amounts in the 2025 Budget are based on the National Security and National Defense strategies and the Department of Defense Future Years Defense Program, which includes a five-year appropriations plan and estimated expenditures necessary to support the programs, projects, and activities of the Department of Defense. After 2029, the Budget reflects outyear growth rates consistent with prior Budgets.

[8] Section 905(c) of division J of the Infrastructure Investment and Jobs Act (Public Law 117–58; IIJA) specified that amounts provided in division J should be considered as emergency discretionary appropriations. The amounts provided as discretionary appropriations in IIJA are summarized here, however, these amounts are kept separate from other discretionary amounts included above that are considered during the regular appropriations process.

Table S–8. 2025 Discretionary Request by Major Agency

(Budget authority in billions of dollars)

	2023 Actual[1]	2024 CR/Likely[2]	2025 Request	2025 Request Less 2023 Actual Dollar	2025 Request Less 2023 Actual Percent
Base Discretionary Funding:[3]					
Cabinet Departments:					
Agriculture[4]	27.2	27.2	29.2	+2.0	+7.4%
Commerce	11.2	11.2	11.4	+0.3	+2.4%
Defense	815.9	817.3	849.8	+33.8	+4.1%
Education	79.2	79.2	82.4	+3.1	+3.9%
Energy (DOE)	47.8	47.9	51.4	+3.6	+7.5%
Health and Human Services (HHS)[5]	129.1	135.6	133.8	+4.8	+3.7%
Homeland Security (DHS):					
HUD program level *DHS program level*	60.9	61.0	62.2	+1.2	+2.0%
Transportation Security Administration passenger fee proposal	....	....	–1.6	–1.6	N/A
Housing and Urban Development (HUD):					
HUD program level	72.1	72.1	72.6	+0.5	+0.7%
HUD receipts	–6.5	–5.0	–6.7	–0.2	N/A
Interior (DOI)	17.0	17.3	17.8	+0.8	+4.8%
Justice	37.6	38.1	37.8	+0.2	+0.5%
Labor	13.6	13.6	13.9	+0.3	+2.3%
State and International Programs[4,6]	64.2	63.4	64.4	+0.1	+0.2%
Transportation (DOT)	28.7	28.7	25.4	–3.2	–11.2%
Treasury[6]	14.2	14.2	14.4	+0.2	+1.2%
Veterans Affairs	134.9	151.7	129.3	–5.6	–4.2%
Major Agencies:					
Corps of Engineers (Corps)	6.3	6.3	5.5	–0.8	–12.6%
Environmental Protection Agency	10.1	10.1	11.0	+0.9	+8.4%
General Services Administration	0.1	–0.4	0.7	+1.0	N/A
National Aeronautics and Space Administration	25.4	25.4	25.4	....	....
National Science Foundation	9.5	9.5	10.2	+0.6	+6.8%
Small Business Administration	1.1	1.1	1.0	–0.1	–7.5%
Social Security Administration[5]	9.6	9.2	9.9	+0.3	+3.4%
Other Agencies	27.4	27.3	29.2	+1.8	+6.6%
Offsets including changes in mandatory programs[7]	–18.6	–15.9	–51.1	–32.6	+175.5%
Adjustments for 2024 Likely Enacted[2]	....	–43.8			N/A
Subtotal, Base Discretionary Budget Authority (BA)	**1,618.1**	**1,602.5**	**1,629.1**	**+11.0**	**+0.7%**
Non-Base Discretionary Funding:					
Emergency Requirements:					
Agriculture	6.0	....	*	–5.9	N/A
Commerce	1.9	....	....	–1.9	N/A
Defense	35.8	....	....	–35.8	N/A

Table S–8. 2025 Discretionary Request by Major Agency—Continued

(Budget authority in billions of dollars)

	2023 Actual[1]	2024 CR/Likely[2]	2025 Request	2025 Request Less 2023 Actual	
				Dollar	Percent
Energy	1.7	......	......	–1.7	N/A
Health and Human Services	6.6	......	3.6	–3.0	N/A
Homeland Security	6.6	16.0	4.7	–1.9	N/A
Housing and Urban Development	5.0	......	......	–5.0	N/A
Interior	2.0	......	......	–2.0	N/A
State and International Programs	19.0	......	......	–19.0	N/A
Transportation	1.0	......	......	–1.0	N/A
Corps of Engineers (Corps)	1.2	......	......	–1.2	N/A
Environmental Protection Agency	1.7	......	......	–1.7	N/A
Small Business Administration	–0.6	......	......	+0.6	N/A
Other Agencies	0.7	......	......	–0.7	N/A
Subtotal, Emergency Requirements	88.4	16.0	8.3	–80.1	N/A
Pending 2024 Supplemental Emergency Requests: [8]					
Agriculture	......	1.2	......	......	N/A
Defense	......	58.3	......	......	N/A
Energy	......	3.0	......	......	N/A
Health and Human Services	......	5.5	......	......	N/A
Homeland Security	......	17.9	......	......	N/A
Justice	......	1.7	......	......	N/A
State and International Programs	......	34.8	......	......	N/A
Federal Communications Commission	......	9.1	......	......	N/A
Other Agencies	......	0.2	......	......	N/A
Subtotal, Pending 2024 Supplemental Emergency Requests	......	131.5	......	......	N/A
Program Integrity:					
Health and Human Services	0.6	0.6	0.6	+0.1	+9.4%
Labor	0.3	0.3	0.3	+*	+5.0%
Social Security Administration	1.5	1.5	1.6	+0.1	+7.8%
Adjustments for 2024 Likely Enacted [2]	0.1	0.1	......	......	N/A
Subtotal, Program Integrity	2.3	2.4	2.5	+0.2	+7.9%
Disaster Relief:					
Homeland Security	19.9	19.9	22.7	+2.8	+13.9%
Small Business Administration	0.1	0.1	0.5	+0.3	+244.1%
Adjustments for 2024 Likely Enacted [2]	......	0.3	......	......	N/A
Subtotal, Disaster Relief	20.1	20.4	23.2	+3.1	+15.5%
Wildfire Suppression:					
Agriculture	2.2	2.2	2.4	+0.2	+8.1%
Interior	0.3	0.3	0.4	+*	+5.9%
Adjustments for 2024 Likely Enacted [2]	......	0.1	......	......	N/A
Subtotal, Wildfire Suppression	2.6	2.7	2.8	+0.2	+7.8%

Table S–8. 2025 Discretionary Request by Major Agency—Continued

(Budget authority in billions of dollars)

	2023 Actual[1]	2024 CR/Likely[2]	2025 Request	2025 Request Less 2023 Actual Dollar	2025 Request Less 2023 Actual Percent
Appropriations Enacted in the Fiscal Responsibility Act of 2023:[9]					
Commerce	22.0	......	......	–22.0	N/A
Health and Human Services	–6.6	......	......	+6.6	N/A
Small Business Administration	–0.8	......	......	+0.8	N/A
Other Agencies	–0.2	......	......	+0.2	N/A
Subtotal, FRA Appropriations	14.4	......	......	–14.4	–100.0%
Exempted Funding:[10]					
Education	0.2	0.2	0.2	......	N/A
Health and Human Services	1.3	0.7	0.4	–1.0	N/A
Justice	0.3	0.3	0.3	......	N/A
Corps of Engineers (Corps)	2.4	2.4	1.7	–0.6	N/A
Environmental Protection Agency	0.2	1.2	2.2	+2.0	N/A
Subtotal, Exempted Funding	4.4	4.7	4.8	+0.4	+9.5%
Subtotal, Non-Base Discretionary Funding	132.2	177.8	41.6	–90.6	–68.6%
Total, Discretionary BA	1,750.3	1,780.3	1,670.7	–79.6	–4.5%

	2023 Actual[1]	2024 CR/Likely[2]	2025 Request	2025 Request Less 2023 Actual Dollar	2025 Request Less 2023 Actual Percent
Memorandum - Comparison by Category:					
Total, Base Discretionary Funding	1,618.1	1,602.5	1,629.1	+11.0	+0.7%
Base Discretionary by Defense and Non-Defense:					
Defense [11]	858.2	886.3	895.2	+37.0	+4.3%
Non-Defense	759.9	716.2	733.9	–26.0	–3.4%
Base Non-Defense, excluding shifted base funding [11]	747.4	703.7	710.7	+7.0	+0.9%
Non-Defense shifted base funding	12.5	12.5	23.2	+10.7	+85.6%
Non-Defense Program Level [12]	759.9	754.9	770.0	+10.1	+1.3%

Table S–8. 2025 Discretionary Request by Major Agency—Continued

(Budget authority in billions of dollars)

	2023 Actual[1]	2024 CR/Likely[2]	2025 Request	2025 Request Less 2023 Actual	
				Dollar	Percent

* Less than $50 million.

[1] The 2023 actual level includes changes that occur after appropriations are enacted that are part of budget execution such as transfers, reestimates, and the rebasing as mandatory any changes in mandatory programs (CHIMPs) enacted in appropriations bills. The 2023 levels are adjusted to add back OMB's scoring of CHIMPs enacted in 2023 appropriations acts for a better illustrative comparison with the 2025 request.

[2] At the time the 2025 Budget was prepared, 2024 appropriations remained incomplete and the 2024 column reflects at the account level enacted full-year and annualized continuing appropriations provided under the Continuing Appropriations Act, 2024 (Division A of Public Law 118–15, as amended) ("the 2024 CR"). The 2024 levels are further adjusted through allowances to illustratively reflect a "likely enacted" level to account for the appropriations topline deal reached by Congressional Leadership in January 2024.

[3] Base funding includes certain amounts designated as emergency requirements that are considered to be for base activities. These amounts are described as "shifted base" in numerous budget materials.

[4] Funding for Food for Peace Title II Grants is included in the State and International Programs total. Although the funds are appropriated to the Department of Agriculture, the funds are administered by the U.S. Agency for International Development (USAID).

[5] Funding from the Hospital Insurance and Supplementary Medical Insurance trust funds for administrative expenses incurred by the Social Security Administration that support the Medicare program are included in the Health and Human Services total and not in the Social Security Administration total.

[6] The State and International Programs total includes funding for the Department of State, USAID, Treasury International, and 11 international agencies while the Treasury total excludes Treasury's International Programs.

[7] The limitation enacted and proposed in the Justice Department's Crime Victims Fund program and cancellations in the Children's Health Insurance Program in HHS and the Nonrecurring Expenses Fund in Commerce make up the bulk of these offsets.

[8] The 2024 column includes several emergency supplemental funding requests that the Administration has submitted to the Congress including all amounts requested in its National Security Supplemental Request for Ukraine, Israel, humanitarian aid, and border and other national security funding that was transmitted on October 20, 2023, as well as additional amounts for domestic needs, including disaster-related funding, that was informally submitted on October 25, 2023.

[9] This columns reflects appropriations enacted in the Fiscal Responsibility Act of 2023 (Public Law 118–5; FRA); these appropriations are considered to be outside of base totals.

[10] The Exempted funds column reflects amounts that are not counted for purposes of budget enforcement which includes 21st Century Cures appropriations in HHS, the Bipartisan Safer Communities Act advance appropriations, certain revenues provided for the EPA Superfund, and the Corps' Harbor Maintenance Trust Fund appropriations. These amounts are not counted as part of base totals.

[11] The defense and non-defense base totals, excluding shifted base funding for 2024 and 2025, tie to the statutory discretionary caps enacted in the FRA.

[12] The non-defense base program level includes shifted base funding and adjusts for certain offsets included in the Budget that are part of the FRA agreement to provide non-defense resources above the FRA caps.

Note: Section 905(c) of division J of the Infrastructure Investment and Jobs Act (Public Law 117–58; IIJA) specified that amounts provided in division J should be considered as emergency discretionary appropriations. The amounts provided as discretionary appropriations in IIJA are not summarized on this table, however, as these amounts are kept separate from other discretionary amounts included above that are considered during the regular appropriations process.

Table S–9. Economic Assumptions

(Calendar years)

	Actual		Projections										
	2022	2023	2024	2025	2026	2027	2028	2029	2030	2031	2032	2033	2034
Gross Domestic Product (GDP):													
Nominal level, billions of dollars	25,744	27,348	28,507	29,640	30,863	32,139	33,466	34,870	36,368	37,947	39,594	41,313	43,110
Percent change, nominal GDP, year/year	9.1	6.2	4.2	4.0	4.1	4.1	4.1	4.2	4.3	4.3	4.3	4.3	4.3
Real GDP, percent change, year/year	1.9	2.4	1.7	1.8	2.0	2.0	2.0	2.1	2.2	2.2	2.2	2.2	2.2
Real GDP, percent change, Q4/Q4	0.7	2.6	1.3	2.0	2.0	2.0	2.0	2.1	2.2	2.2	2.2	2.2	2.2
GDP chained price index, percent change, year/year	7.1	3.7	2.5	2.1	2.1	2.1	2.1	2.1	2.1	2.1	2.1	2.1	2.1
Consumer Price Index,[1] percent change, year/year	8.0	4.2	2.9	2.3	2.3	2.3	2.3	2.3	2.3	2.3	2.3	2.3	2.3
Interest rates, percent:[2]													
91-day Treasury bills	2.0	5.1	5.1	4.0	3.3	3.1	2.9	2.8	2.8	2.7	2.7	2.7	2.7
10-year Treasury notes	3.0	4.1	4.4	4.0	3.9	3.8	3.8	3.7	3.7	3.7	3.7	3.7	3.7
Unemployment rate, civilian, percent[2]	3.6	3.6	4.0	4.0	3.9	3.9	3.8	3.8	3.8	3.8	3.8	3.8	3.8

Note: A more detailed table of economic assumptions appears in the "Economic Assumptions and Overview" chapter of the *Analytical Perspectives* volume of the Budget.
[1] Seasonally adjusted CPI for all urban consumers.
[2] Annual average.
[3] Average rate, secondary market (bank discount basis).

Table S–10. Federal Government Financing and Debt

(Dollar amounts in billions)

	Actual 2023	Estimate										
		2024	2025	2026	2027	2028	2029	2030	2031	2032	2033	2034
Financing:												
Unified budget deficit:												
Primary deficit	1,035	971	816	533	438	437	293	400	313	304	373	192
Net interest	658	889	965	1,013	1,072	1,136	1,190	1,241	1,301	1,367	1,428	1,485
Unified budget deficit	1,694	1,859	1,781	1,547	1,510	1,573	1,483	1,640	1,614	1,671	1,801	1,677
As a percent of GDP	6.3%	6.6%	6.1%	5.1%	4.7%	4.7%	4.3%	4.6%	4.3%	4.3%	4.4%	3.9%
Other transactions affecting borrowing from the public:												
Changes in financial assets and liabilities:[1]												
Change in Treasury operating cash balance	21	143	......	......	......	......	......	......	......	......	......	......
Net disbursements of credit financing accounts:												
Direct loan and Troubled Asset Relief Program (TARP) equity purchase accounts	259	–102	43	104	97	66	63	54	37	33	32	36
Guaranteed loan accounts	37	22	3	6	4	5	4	5	5	5	5	5
Net purchases of non-Federal securities by the National Railroad Retirement Investment Trust (NRRIT)	1	–1	–*	–*	–1	–1	–1	–1	–1	–1	–1	–*
Net change in other financial assets and liabilities [2]	–30	......										
Subtotal, changes in financial assets and liabilities	288	61	47	109	100	70	66	58	41	36	36	40
Seigniorage on coins	......	–*	–*	–*	–*	–*	–*	–*	–*	–*	–*	–*
Total, other transactions affecting borrowing from the public	288	61	47	109	100	70	66	58	41	36	36	40
Total, requirement to borrow from the public (equals change in debt held by the public)	1,982	1,921	1,828	1,656	1,610	1,643	1,549	1,698	1,655	1,707	1,837	1,716
Changes in Debt Subject to Statutory Limitation:												
Change in debt held by the public	1,982	1,921	1,828	1,656	1,610	1,643	1,549	1,698	1,655	1,707	1,837	1,716
Change in debt held by Government accounts	168	198	161	288	138	31	155	49	33	–16	–135	–35
Change in other factors	51	–1	–2	–2	–1	*	1	*	1	1	2	2
Total, change in debt subject to statutory limitation	2,201	2,118	1,986	1,941	1,747	1,674	1,705	1,748	1,689	1,692	1,703	1,683
Debt Subject to Statutory Limitation, End of Year:												
Debt issued by Treasury	32,968	35,086	37,071	39,012	40,758	42,431	44,135	45,883	47,572	49,264	50,967	52,649
Adjustment for discount, premium, and coverage [3]	102	103	104	105	106	106	106	106	107	107	107	108
Total, debt subject to statutory limitation [4]	33,070	35,189	37,175	39,116	40,863	42,537	44,241	45,989	47,679	49,371	51,074	52,756
Debt Outstanding, End of Year:												
Gross Federal debt: [5]												
Debt issued by Treasury	32,968	35,086	37,071	39,012	40,758	42,431	44,135	45,883	47,572	49,264	50,967	52,649
Debt issued by other agencies	21	22	25	27	29	30	30	30	29	28	27	26
Total, gross Federal debt	32,989	35,108	37,096	39,040	40,788	42,461	44,165	45,912	47,601	49,292	50,993	52,674
As a percent of GDP	122.3%	124.3%	126.4%	127.8%	128.2%	128.2%	128.0%	127.6%	126.8%	125.8%	124.7%	123.5%

Table S–10.　Federal Government Financing and Debt—Continued

(Dollar amounts in billions)

	Actual 2023	Estimate 2024	2025	2026	2027	2028	2029	2030	2031	2032	2033	2034
Held by:												
Debt held by Government accounts	6,753	6,952	7,113	7,400	7,538	7,569	7,724	7,773	7,806	7,790	7,654	7,619
Debt held by the public[6]	26,236	28,156	29,984	31,639	33,250	34,892	36,441	38,139	39,795	41,502	43,339	45,056
As a percent of GDP	97.3%	99.6%	102.2%	103.6%	104.5%	105.3%	105.6%	106.0%	106.0%	105.9%	106.0%	105.6%
Debt Held by the Public Net of Financial Assets:												
Debt held by the public	26,236	28,156	29,984	31,639	33,250	34,892	36,441	38,139	39,795	41,502	43,339	45,056
Less financial assets net of liabilities:												
Treasury operating cash balance	657	800	800	800	800	800	800	800	800	800	800	800
Credit financing account balances:												
Direct loan and TARP equity purchase accounts	1,598	1,496	1,539	1,643	1,740	1,806	1,869	1,923	1,960	1,993	2,025	2,061
Guaranteed loan accounts	83	104	108	114	118	122	127	131	136	141	145	150
Government-sponsored enterprise stock[7]	240	240	240	240	240	240	240	240	240	240	240	240
Air carrier worker support warrants and notes[8]	12	12	11	10	10	9	9	5	*	*	*	......
Emergency capital investment fund securities	3	2	2	2	2	2	2	2	2	2	2	1
Non-Federal securities held by NRRIT	24	23	23	22	21	20	19	18	17	17	16	16
Other assets net of liabilities	–109	–109	–109	–109	–109	–109	–109	–109	–109	–109	–109	–109
Total, financial assets net of liabilities	2,508	2,569	2,614	2,722	2,822	2,891	2,956	3,010	3,047	3,083	3,119	3,159
Debt held by the public net of financial assets	23,728	25,587	27,370	28,917	30,428	32,001	33,485	35,129	36,748	38,419	40,220	41,897
As a percent of GDP	88.0%	90.6%	93.3%	94.6%	95.6%	96.6%	97.0%	97.6%	97.9%	98.1%	98.4%	98.2%

* $500 million or less.

[1] A decrease in the Treasury operating cash balance (which is an asset) is a means of financing a deficit and therefore has a negative sign. An increase in checks outstanding (which is a liability) is also a means of financing a deficit and therefore also has a negative sign.

[2] Includes checks outstanding, accrued interest payable on Treasury debt, uninvested deposit fund balances, allocations of special drawing rights, and other liability accounts; and, as an offset, cash and monetary assets (other than the Treasury operating cash balance), other asset accounts, and profit on sale of gold.

[3] Consists mainly of debt issued by the Federal Financing Bank (which is not subject to limit), the unamortized discount (less premium) on public issues of Treasury notes and bonds (other than zero-coupon bonds), and the unrealized discount on Government account series securities.

[4] Legislation enacted June 3, 2023 (Public Law 118–5), temporarily suspends the debt limit through January 1, 2025.

[5] Treasury securities held by the public and zero-coupon bonds held by Government accounts are almost all measured at sales price plus amortized discount or less amortized premium. Agency debt securities are almost all measured at face value. Treasury securities in the Government account series are otherwise measured at face value less unrealized discount (if any).

[6] At the end of 2023, the Federal Reserve Banks held $4,952.9 billion of Federal securities and the rest of the public held $21,282.7 billion. Debt held by the Federal Reserve Banks is not estimated for future years.

[7] Treasury's warrants to purchase 79.9 percent of the common stock of the enterprises expire after September 7, 2028. The warrants were valued at $4 billion at the end of 2023.

[8] Portions of the notes and warrants issued under the Air carrier worker support program (Payroll support program) are scheduled to expire in 2025, 2026, 2030, and 2031.

OMB CONTRIBUTORS TO THE 2025 BUDGET

The following personnel contributed to the preparation of this publication. Hundreds, perhaps thousands, of others throughout the Government also deserve credit for their valuable contributions.

A

Allison Abbott
Andrew Abrams
Chandana L. Achanta
Laurie Adams
Jeffrey Adarkwa
Olukayode Adeyemo
Abby Admete
Shagufta Ahmed
Benjamin Aidoo
Lina Al Sudani
Erin Cheese Alejandre
Jason Alleman
Emma S. Almon
Katherine S. Aloisi
Raymond Y. AlQaisi
Aaron Alton
Marc Alvidrez
Samantha Ammons
Starlisha Anderson
James L. Anthony
Lisa Anuszewski
Alejandra Apecechea
Kristine Arboleda
Fiama P. Arce
Rachel Arguello
Alison Arnold
Anna R. Arroyo
Emily Schultz Askew
Lisa L. August
Jeffrey Auser
Viraj Ayar

B

Eileen Baca
Drew Bailey
Jessie W. Bailey
Paul W. Baker
Melinda J. Baldwin
Carol A. Bales
Pratik S. Banjade
Carl Barrick
Avital Bar-Shalom

Amy Batchelor
Sarah Belford
Alexandra Bell
Jennifer Wagner Bell
Joseph J. Berger
Samuel Berger
Danielle Berman
Elizabeth A. Bernhard
Katherine Berrey
Jalen K. Berrian
William Bestani
Karuna Bhimagouni
Samuel J. Black
Kathleen M. Blackwell
William M. Blais
Mathew C. Blum
Brandon Bodnar
Amira C. Boland
Melissa B. Bomberger
James R. Boohaker
Charles J. Borges
Alexandra S.
  Bornkessel
Matthew Bowen
Michael E. Boyce
Michael D. Branson
Alex M. Brant
Jon Paul Brazill
Victoria Bredow
Joseph F. Breighner
Nicholas Brethauer
Candice M. Bronack
Ashley A. Brooks
Katherine W. Broomell
Dustin S. Brown
Michael T. Brunetto
Brandon Bryan
Tom D. Bullers
Coulton Bunney
Jinee Burdg
Scott Burgess
Elisha M. Burke
Samantha M.
  Burkhart

Michael D. Burstein
John C. Burton
Cinnamon L. Butler
Sean Butler

C

Steven Cahill
Edward A. Calimag
Samuel F. Callahan
Gregory J. Callanan
Amy Marie Canfield
Eric D. Cardoza
Joseph Carlile
Laura Carollo
Kevin Carpenter
Christina S. Carrere
Scott D. Carson
Mariah L. Casimir
Mary I. Cassell
David Cassidy
Trisha Castaneda
Sam P. Cathcart
Dan Chandler
David Chang
Laura K. Chang
Suzanne Chapman
William W. Chapman
Anthony Chase
James Chase
Nida Chaudhary
Anita Chellaraj
Fonda Chen
Amy Chenault
Douglas G. Cheung
Zachary A. Child
Dana Chisnell
Sophia Choudhry
Colin D. Christensen
Lisa Chung
Michael J. Ciccarone
Alex Ciepley
Ashley N. Clark
Jaimie N. Clark

Louise A. Clark
Michael Clark
Rachel Claude
Christopher Clavin
Christopher L.
  Clayton
Alyssa Cogen
Jesse A. Cohen
Kristy L. Colbert
Nani A. Coloretti
Kelly T. Colyar
Kathleen B. Comando
Jose A. Conde
Christine M. Connolly
David C. Connolly
Kyle Connors
LaTiesha B. Cooper
Nicole Cordan
Drew W. Cramer
Ayana Crawford
Tiffany N. Crawford
William E. Creedon
Jefferson Crowder
Albert Crowley
Juliana Crump
Lily Cuk
Pennee Cumberlander
C. Tyler Curtis
Patricia Cusack

D

Nadir Dalal
Shaibya L. Dalal
D. Michael Daly
Rody Damis
Neil B. Danberg
Kristy L. Daphnis
Joanne C. Davenport
Kelly Jo Davis
Kenneth L. Davis
Margaret B. Davis-
  Christian
Karen De Los Santos

David A. del Cuadro-Zimmerman
Emily L. DeLancey
Tasha M. Demps
Paul J. Denaro
Catherine A. Derbes
Christopher DeRusha
Maggie A. DeSisto
Selene Diaz
John H. Dick
Rachel M. Diedrick
Rachael E. Dietkus
Cle Diggins
Jean Diomi Kazadi
Katie Webb Doerge
Angela Donatelli
Paul S. Donohue
Tobias A. Dorsey
Clara Marian Downey
Celeste Drake
Megan Dreher
Angela Driscoll
Lisa Cash Driskill
Adrian Drummond
Vanessa Duguay
Daphney Dupervil
Nathaniel Durden
Ryan R. Durga
Javier R. Dutan
Dominique M. Duval

E

Maureen E. Earley
Jeanette Edwards
Peter S. Eggerding
Melissa Eggleston
Matthew Eliseo
Jeffrey M. Elkin
Michelle Enger
Diana F. Epstein
Paul R. Eriksen
Celeste Espinoza
Jose A. Estrada Ramirez
Erica Evans
Gillian Evans
Patrick Evans

F

Farnoosh Faezi-Marian
Edna Falk Curtin
Hunter Fang

Kara Farley-Cahill
Luke M. Farrell
Louis E. Feagans
Kelsi Feltz
Agatha Fenech
Matias C. Fernandez
Saverio V. Feudo
Lesley A. Field
Tess E. Fields
Jonathan R. Finch
Mary S. Fischietto
John J. Fitzpatrick
Ashlie B. Flegel
Cleones Fleurima
Maria Christina J. Foreman
Mary Frances Foster
Daniel G. Fowlkes
Steven D. Frankel
Nicholas A. Fraser
Katherine L. Friedman
Carlos A. Fuentes Cruz
Laurel D. Fuller
Steven Furnagiev

G

Noha Gaber
Kelley J. Gallagher
Christopher D. Gamache
Joseph R. Ganahl
Jacob A. Garcia
Kyle Gardiner
Mathias A. Gardner
Marc Garufi
Alex Gaynor
Jeremy J. Gelb
Marc Geller
Anna M. Gendron
Laura Gerhardt
Mariam Ghavalyan
Daniel M. Giamo
Carolyn Gibson
Laura Gillam
Brian Gillis
Janelle R. Gingold
Jacob Glass
Porter O. Glock
Christopher Glodosky
Tyler Glotfelty
Andrea L. Goel
Jeffrey D. Goldstein
Christopher Gomba

Anthony A. Gonzalez
Oscar Gonzalez
Alex Goodenough
Colleen M. Gravens
Kathryn Green
Aron Greenberg
Elyse F. Greenwald
Robin J. Griffin
Justin Grimes
Hester C. Grippando
Adam A. Grogg
Benjamin Guhin

H

Michael B. Hagan
James R. Hagen
William F. Hamele
Christine E. Hammer
Rachel Han
Anastasia K. Hanan
Brian J. Hanson
Jennifer L. Hanson
Christine J. Harada
Dionne Hardy
Ashley Harris
Noah Harris
Deidre A. Harrison
Paul Harvey
Homa Hassan
Julian Hasse
Joseph Hatzipanagiotis
Glinda R. Hawkins
Mark Hazelgren
Kelly A. Healton
Noreen Hecmanczuk
Margaret Z. Heimann
Gary Hellman
Sherita J. Henderson
Natalie D. Hengstebeck
Tonya R. Henley
Catherine M. Hensly
John David Henson
Mitchel Herckis
Nathalie S. Herman
Jacobo Hernandez
Rachel Hernández
Michael J. Hickey
Michael Hildner
Amanda M. Hill
Jennifer E. Hoef
Stuart Hoffman

Anthony Hokayem
Jayla R. Hollie
Shavonne U. Holman
Michele Holt
Michael Holtje
Nicholas Holtz
Camille T.D. Hopkins
Christopher Hoppel
Benjamin Hosmer
Clinton T. Hourigan
Danielle S. House
Devany M. Howard
Peter Hoy
Mina Hsiang
Grace Hu
Julia Bickett Hubbell
Samantha Hubner
Kathy M. Hudgins
Zachary M. Huebschman
Thomas Huelskoetter
Shristi Humagai
Ashley Hungerford
Sally J. Hunnicutt
Alexander T. Hunt
Ginny Hunt
Lorraine D. Hunt
James C. Hurban

I

Tae H. Im
Shelley Irving
Matthew Ishimaru
Maya Israni

J

Alfred Jackson
Sharease M. Jackson
Theodore R. Jackson
Aryeh Jacobsohn
Daniel Jacobson
Manish Jain
Natasha A. Jamal
Yejin Jang
Joseph C. Jankiewicz
Ames R. Jenkins
Carol Jenkins
Juan G. Jimenez
Michael J. Joannes
Carol Johnson
Gregory Johnson
Michael D. Johnson

Suraju O. Jolaoso
Andre A. Jolivette
Denise Bray Jones
Joshua Jones
Karianne M. Jones
Lauren H. Jones
Lisa M. Jones
Shannon Maire Joyce
Hursandbek
  Jumanyazov
Hee Jun

K

Jason Kahn
Riyad Kalla
Benjamin J. Kallos
Jennifer Kam
Daniel T. Kane
Jacob H. Kaplan
Steven Kappel
Jenifer Liechty
  Karwoski
Florence Kasule
Natalie Kates
Jason Kattman
Regina L. Kearney
Ariel L. Keller
Mary W. Keller
Natonne E. Kemp
Nancy B. Kenly
Kameron Kerger
Arianna Khan
Alexander J. Kharbush
Meen Khatri
Amy J. Kim
Maria Kim
Nathaniel Kim
Rachael Y. Kim
Kelly C. King
Kelly A. Kinneen
Jessica Elizabeth
  Kirby
Cheryl A. Klein
Robert T. Klein
Hank Knaack
Sreeja Kondeti
Clair A. Koroma
Andrea G. Korovesis
Megan Kosai
Anneli Faride Kraft
Charles Kraiger
Jennifer O. Kramer
Lori A. Krauss

Alyssa Kropp
Megan K. Kruse
Steven B. Kuennen
Jennifer J. Kuk
Anshul Kumar
Tara Kumar
Sara Kuncaitis-Wall
Christine J. Kymn

L

Christopher D. LaBaw
Leonard L. Lainhart
Chad A. Lallemand
Kristine Lam
Lawrence L. Lambert
Michael Landry
Katrina M. Langer
Rachel S. Lanman
Daniel LaPlaca
Eric P. Lauer
Shelby K. Lauter
Jessie L. LaVine
Daniel Lawver
Jessica K. Lee
Susan E. Leetmaa
Jacob Leibenluft
Stephen Leibman
Bryan P. León
Annie M. Leonetti
Kerrie Leslie
John C. Levock-
  Spindle
Andrew Lewandowski
Kali M. Lewis
Benjamin Lidofsky
Andrew Lieberman
Jennifer Liebschutz
Jane C. Lien
Ming Ligh
Kristina E. Lilac
Erika Liliedahl
John E. Lindner
Jennifer M. Lipiew
Adam Lipton
Luanne Lohr
Tanner L. Long
Sara R. Lopez
Zuzana Love
Adrienne E. Lucas
Alisa Luu
Kelvin T. Luu

M

Steven Mackey
Sarah Mackintosh
Ryan MacMaster
Joshua H. MacNeill
Brett Maden
Sophie Maher
Claire A. Mahoney
Dominic Maione
Bianca Majumder
Nancy Makale
Kathryn E. Maloney
Dominic J. Mancini
Emily J. Mann
Noah S. Mann
Iulia Z. Manolache
Christopher Steven
  Marcum
Madeline R. Marquez
Nicole Martinez Moore
Clare Martorana
Stephen Massoni
Monica Mata
Ankit Mathur
Kimie Matsuo
Maya Mau
Joshua May
Jenna J. Mayer
Mitzi Mayer
Maxwell R. Mazzocchi
Jessica Rae McBean
Alexander J.
  McClelland
John L. McClung
Elisabeth L. McClure
Daniela McCool
Jeremy P. McCrary
Anthony W. McDonald
Christine A. McDonald
Katrina A. McDonald
Renford McDonald
Benjamin L. McGuire
Lewis A. Mcilwain
Katherine E. McKenna
Kellie McManamon
Michael McManus
Frank McNally
Amy L. McNary-
  Bontrager
William McNavage
Christopher McNeal
Maya Mechenbier
Edward Meier

Flavio Menasce
Gabriel A. Menchaca
Andrew G. Mendoza
Margaret Mergen
P. Thaddeus
  Messenger
Daniel J. Michelson-
  Horowitz
Jaden A. Mikoulinskii
Frank W. Milbourn V
Leah Milhander
Eric Mill
Jason Miller
Kimberly Miller
Leanna M. Miller
Sofie Miller
Morgan Mills
Susan M. Minson
Angela L. Mitchell
Chance Mitchell
Terrance D. Mitchell
Kira Mickie Mitre
Katherine Mlika
Elizabeth E. Molle-
  Carr
Kirsten J. Moncada
Allyce Moncton
Claire E. Monteiro
Andrea J. Montoya
Julia C. Moore
Natalie Moore
Amy A. Morath
Mary J. Moreno
Anne M. Morgan
Karen M. Moronski-
  Chapman
Peter D. Morrissey
Savannah M. Moss
Zoriana Moulton
Siddharth Muchhal
Robin McLaughry
  Mullins
Tracey C. Mulrooney
Angela Lum Mundi
Ian Munoz
Daenuka
  Muraleetharan
Susan R. Murphy
Paul-Donavon Murray
Christian G. Music
Hayley W. Myers
Heather Myers
Kimberley L Myers
Drew Myklegard

N

Andrew Nacin
Jeptha E. Nafziger
Larry J. Nagl
Barry Napear
Robert Nassif
Beverly Nelson
Kimberly Nelson
Michael D. Nelson
Anthony Nerino
Melissa K. Neuman
Travis Newby
Joanie F. Newhart
Sheila Newman-
  Rogers
Annie Nguyen
Hieu Nguyen
Ella M. Nicholson
Brieanna Nicker
Thomas Nielsen
Yu Ning
Julia Nonnenkamp
Sharanda D. Norman
Jennifer Nou
Greg Novick
Janice M. Nsor
Nagela Nukuna
Tim H. Nusraty
Joseph B. Nye

O

Erin O'Brien
Mary O'Brien
Kevin R. O'Connor
Wayne T. O'Donnell
Matthew O'Kane
Tyler Olsen
Cassandra Olson
Kathryn Olson
Alison O'Mara
Brendan J. O'Meara
Jessica L. Ondusko
Stephanie D. O'Neill
Matthew Oreska
Karin A. Orvis
Joe Osborne
Timothy F. O'Shea
Jared Ostermiller
James Owens
Leticia C. Oxley

P

Heather C. Pajak
Farrah N. Pappa
Amy Paris
Eric L. Parks
Breanna L. Parra
John C. Pasquantino
Matthew Pastore
Mira D. Patel
Swati A. Patel
Kareema N. Patton
Brian Paxton
Casey Pearce
Liuyi Pei
Zoe W. Pennington
Sean Pennino
Amanda Y. Perez
Patricia C. Perozo
Michael A. Perz
Sean E. Peters
William C. Petersen
Andrea M. Petro
Amy E. Petz
Stacey Que-Chi Pham
Brian Pickeral
Joseph Pipan
Megan Policicchio
Marc A. Poling
Nicholas Polk
Mark J. Pomponio
Ruxandra Pond
Imani Pope-Johns
Bev Pratt
Jamie M. Price
Grant Procopio
Alanna B. Pugliese
Robert B. Purdy
Hannah Pyper

Q

Syeda A. Quadry
Kathleen J. Quinn
Angie B. Quirarte

R

Lucas R. Radzinschi
Mary Raglin
Makaila Ranges
Zahid Rashid

Johnnie Ray
Alex Reed
Maurice Reeves
Heather Regen
Thomas M. Reilly
Cody Reinold
Andrew R. Reisig
Bryant D. Renaud
Richard J. Renomeron
Richard L. Revesz
Marta A. Reyes
Kharl M. Reynado
Charles R. Rhodes
Cheredith Rhone
Keri A. Rice
Michael P. Richard
Robert B. Richardson
Kyle S. Riggs
Glorimar Ripoll Balet
Rahish Risal
Tina Roberts Ashby
Sean M. Robertson
Donovan Robinson
Lamar R. Robinson
Whitney R. Robinson
Marshall J. Rodgers
Jose Antonio
  Rodriguez-Arroyo
Samantha Romero
Meredith B. Romley
Nichole M. Rosamilia
Andrea L. Ross
Katy Rother
Alicia Rouault
Rachael M. Roueche
David J. Rowe
Amanda Roy
Brian Rozental
Todd W. Rubin
Erika H. Ryan

S

Muhammed Saeed
Elana L. Safran
Jennifer Saindon
Faisal G. Salad
John Asa Saldivar
Zohaib Sameer
Aziz K. Sandhu
Mark S. Sandy
Mi-Hwa Saunders

Ruth Saunders
Joel J. Savary
Jason K. Sawyer
Tricia Schmitt
Eric A. Schroeder
Loren DeJonge
  Schulman
Benjamin E. Schwartz
Vanessa G. Schwartz
Mariarosaria
  Sciannameo
Kristi Scott
Jasmeet K. Seehra
Owen Seely
Andrew Self
Anna Setzer
Megan Shade
Vimal Shah
Andrea N.
  Shahmohammadi
Shabnam
  Sharbatoghlie
Ishan K. Sharma
Amy K. Sharp
Dionna Sharp
Pooja Shaw
Paul Shawcross
Parag A. Shende
Kartik Sheth
Livia Shmavonian
Gary F. Shortencarrier
Matthew Sidler
Julie Siegel
Leticia Sierra
Sara R. Sills
Alexa Simmons
Celeste Simon
Daniel Liam Singer
Sarah L. Sisaye
Robert Sivinski
Benjamin J. Skidmore
Vanessa R. Sloane
Curtina O. Smith
Jasmine R. Smith
Matthew Smith
Patrick C. Smith
Stannis M. Smith
Tatiana Y. Smith
Joshua Solomon
Roderic A. Solomon
Timothy Soltis
Ki Suk Song

Suzanne Soroczak
Valerie Souffront
Amanda R.K. Sousane
Megan Sowder-Staley
Rebecca L. Spavins
Samara M. Spence
Valeria Spinner
Christopher Spiro
John H. Spittell
Sarah Whittle Spooner
Deneen Spruill
Travis C. Stalcup
Scott R. Stambaugh
Nathan A. Steele
Nora Stein
Benjamin M. Stern
Brittany M. Stewart
Meredith Stewart
Aaron M. Stienstra
Ryan Stoffers
Gary R. Stofko
Robert B. Stone III
Conrad D. Stosz
Nathan T. Stowes
Paul D. Strande
Terry W. Stratton
Vanessa Studer
Thomas J. Suarez
Elizabeth G. Sukut
Kevin J. Sullivan
Patrick Sullivan
Abe Sussan
Katherine M. Sydor

T

Jamie R. Taber
Diane Thanh Nhu
  Talaber
Shelby Ann Talton
John T. Tambornino
Naomi S. Taransky
Patrick Tarasiewicz

Stephanie J. Tatham
Kelly Taylor
Myra L. Taylor
Whitney Teal
Jay F. Teitelbaum
Stephanie Teller-
  Parikh
Emma K. Tessier
Lan H. Thai
Amanda L. Thomas
Barbara E. Thomas
Jennifer Thomas
Judith F. Thomas
Payton A. Thomas
Will Thomas
Serita K. Thornton
Matthew B. Tibbitts
Parth Tikiwala
Thomas Tobasko
Allison C. Toledo
Erika Tom
Gia Tonic
Susanna Troxler
Patrick Trulock
Ariana C. Tuckey
Austin Turner

U

Regina A.
  Udomratanavasi
Shraddha A.
  Upadhyaya
Darrell J. Upshaw

V

Matthew J. Vaeth
Saratkumar Varanasi
Areletha L. Venson
Alexandra Ventura
Jesus Vidaurri
Genna Kate Viggiano

Merici Vinton
Megha Vyas

W

James A. Wade
Shelby Wagenseller
Brett Waite
Nicole Waldeck
Joseph Waldow
Eric C. Waller
Heather V. Walsh
Gang Wang
Sonia Wang
Suzy Wang
Tim Wang
Ben A. Ward
Michelle Ward
Jhavoiya Washington
Gary Waxman
Bess M. Weaver
Emily M. Weaver
Daniel Week
David M. Weisshaar
Philip R. Wenger
Max West
Elizabeth Whitcomb
Arnette C. White
Ashley M. White
Curtis C. White
Kim S. White
Sherron R. White
Timothy White
Alison Whitty
William G. Wickett
Brian A. Widuch
Christina Wilkes
Avery D. Williams
Carl Christian
  Williams
Jamie S. Wilson
Kevin Wilson
Kimberly C. Wilson

Kristen H. Wilson
Christine A
  Winchester
Stephanie Winker
Catherine Winters
Jeffrey A. Wojton
Wintta M.
  Woldemariam
Ephrem Woldetsadik
Brittany J. Wolford
Henry K. Wolgast
Minzy Won
Nicholas J. Woroszylo
Christopher Wren
Jazmine P. Wright
Sophia M. Wright
Bertram J. Wyman

Y

Melany N. Yeung
David Y. Yi
Wesley Yin
Christian T. Yonkeu
Jinha Yoon
Xia You
Rita Young
Shalanda D. Young

Z

Nadia K. Zahir
Elizabeth Zahorian
Erica Zamborsky
Corinna J. Zarek
Eliana M. Zavala
Bin Feng Zheng
Olivia D. Zhu
Erica H. Zielewski
Timothy Ziese
Morgan E. Zimmerman
Jeremy Zitomer